Dear Aunt Foster,
I wish we might see one another once more before we die, but if not, join with me in writing. It seems the only satisfaction we can have here.

... a 15 year old immigrant to the Ottawa Valley writing to his aunt, 1823.

They left their homes, never to return, with a dream of living a better life.

They found themselves on the other side of the ocean, in a completely unknown wilderness, struggling to survive.

This book peels away romanticized notions of what everyday life was really like for early settlers in the Ottawa Valley.

It is the story of ordinary people confronted with loss, isolation, unforgiving winters, and deprivation, who find their endurance and willpower tested to the limits.

Through letters and true accounts the great-great-granddaughter of these two families reveals what it was like for them to pursue their quest.

Living Out The Dream

Olive Caldwell Lee

Published by

William Jenkins

2106-1200 Alberni Street
Vancouver BC V6E 1A6 Canada

williamhenryjenkins@gmail;com
http://www.williamjenkins.ca

Telephone: 1-604-685-4136
Cell: 1-778-953-6139

Edition 1

ISBN 13: 978-1500804077
ISBN 10: 150080407X

.

for my parents
Wesley Caldwell and *Emma Argue*
with gratitude

ACKNOWLEDGEMENTS

Margaret Caldwell James, Allan Caldwell, Ernest McCallum and Herbert Argue provided stories, research and genealogies. Herbert Argue knew his great grandfather, Andrew Argue, heard the migration story directly from him and was wise enough to write it down. Valuable research from the Goulbourn Township Historical Society kept me on track.

Support and helpful advice came from Helen Tape, Sharon McInnes, Dennis Johnston, Corinne Saunderson and Thyrza Cohen, Susan Lindenberger and Margaret McIntyre. The cover design was done by Claire Marchand and Andrew Lee.

Bill Jenkins gave freely of his time to direct the editing and self-publishing process, support that was essential to the final product.

Finally, thanks to my husband. He is a great cook and exhibited remarkable patience throughout this whole process.

Bibliography:

Kee, Robert, Ireland, A History, London, Little brown &Co. 1995
Walker, Harry and Olive, The Carleton Saga, Ottawa, The Runge Press, Ltd, 1968
Elliot, Bruce, Nepean, The City Beyond, Ottawa, Tri-graphic Printing, 1991
Finnigan, Joan, Giants of Canada's Ottawa Valley, Renfrew General Store Publishing House, 2005
MacDonald, Ervin A., The Rainbow Chasers, Vancouver, Douglas & McIntyre, 1982.

Table of Contents

PROLOGUE: IRELAND IN THE 18TH CENTURY

This story follows the real life experiences of two Protestant families who emigrated from Ireland in the early part of the 19th century to make a new life in British North America. To understand their reasons for this momentous decision it is helpful to acquaint oneself with the history and character of Ireland at that time.

George Argue and Forest Caldwell were born into a country that was a cauldron of anger and fear, the genesis of which goes far back into Irish history to a time when the King of Leinster invited a Welsh warlord to come over to Ireland to help subdue his rival. Once the Welshman, known as Strongbow, established himself with the aid of the Vikings, King Henry II came along to subdue Strongbow who, Henry thought, was getting too strong. From there, by degrees, England made Ireland their business. It was not a quiet affair! The Irish warlords resisted strongly and persistently until English kings decided it would be best to take over the whole country and put an end to their rebelliousness. To skip a few kings and several centuries of turbulence we come to that well-known knave Henry VIII. He decided to end the uproar by confiscating all clergy-owned land for the English Crown. He had done that fairly effectively in England, and thought it would be an equally good plan in Ireland. He then proceeded to give the land to the Crown's favourites in return for their homage and loyalty. The Irish Lords did not know when to bend their knee and it did not go smoothly. One rebellion followed another.

Elizabeth I, a queen regarded with some admiration by her countrymen, but not equally so by the Irish, gave orders that the rude, rascally and barbaric Irish had to be broken before they could be ruled. Any sign of resistance was met by widespread slaughter of the Irish, including women and children, the armed and the unarmed. These atrocities, which were horrific even by the standards of that day, laid the seeds of Irish hatred for all things British, a hatred that remained deep in Irish consciousness for many centuries.

1

Early in the 17th century the British Crown established Protestant settlers in the Province of Ulster, that is, in the northern counties of Antrim, Tyrone, Donegal, Derry, Armagh, Fermanagh, Monaghan and Cavan. Land was taken from the Irish and given to Protestant settlers, English, Scots and even Huguenots, indeed anyone who swore to fight for the British Crown. This process was called the Irish Plantations. Previous attempts to plant Protestants among the native Catholics had failed and this one had only tenuous success, except in the County of Antrim, which became predominantly Scots. In other parts of Ulster the new settlers were planted in amongst Catholic tenants and relations between the two groups continued to be predictably volatile.

To add further cause for rebellion, the English Parliament imposed a series of Penal Laws in the first half of the 18th century, the most grievous of which are listed below.

The Penal Laws

Roman Catholic priests and members of the religious orders were banned; the intention was to gradually destroy the Roman Catholic Church.

No Catholic could receive an education. There were to be no Catholic schools, no instruction in their language, their history or their literature. No Catholic could become a schoolteacher.

They could not vote, nor sit on a jury, nor hold public office either by appointment or election. They could not become a lawyer or a Member of Parliament.

They could not bear arms, except as privates in the English army where they were considered to be good cannon fodder the same as an English or Scots peasant, but none could rise above the rank of private without becoming a Protestant.

A Catholic could not buy land. A Catholic farmer had to divide his land among all his sons equally on his death. An eldest son of a Catholic landowner could inherit all of his father's land only by becoming a Protestant.

A Protestant could take possession of a horse belonging to a Catholic, whatever its value, for five pounds.

Many of the Penal Laws were so draconian that they were never enforced, but one particular law, made to ensure that Catholics would lose ownership of their land, was enforced. A Catholic could not purchase land and if he had owned land prior to the Penal Law, then he had to divide the land equally amongst all his sons, thereby ensuring that the holding became smaller with each generation until eventually it would not be big enough to support a family. Then he became a tenant, and if unable to pay his rents, which were considerable, he could be evicted. The Protestant landowner could leave all his land to his eldest son.

This particular provision made its mark. By the end of the 18th century, less than five percent of the land of Ireland belonged to Catholics.

Another big factor leading to the pressure to leave Ireland was an unprecedented population explosion. From 1687 to 1725 the number of people living in Ireland increased from 2.1 million to 3 million; by 1785, to 4 million. By 1821, there were 6.8 million and by 1841 Ireland was bursting at the seams with a population of 8.2 million. The Protestants as well as the Catholics were involved in this population boom. From 1772 to 1821, the years we are examining especially, there had been a population growth of 3 million, not quite doubling the population but a truly tremendous and alarming rate of growth. Even today, Ireland has fewer people than it had in 1821.

The Protestant farmer, who was very well off compared to his Catholic neighbour, was on his own as far as help from the authorities was concerned. He had to defend himself against huge numbers of Catholic peasants who were willing to lose their lives in order to avenge themselves against the hated Protestants. Since no open form of protest was possible, the Catholics formed secret societies, the RightBoys and later the Defenders. The Protestants formed the Protestant Boys and the Loyal Orange Order. Most were forced into belonging to one side or the other. Neutrality and peaceful co-existence had no place in Ireland of that day.

The origin of the Argues is not documented; they were most likely to have been Huguenots who fled France and arrived in Ireland by way of Scotland or they may have been an Irish clan of a similar name, 'Argee', who converted to the Protestant faith out of prudence. The Caldwells, whose origins are equally unclear, claimed membership in the Church of Ireland when this

3

story begins. By the middle of the 18th century both families considered themselves Irish.

George Argue, born in 1772 and Forest Caldwell in 1780, were each from a family of seven, a modest sized family in those days. In their formative years they received vivid lessons about their world. By the time George was eleven, the American colonies had challenged the mighty British forces for their independence and ultimately defeated them! In 1789 the French Revolution began; the people of Paris watched as the guillotine sliced the heads off people all day, every day, until the streets ran red with blood. Chaos and murder by mobs killed both the guilty and the innocent, and the mayhem continued for most of the 1790's.

When you think of what was happening in the world outside Ireland and the fact that Ireland itself was seething, bubbling and letting off steam, is it any wonder that a rational person would wish to escape? The most dangerous places in Ireland were the regions where numbers of Protestants and Catholics differed by only a very small margin. This was the case in County Cavan and a few adjacent counties.

Finally in the year 1798 there were scattered uprisings by the Catholics ending in a blood bath of major proportions. In that year, George Argue was 26 and Forest was 18. The outlook in Ireland promised more of the same and worse. A growing number of English and Irish politicians were advocating the repeal of the Penal Laws and granting more privileges to the Irish Catholics. With hindsight one can see that these ideas were wise, but at that time any hint of appeasement frightened the Protestant minority out of their collective wits. They fully expected to lose both their lives and their lands.

Hopes for religious freedom and land ownership were frequently the major factors in decisions to immigrate to North America. For many, the simple desire for peace and safety for one's family was perhaps the greatest factor of all. For each man one reason would have weighed more heavily than another. For some it may simply have been a desire for adventure. For men in their forties with large families to support, adventure may have been as much a deterrent as a pull.

Catholics, who never regarded the 'planted Protestants' as Irish, had stronger reasons to emigrate and greater

4

ambivalence. They felt forced to leave their beloved homeland in order to survive.

Around 1818, there was an important shift in immigration policy by the Colonial Office. Following the War of 1812, the British Government had encouraged the immigration of young men who could serve the dual purpose of clearing the land and defending the colony. They learned fairly quickly that young single men did not fare well as settlers. When this story commences, the Government preferred to sponsor groups of families to settle Upper Canada.

ARGUE

THE DECISION 1820-21

Clusters of women sat on crates on the wharf, surrounded shoulder high by more boxes and barrels. Young children scampered past them, racing up and down the wharf, scarcely heeding the cries of their mothers who sat anxiously guarding their precious belongings. Older children and youths promenaded more sedately to and fro, trying to contain their excitement about the adventure that was to be their new life. The men stood a little apart, saying little or saying much as was their individual habit, but all had the same need: to bolster their courage for the venture to which they had committed themselves and their families, to leave Ireland and sail to the New World.

Two women, one in her thirties and the other about sixty, sat huddled together on a large wooden crate; they were dressed entirely in black except for the white pinners[1] under their black bonnets. For the most part they were silent. There was no need for words between them. From time to time the elder woman cast a keen eye over their chattels, then, reassured that all was well, she returned to her own thoughts. The younger woman was Mary Argue; the other was Anne Wilson, her mother. It was the first time in many days that Mary had taken time to sit, and now that opportunity for reflection presented itself, she dreaded it. As she gazed at the pitifully few reminders of their homes they had been allowed to take with them, waves of near panic flooded over her at the irrevocable step they were taking. Here

---

[1] Pinner is an 18th century headdress which matrons wore under their bonnets. Older women still wore them late in the 19th century.

7

they were on a wharf in Belfast, about to say goodbye to everything they knew and cherished, to the graves of their fathers, to the graves of their children, now to board a ship, never having laid eyes on one before, and sail across an ocean to a new land about which they knew nothing. Their decision now seemed to be madness.

She looked at her family. For William, 17, and Andrew, 14, this seemed to be one big adventure; Robert at 12, tried hard to imitate his older brothers. Her daughters, Anne and Jane, and their youngest son, John, looked a little more fearful; perhaps they were taking their cues from her. She forced herself to sit upright and try not to show any weakness or doubt. Her husband George, who had been chosen to lead this group, had the welfare of so many on his shoulders, or at least he felt that he had, and no reasoning would remove a jot of it. All the families had come to this place of their own free accord. The other men were able to take full responsibility for their own decisions, of course, but still, George felt the greater weight of it. Without him or another leader like him, none of them would be in this place, leaving all they knew to try their fate in a new country.

Mary's ruminations continued: when did it all begin? Was it when her youngest brother James Wilson and their neighbour John Scott, left for the New World, so confident in themselves and their future? That had been only two years ago, April 1st, 1819. No, it had begun long before that. Who could trace its beginnings? When had discontent become virulent? As long as Mary could remember there had been crosscurrents of fear and bitterness in Redhills, Cavan. But she had understood that was just a part of life, not the whole of it and as such she had not questioned it. She recalled weddings, births, harvest celebrations, so many happy times with her family when she was a young girl. She had not taken a gloomy view of her life.

Then she met George Argue. She was at a county fair in Cavan with her father, William Wilson, her older brothers, Gideon and Moses, and her older sister, Eliza. John and Amy had remained home with Mama and baby James. Mary found the fair enchanting, loved visiting the stalls where village women and storekeepers sold their cloths, ribbons, toffees and candies. If there were money enough at the end of the day sometimes the little ones were allowed to toss a ball at a small doll, maybe win a doll for their very own. Their father saw only the potential for trouble and kept a watchful eye on his children.

For most of the day, Mary and Eliza stayed with their father at the back of his cart where he sold his butter, eggs and the linen cloth he had woven. They contented themselves watching the crowds, but as the noon hour crept past Mary persuaded her father to let her wander about a little with Gideon and Moses. Eliza remained behind with their father for she found the fair with its hustle and noise a little frightening without his solid presence. Mary's brothers were warned to look out for her, a serious injunction laid upon them by their father. County fairs were well known for the fights that could erupt towards the end of the day. Protestants and Catholics, aided by strong drink and pitchforks, were unstable combinations. Mary's brothers were as like as not to be in the thick of it if a fight broke out, and her parents were most reluctant to entrust the welfare of their eldest daughter to their care.

By mid-afternoon Mr. Wilson had sold all but one length of linen. Glad to leave for home, he gave Gideon and Moses permission to remain at the fair for a few more hours. Mary, seeing her father to be happy with his sales that day, wheedled and begged to be allowed to stay with them.

"Please, Father, just a few more hours. Let me stay with Moses and Gideon. They will look out for me, they will."

"We-ell," he said slowly, "you will have to promise to leave the fair by five o'clock in order to be home by dark, before the roads become unsafe."

"Yes, yes, I'll stay right close to their sides and we will surely be home before dark." And so with the promise obtained from Mary and her brothers, Mr. Wilson with Eliza seated proudly beside him, turned his horse and cart and headed for home. This was nearly ten miles away but neither Mary nor her brothers gave any thought to a ten-mile walk at the end of the day.

All went smoothly and Mary was having quite the best time of her life visiting the many stalls and trundling after her brothers who, out from under their father's eye, soon met up with a few of their friends. Their party grew larger but they still gave thought for Mary's welfare. Two of the young men who joined them were George Argue and his cousin Albert. George was a little older than the Wilson lads but he joined them willingly

9

enough for the chance to further his acquaintance of their sister Mary. He remembered Mary from years ago at a campground meeting when she was still a young girl. She had been there with her family and at the time George had no more than registered the fact that the Wilson boys had a younger sister; his mind had been on more serious matters. When George saw her again that day at the fair, he was determined to get properly introduced. Indeed, he could see straight off that he was not the only one to have such a determination. He thought it likely that Moses and Gideon had never had so many friends willing to join them until they appeared with Mary.

Mary was a beauty; petite and well-rounded in figure, her real beauty lay in her colouring, glossy auburn curling hair, rose and cream complexion and saucy brown eyes. Her appeal for George did not end with her physical attributes, as vital as they were. Mary's family attended chapel too and George, a newly converted follower of John Wesley, was lost at once.

George, a comely man, above medium height, with jet-black hair, dark complexion and grey eyes, could easily be passed by in a crowd, for there was nothing in his manner to make you look twice, not until you looked into his eyes. They were startlingly direct and keen in their gaze. Mary was noticed immediately. She dressed modestly; yet one did not see her as a modest maiden. Where George was sober, she was gay; where he was good-looking, she attracted looks. The difference seemed to lie in her manner. While she regarded herself to be a committed Christian and member of the chapel, she could never understand the need for the sombreness that some of her brothers and sisters had in abundance. That day at the fair, with so many wonderful things to see and do, she cast aside all inhibitions and her lively manner and natural beauty won George's heart and firmed his resolve to make Mary his own.

His major problem was how to see more of her. Of course he could approach her father directly for permission to court her, but George wanted to know if Mary would welcome his courtship. So he planned how he might walk her home that night, even if he had to do so in the company of her two brothers. Providence was with him. As soon as he offered to walk Mary home, Gideon and Moses argued which of them could then stay at the fair and which was to go home with Mary. After their promise to their father they knew they dared not leave her, even

10

with someone as reliable as George Argue. Gideon, the older, got the short straw and declared himself ready to do his duty. He knew it boded well for any future consent to attend a fair or anywhere else that they keep their promise to their parent. After they shared a couple of pasties and a sup of water at one of the stalls they set out to walk the distance home.

It was as well that they did so, for little more than an hour later, as dusk was drawing nigh, a group of young men who had been drinking and were looking for an opportunity to settle a few scores, arrived at the fairgrounds and a scuffle broke out. Soon it escalated from fists to sticks, from sticks to stones, to more sticks, to more people and finally, a few pitchforks were being wielded about and half the fairground was in an uproar. Moses escaped with only his jacket torn and Albert a lump over one eye. Both struck out for home, congratulating themselves on their getaway when they heard some commotion behind them around the bend of the road. They hid in the ditch until heavy footsteps of at least four men thudded past and then returned. It was a close call. Dangerous enough to be caught in a crowd with fists and stones flying about, it was a great deal worse to be caught out alone on the road in the dark with no one to witness who did what to whom. And so they kept to the ditch, making as little sound as possible for another half mile before getting onto the road again.

Moses got home well after dark, having had to walk most of those miles in wet boots. Albert parted from Moses shortly after they got on the road again and walked another seven miles to his home. Tomorrow was the Sabbath Day and staying too late at the fair was not an acceptable excuse for failing to rise and attend church on the Sabbath.

All of these happenings contrived to put George Argue's suit in a good light as far as Mary's parents were concerned. Here was a man who had shown the good sense to leave the fairgrounds at a "daicent" hour. That very night he asked her father's permission to call upon her the following Sunday afternoon. Permission was granted. He was first and most importantly a chapelgoer; he seemed to be healthy, hard-working, intelligent, and old enough to look after Mary. Mary voiced no objection although privately she hoped that with time and more familiarity he might become less serious.

When George started to court Mary he was twenty-six years old, no longer a broth of a lad, and the middle of six sons. With no inheritance staring him in the face, he put the bit between his teeth and worked like a draft horse. It took five long years before he was satisfied that he could provide for Mary and on New Year's Day 1803, George and Mary were married.

For Mary, the years since 1803 were marked mostly by the arrival of their children. Apart from the death of one child to measles as an infant, Mary counted herself to be the most fortunate of women. George, likely the more rational of the two, worried more with the addition of each child. There was little to be complacent about in Ireland in the first part of the century. Unrest and flagrant injustices were everywhere: barns continued to burn down mysteriously; livestock vanished; life itself was precarious. Then there was the war with France. The litany of problems never left George. Mary urged him to have more faith and less worry but her words might as well have been spoken to the wind, for George harboured a dream of leaving Ireland's woes and sailing to the New World, a dream he had not confessed to anyone for he saw no hope of being able to afford to go even if Mary were willing. The birth of each child rooted him ever more deeply into the soil of Cavan.

Then, in 1817 and 1818, rumours of free land being opened up to immigrants in British North America slowly filtered down to Redhills and Clara. It quickly became the Land of Hope and Glory for all the young men of the district. There had been a steady if small trickle of young men leaving to try their fortunes in the newly formed United States of America, but these stories told of free land in the Colony of Upper Canada being offered to settlers from the British Isles. After 1815, with the war against the French and Napoleon over at last, where better for young men eager for adventure and opportunity to go but to the New World?

Now as she sat on the wharf, Mary reflected that this had been the moment when the mounting dissatisfaction she had sensed in her husband gained momentum. But it was not the final catalyst.

Indeed she was quite right. George heard this news with longing in his heart. How he wished he were a young man. Not that he wanted any other life than his life with Mary, and of course he was properly thankful for so many healthy children, but to own your own land and to own so much of it that you never had to worry about feeding your family. That was his dream, a dream well beyond his grasp in Ireland.

Of those who heard the news and responded with speed were Mary's youngest brother James Wilson, and John Scott, close kin of their good neighbour, Archibald Scott. James and John were among the first to go from County Cavan and opinion in the County was evenly divided. Were they fools or wise men? Their mission was to explore the land and tell their friends if they should leave their homeland for Upper Canada.

When James and John came to take their leave of Mary and George one Sunday night at the end of March, 1819, George took James aside quietly and asked him to, "Write as often as you can. It will ease your mam's mind you know. And look about you to see if an older man with a family to support can find his way over there. And if that be so pray let me know as soon as may be. I have a strong will to join you but I cannot ask Mary to step out into the entire unknown now, can I?"

They set sail from Belfast on April 1, 1819 on the sailing brig *Sally*. Their letters were eagerly awaited and a long wait it was too. For months no one knew if they were alive or dead. Then in the spring of 1820, a full year after they left, came the first letter.

Dear Families and Friends

We are in good Heart and Health and vitals. We have both found work in a lumber camp north of the Ottaways River. There be lots of work to be had and all that would make life better would be to see old friends and neighbours join us here to work for a Better Life We must make haste to send this letter with a friend who is off to Montreal now We have no address for you to write to us except you send it in C/o James Hawes and Co. at Bellow's Landing, Upper Canada. When we get there we will look for news of you and hope to hear you are Coming to us Soon.

Your brothers in the Lord,
John Scott and James Wilson.

The welcome letter received varied reactions. Where was the information the women wished to hear? Everyone wanted news of the voyage, but there was not a word about it.

13

Did that mean anything? After so many months of waiting, it was bitterly disappointing to hear so little. But, thank God for it, they were well.

The following is the Ship's Notice for the Sally on which John Scott and James Wilson sailed to British North America on April 1, 1819.

SHIP'S NOTICE

Ships for America[4]

FIRST SPRING SHIP FOR QUEBEC

To Sail 1st April

THE BEAUTIFUL FAST SAILING

COPPRED BRIG,

SALLY,

SAMUEL BALL, Commander

Burthen 500 Tons

(A Regular Trader)

This first class Vessel is built of the very best Materials, is particularly well calculated for the ease, comfort, and accomodation of passengers, being the regular height for Troops between decks, and sell known as a swift sailer.

Captain BALL's abilities as a seaman, his prompt and unremitting attention to the comforts of his Passengers, and humane

---

[4] The Brig Sally for Quebec
SOURCE The Irishman, Vol. 1 1819-22, Friday, 4 February, 1820.
ARCHIVE The Linenhall Library, Belfast
KEYS #SERIAL = 9312095, #DATE = 31:01:1820, #TYPE=ADV

treatment of them during the voyage, render this a most desirable conveyance for persons wishing to cross the Atlantic in safety.

For Freight of Passage, please apply to

ALEX McCLOY

7, Chichester-Quay, Belfast.

January 31, 1820.

Quebec,

June 7, 1819.

We the undersigned PASSENGERS on board the brig SALLY, SAMUEL BALL, Master, from Belfast, on Behalf of ourselves and all other Passengers, being the appointed Committee, return our most grateful thanks to the said Captain BALL, for his gentlemanly conduct and humane attention to us during the voyage; and are strongly recommend all our Irish Friends, who intend to emigrate to America next season to give the SALLY a decided preference, she being a safe and comfortable vessel.

> *Owen McDonald, Ballyhaise, Near Cavan.*
>
> *Benjamin Workman, Lisburn.*
>
> *John Loreman, Carncastle.*
>
> *James Wilson, Ballyhaise, Near Cavan.*
>
> *John Scott, Ballyhaise, Near Cavan.*
>
> *Richard Long, Lisburn.*
>
> *Samuel Bowman, Carrickfergus.*
>
> *John McAdorey, Larne.*
>
> *Neal McNeill, Cushedndall.*
>
> *Henry Whitely, Ashfield, near Coothill.*
>
> *William McMin, Ashfield, near Coothill.*

In Cavan a significant change had occurred during the past year. Old Lord Dansy had died at Christmastide 1819, and his heir was now in charge. George had heard rumours of the new lord, but had not seen him since he was a wee lad when he had been sent off to school in England and then to travel on the Continent. Rumours said he had not gotten on well with his father. They were too unalike in temperament and that was not a good thing either, for the elderly Lord Dansy had been well liked. Rumours, rumours. George tried to ignore them.

For once rumours did not exaggerate. It soon became apparent the new Lord Dansy was going to govern the tenants with a strong fist. He had been heard to rant, 'Right now these blasted tenants act as if they own the land.'

He admitted they performed their duties according to the letter of their agreement, but failed to regard him with the respect and awe he felt was due him. They would soon find out he intended to run things differently; he planned to buy up any lease that he could and settle a new tenant on much shorter leases. There would be no more lifetime leases. If a new tenant failed to please, he would cancel the lease and hire men to work by the day instead. He was their Lord and he would act as Lord.

Then came the day which decided George's fate. It is odd how often one's destiny is decided by an incident. Rational thinking frequently fails to provide sufficient impetus for a major change. Certainly George had not yet succeeded in persuading Mary to leave Ireland and all she loved, and migrate with her family to a new country. George might not have left Ireland at that time, but for what happened at the pit the last day of September.

That day he was to bring in peat for Lord Dansy, a labour he owed to his landlord. The money obtained from selling the peat was used to pay the workers down at the same mine at which George had worked as a young man. To his surprise, when he arrived at the pit early enough by his standards, he saw that his neighbours had already begun working. Oddly, they did not raise their heads to acknowledge his arrival, but kept steadily to their work. Then he saw a man in vivid blue riding pants topped by a well-fitted, dark yellow jacket ride up on a magnificent white horse. George, thinking it just as well not to stare, bent his shoulders to digging the peat into blocks. His son Andrew was his helper this day. Now twelve, he was old enough to handle the job of picking up the blocks of peat and laying them alongside for drying. They had barely begun their work when they heard horses hooves close behind them. Andrew turned to look and then stared open-jawed. Never had he been as near to nobility before nor seen a man so finely dressed out at the pit acting as an overseer. The man held his long thin body erect on his big horse, making himself as tall as possible. His features were thin, pointy and inflamed with rage; below his tricorn were wisps of blazing red hair.

From the expression on Andrew's face, one would think he had seen the devil himself. At a word from his father he quickly shut his mouth and turned to pick up a block of peat. Without warning, there was a whistle of air and the riding crop came down on Andrew's shoulders. George's head jerked up in disbelief.

He said quietly, "There was no call for that. He's just a lad." To Andrew he said, "That's enough. We'll go home now."

Then George got into the cart, wheeled it about slowly and left the pit. Those close by witnessed everything, but put their heads down, not wanting Lord Dansy to know they had seen any of it. Dansy's face was purple. It did not look good for Argue. What could have come over the man?

Indeed it wasn't like the George Argue most of them knew. He was a man slow to anger, slow to speak, never impulsive and up to this point, a man who conducted himself most humbly, as befitted a member of chapel. But Lord Dansy had found George's Achilles' heel — his loathing of injustice. So surprised was George that he had no time to put a screen between his feelings and his action. Once the words had left his mouth, dignity demanded that he depart. In almost the same length of time, he decided that this place was no longer a place for his sons. The die was cast. He and his family would go to Upper Canada. It did not take long for George to realize that he had not acted as the Bible recommended toward those in authority over him. He had not submitted meekly. He was prepared to ask the Lord Jesus to forgive him for his stiff-necked pride, but nothing could alter or lessen his resolve to leave behind him Ireland and all its lords. In his life there was only one Lord, and His name was not Dansy.

When he arrived home early in the morning and told Mary what had happened, she knew then they were going to Upper Canada.

A couple of months later, when the autumn air was chill and the evenings black, the second letter came. Mary sent word immediately to friends and family to come round that evening to hear the letter. Everyone in the whole of Redhills knew of the letter and the slightest delay would have been unpardonable. Archie Scott, Mary's three brothers, Gideon, Moses and John, and their uncle, John Wilson Sr., arrived together. Close behind were James Blair and Robert Mitchell.

The letter was brought forth and smoothed out on the table. It looked well travelled. George offered it to Archie to read aloud.

Archie waved it away impatiently, "Get on with it, George".

Gooldbourn,[2] Upper Canada,   Oct 24th, 1820.
Dear Mother Wilson, Father and Mother Scott, George and Mary, friends and family,
This letter finds us well and never better and we trust that you are well too as you were when you wrote to us We have at this time but one letter from home and are eager for more news of you all Why has Amy not written, and cousin Thomas too? But what would bring us the Greatest Joy is to hear that you are making ready to come to this country Give up the pain of Ireland and come to Upper Canada. Here no man is your master but your own self Every man 18 years of age and over can have 100 acres granted to him by the Crown. All you have to do to claim this land is to clear ten acres and use the wood to build a house This any man with the Will to Work can do We have already laid claim to 100 acres in the Township of Gooldburn, near Richmond We have been told the land is rich and good and we will have three years to clear ten acres and then it is ours. Do give joy to our hearts to hear news of your coming.
Your brothers in the Lord, James Wilson and John Scott.

---

[2] The spelling of Goulbourn changes frequently throughout the text; this is intentional. Words were spelt according to how they sounded to the writer. There was no sense of right or wrong spelling.

When George finished reading, an expectant hush fell on the room. Then he leaned toward them and said, "I've a mind to go to Upper Canada." He sat back and waited. Their voices were loud in approval.

"Sure an' you know well we've been waiting and wanting to hear you that say just that, that we have," Archibald Scott proclaimed.

George nodded. He did not explain or tell them of the incident which had occurred. He had no need to tell them for everyone knew about it to the last detail.

The talk instantly became boisterous. From James Blair, "We're with you all the way and the sooner we leave this accursed land the better."

And from the others, "Aye, Aye. You well know we're all for it."

George replied, "Yes I've known for some time that ye are all for it, but how about your families?"

Archibald Scott said, "What we decide our wives will follow. What is there to discuss about that?"

"We have heard from two young men who speak of the new land as the Promised Land, but not a word about how the women might fare. Do ye think your wives will be up to it?"

"Our women are all God-fearing, sober women," Moses Wilson huffed. "They need not a lot of gewgaws and fripperies to make them content. They have their contentment in the Lord".

"Well spoken Moses, and I am confident it may be so, but I think it would be good to bring your wives to our meeting tomorrow night and hear from everyone what their decision will be."

"Tomorrow night is chapel meeting, George."

"Aye, so 'tis. And a good time it will be to put this plan before the Lord."

Oh yes, Mary recalled every detail.

The next evening the group was so large it was a tight squeeze to fit into the large kitchen. Women who often stayed home with the young'uns fetched them along, determined to ask their own questions and have their own say. Chapel commenced as usual with a prayer by Moses and a scripture reading by George. What followed was not the usual discussion of the Word

19

and a laying bare of souls with the brothers and sisters; instead George laid aside the Bible and spoke.

"I have read to you from Nehemiah and from Psalm 127 where the Lord enabled His people who were in exile in Babylonia to return to their homeland, and to rebuild the temple at Jerusalem. They had the heart to undertake this great venture because they believed that He would be with them as they went. Each one of you here tonight knows that we have gathered together to discuss leaving our homeland and going to a place called Upper Canada, a place as close to total wilderness as any we know of in this world. For those who go, there will be no coming back. No matter how much we are told, there will be much we do not know, and we cannot know how it will be for each one of us. I ask you now to consider the scripture, Psalm 127, vs. 1: *Except the Lord build the house, they labour in vain who build it: except the Lord keep the city, the watchman waketh but in vain.*

George paused, then, looking around, said, "Unless the Lord is with us in this endeavour, we who make the journey make it in vain. I have prayed on my own behalf and on that of my family and we are set upon this course. But I beg of you not to make the decision in haste."

He folded his hands and waited. This time there was no immediate burst of sound. Each man kept silent. And not a few of the women thought as Mary did, that they were not venturing to return to their homeland, to their Jerusalem, but rather to leave their homeland and go to a strange land.

They all knew by heart the first letter sent from John Scott and James Wilson. After a moment George said, "As you no doubt know, there has been another letter from James and John. Would you like to hear both letters now?" A few of the women nodded. And so both letters, well worn from reading, were brought forth; the words themselves, printed into their memory.

Give up the pain of Ireland and come to Upper Canada Here no man is your master but your own self. Every man 18 years of age and over can have 100 acres granted to him by the Crown. All you have to do to claim this land is to clear ten acres and use the wood to build a house. This any man who has the Will to Work can do.

It sounded good, too good, a hundred acres, free! Did they not know how to work? Could they not teach ten men how to go about it? The women noticed that there was no news of how they lived from day to day, what food they ate, or where they slept, nothing even about the climate and what ailments one could expect in that part of the world. But all who knew these two young men had expected little in the way of words from either of them. There was only one message:

Make haste to come to British North America, to Upper Canada, and be your own man.

The men who received these letters were neither so freely placed nor as young as James and John. George was in his mid-forties, a man with a wife to consider and children both young and nearly grown; his mother-in-law, Anne Wilson, who lived with them, was nigh on sixty. So was the case with many of the men he spoke to that night. Again he was greeted with silence. Then he saw his brother-in-law Robert Mitchell look to his wife Amy who gave the slightest inclination of her head. He turned and said, "We would go, me and mine." Then John Wilson Sr. said that he and Maude were of a like mind. And after that, one after the other without further discussion said they wished George to put their names down too, and asked him to do all that was necessary to endeavour to get this free passage.

When all but Mary's oldest brother Gideon had signalled their intention to join the group, George turned to him. Gideon said, "No, I think Agnes and I will bide here in Ireland. I know she's not over keen and someone has to stay and look after our Maw. She will be welcome in our home if you have a mind to go, George."

Anne Wilson spoke out clearly. "You have no need to tarry here on my account, Gideon, for I've made up my mind. I'm going too."

This met with only a little surprise by the members of the group. Since her husband had died, Anne had made her home with her daughter Mary, taking care to go for frequent visits to her other daughters' homes as well. But she rarely spent the night in the homes of her daughters-in-law. Few could imagine this woman, who was the matriarch of nearly the whole assembly, biding her time happily by the hearth of her eldest son's wife. Agnes was a good woman and so said everyone. And then they

21

said no more. To say her mouth drooped and twisted down at the sides and that she was ever discontent would not be charitable; best to say nothing. But no one could see the two of them rubbing along well together. Anne was too spirited to take a back seat to anyone and her daughters were used to her ways. The journey would be hard on her but, with nearly all her children departing, no one was truly surprised that she was set on going too.

There was a little pause and then Archie, thinking it wise to shift attention from this domestic issue, said, "Free passage or not George, our minds are made up. Do your best and we'll be with you."

As far as Mary was concerned her fate was sealed. George had put himself in such a position with his landlord that he had to leave. Her heart cried out in protest and her cries were all the stronger for being muzzled before they could break forth. What irony to hear George speak and advise the other men that they were to make sure their wives agreed to uproot themselves, to leave the green hills, to leave the green graves in the churchyard, to leave — no, she was not being fair. George had to go. She understood it, but to say that she accepted it, that she was wholehearted and willing to go, was far from truthful. George got around this very carefully by saying, "We are determined to go." And the die was cast.

Once set upon a course it was not George's way to be imprudent. He had no intention of frittering away the passage money if it could be had for naught, and so he brought forth a letter he had written to Lord Bathurst at the Colonial Office in London.

"A while back I spoke with Bailiff Briggs to find out how to get this free passage and learned we have to write to the Colonial Office in London. If we can obtain their blessing then the Government will supply the passage."

Everyone knew it was a bit more complicated. The funds for free passage were to be raised within the parish, with large donations to be expected from the landlord and the nobility. This procedure would take some time, and they doubted strongly that their landlord would lift a finger to help any of them, let alone contribute a shilling, unless it were to his own advantage to do so. But then perhaps Lord Dansy would like to be rid of the whole lot of them.

22

George continued, "I think it's just as well to impress the Colonial Office with our loyalty to the Crown, something that might not be taken for granted from an Irishman. The Crown wants to fill up the empty spaces in Upper Canada with English speaking yeomen who are prepared to defend the Colony against the Americans. Right after the war in the colonies, Americans loyal to the Crown flowed into Upper Canada and were well rewarded with prime land on the waterways. But more and more settlers kept on coming across the border, many of them only after free land, much like ourselves. Now the Crown wants no more Americans, just settlers from Great Britain. They have been offering 200 acres of free land to any soldier who is prepared to remain in Upper Canada and farm, and now they are opening up the land to settlers such as ourselves."

He paused and looked around, "We hope to go to the Military Fort at Richmond where James and John have their land grants. All that remains is for those who are going to put their names on the other side of the page and to include the number in each party."

Dec 28, 1820
To Earl Bathurst Colonial Department London
We the undersigned having a few days ago Rec'd Letters Dated at Gooldburn the 24th of October last in British America from Two of our Friends (John Scott and James Wilson by name) who have left this Country and have Settled there who have given us the utmost encouragement to make application to your Hon'bl Person for Instructions How we may prepare and proceed for a Free Passage to that good Country as is represented by them.

Therefore we take the Liberty of Laying before Your Honour not Presuming in any respect an Intrusion on your Dignity the Measures that have been laid before us by our above named Friends to have us and our Respective familys Brought over to Canada that is that (sic) they got our Names and Families Enroll'd with the Commissary under a petition which by us making Application unto you Sir that you would furnish us with every Credential that might enable us to prepare for the Voyage which is our Object at Present So now we take the Liberty of Sending a list of Ourselves and our families who prays

23

to be landed at Quebec from there to the Township of Richmond
in the following manner

On the Other Side (of the page)

Families	#	Sons	Daughters
Mosses Wilson	7	4	1

Anne Wilson (Mother of Mosses and John Wilson and
mother-in-law to Geo. Argue, Jas. Blair and Robt Mitchell and
Mother to Jas. Wilson who is resident at Gooldburn in Canada

John Wilson	5	3	-
Geo Argue	9	5	2
James Blair	4	1	1
Robert Mitchell	4	1	-	1
John Wilson Sen'r	8	3	3
John Graham	3	-	1
Archibald Scott	9	4	3
John Foster	8	3	3
Will'm Foster	9	1	6

These (three) are Brothers in law to John Scott who is
resident or Convenient to the Township of Richmond

Thomas Buck	3	1	-

(Thomas Buck also wishes to bring) two orphan
children. Thomas Buck is father-in-law to Archibald Magee who
is resident in British America.

Samuel Halliday is an Excellent Carpenter and friend to
the aforenamed Archibald Magee prays for free passage for
himself his wife and Two sons and likewise George Argue for
John McFadden his Serv't Boy Every Man in the foregoing list
are Loyalists and have Ser'd Several years in the Yeomanry.

We request an Immediate Answer Directing to George
Argue Castle Roe to the Care of Francis Whyte Esq.'re,
RedHills, Large, Co Cavan, Ireland.[3]

---

[3] Public Archives Canada. (PAC) Reel B 881 C.O. (Colonial Office) 384/7
Folio 615

To Earl Bathurst Colonial Department 615

London 1237

We the undernam'd, Having a few days ago rec'd Letters
Dated at Gooldsboro in the 24th of October last in British America
from Two of our Friends (John Scott and James Wilson by name)
who have left their Country and have Settled there who have given
us the utmost encouragement to make Application to your
Hon'bl; person for Instructions How we may prepare or proceed
for a Free passage to that good Country as is Represented by them

Therefore we take the Liberty of Laying before Your Honour not
presuming in any Respect an Intrusion on Your Dignity the
measures that have been laid before us by our above nam'd
Friends to have us and our respective families Brought over to
Canada that is that the they got our Names and Families Enroll'd
with the Commissary under a petition which by us making
Application unto you Sir that you would furnish us with
Every Credential that might enable us to prepare for the
Voyage which is our Object at present So now we take
the Liberty of Sending a list of Ourselves and our families
Who prays to be landed at Quebec from thence to Township
of Richmond in the following manner Viz;

On the Other Side

... a Families ...	Number of families	Sons	Daughters
...		2	3
Moses Wilson	7		and Mother in law to
Anne Wilson Mother of the s[ai]d Moses & John Wilson			0	George Argue Jas Blair
John Wilson Jun[r] ---- 5		3	and Robert Mitchell
George Argue ---- 9		5 -- 2	and mother to Jas
James Blair ---- 4		1	1	Wilson who is [...]
Robert Mitchell --- 4		1	1	at Goolboure in [...]
John Wilson Sen[r] --- 8		3	3
John Graham --- 3		0	1
Archibald Scott --- 9		4	3
John Foster --- 5		3	3
Will[m] Foster --- 9		1	6

These are Brothers in laws to John Scott who is resident or Commissa... to the Townshile of Richmond

| Thomas Buck -- 3 ---- 1 ---- 0 | | | |

and Two Orphan children

Thomas Buck is Father in law to Archibald Magee who is resident in British America

Samuel Halliday who is an Excellent Carpenter and friend to the fore named Archibald Magee prays for a free passage for himself his wife and Two Sons and likewise George Argue for John M[...] Goddelin his Serv[t] Boy — Every man in the foregoing List are Loyalists and have serv[d] several years in the Yeomanry

We request an Immediate Answer Directing to George Argue Castle Roe to the care of Francis Whyte Esq[r] Rednhill Lodge to Cavan Ireland

The letter was dispatched the very next day. From this point onward all communication from the Colonial Office would be directed to George Argue. He began to feel the weight of the responsibility right away, as he had known he would.

Word got about by the next day of what was afoot. By the following day George was approached by two men, not chapel members, who wanted to go with the group. This was a development that George had scarcely thought of, and when he inquired from Sir Francis Whyte about what he was to do, he was told bluntly,

"You don't have the power of refusal. The Colonial Office is not providing just for you and your friends, you know."

Yet it gave a whole new flavour to the matter, one he didn't much care for. He took it to chapel meeting on Wednesday night. The first reaction was shock and dismay.

"We thought to get away from Ireland, not to take it with us," came from James Blair, as usual the first to express what was in everyone's mind.

Then from George, "We cannot say naught. The ship does not arrange to sail for our benefit, nor is free passage only for chapel goers."

"Aye, but cannot these others make their own arrangements, find their own leader?"

George replied, "Squire Whyte tells me that the Colonial Office expects only one group from each parish and right now ours is the one from Ballyhaise. I have had but the two requests 'til now, but there will be more. The names are Tim Wiggins and Jeremiah Scott and their families. I ask you to pray on this matter. If any of you know these persons well, you can speak with them to test out the firmness of their commitment. Dissatisfaction with what we now have cannot be the only requirement for planning to take this step. What will be, will be, as the Lord arranges."

They went home, the first blush of their euphoria waning.

Several more men showed up on George's doorstep to ask George to let them know what it would be like for them to uproot their families and follow in his footsteps. George could well understand their need to know as much as possible about such a big step, but warned them that the mails were slow, perhaps unreliable; nevertheless he promised to do his best to send a letter after he arrived in Upper Canada. He suggested that perhaps they could share a letter amongst them.

George now started to set his house in order. He and most of his friends were tenant farmers and some owned a small freehold as well. A tenant was usually granted a lease for a lifetime or in some cases two lifetimes. Although George expected no trouble in finding someone who would take over his tenancy, he did not intend to wait until the last moment. And so in full confidence of a favourable reply from London, he let it be known he was willing to sell his own freehold, and relinquish the rights to his tenancy. Lord Dansy had the first right to the tenancy of course. No tenant could dispose of his lease until his landlord had first refused it.

Lord Dansy was their first real stumbling block. Inevitably it had been that pivotal meeting with George Argue which had aggravated Dansy's temper and hardened his attitude. When he learned they wanted to sell their leases he decided that, despite the fact he wanted to buy their leases, it would be pleasant to let them fret awhile before letting them know his intentions. In particular, he felt he had a score to settle with Argue. The man had actually dared to speak back to him one day. It was all he could do not to take his whip to the man, but something about the man had stayed his hand. He still didn't know exactly what it was; certainly Argue was not imposing to look at, a little over medium height, but not someone in any way noticeable in a crowd — not until you looked into his eyes. Dansy was not used to these peasant farmers looking him straight in the eye. He had no intention of getting used to it. He would be glad to see the back of them.

Indeed it had been this same meeting with Lord Dansy which George kept firmly in mind as he went about the business of leaving all that was known and much that was dear to him. He needed always to maintain a firm resolve. Any wavering would be a disaster for the whole group. Word had filtered back that some people had found the voyage a dreadful business from start to finish. John and James had not spoken of the journey at all and perhaps this was even more ominous. It could only mean that it had been very bad; otherwise they would have sought to reassure on this point. No, it would not do for George or any of his family to show doubt about the course that was set before them.

By the middle of January George was no further ahead in his knowledge of what Lord Dansy intended to do.

It was at this point that Mary's thoughts shied and sheered off at a tangent, but herein lay the explanation for their black clothing. A tragedy fell upon the Argue household before they left their homeland. Their fourth son, George, aged eight, was tagging along after his older brother William one day as he tended to their animals. William had just laid down the pitchfork, which he had been using to clean out the cow's stall, when young George ran right on top of it. The prong of the fork went right through his foot. The injury was not too painful, surprisingly enough, and he was treated with all the care that was known in those days. This mainly consisted of wiping the wound, applying a poultice and binding the wound in cloths. It had not been too many years since doctors were treating cuts with concoctions of mare's urine and cobwebs and occasionally dung poultices mixed with sundry plants. Such wonders were not applied to George's foot, but despite the remedies used after a few days his foot began to swell, and the wound festered. In less than a week, young George died of blood poisoning. The entire household was stricken, but Mary was rigid with shock and grief. Her constant thought night and day was, "I cannot leave him here alone in his small grave. I cannot".

She received counseling on all sides to regard her son as being in heaven with the Lord. She withdrew from them all. It was more than she could cope with to think of uprooting herself from her home; indeed she could scarcely think at all. Part of her wanted to run far away and hide her eyes from the cot where he had died.

It was no easy time for George either. He would have been ready to bide in Ireland and try to go at a later time but he had given his word to such a large group of his friends to be their leader and there was a more practical consideration as well. He still had not sold his lease but he was sure that Dansy was only biding his time to make things more difficult. He and all of his friends were now committed to leave Ireland.

Bailiff Briggs had no news for them. Dansy was still trying to figure out a means of revenge for Argue. Then of a sudden he thought that the best revenge was to put all of them off their lands and so, by the last day of January, he communicated through Bailiff Briggs that he expected them to be gone by the end of February.

Unfortunately for the men who were preparing to leave, they had not yet received an answer from the Colonial Office, a fact well known to the whole village and to Lord Dansy too, for it was Dansy who had received the reply from Colonial Office. The letter instructed him to make suitable preparations to facilitate any would-be emigrants from the Parish of Ballyhaise and the country roundabout, but he had not passed this word on to his tenants. Let them stew.

Another meeting was held at George's home and all agreed that it was time to send another letter to the Colonial Office, this time omitting to address it to Lord Bathurst.

> *Clara, Feb'y 3 1821*
>
> *Sir*
>
> *We take the liberty of Informing you that we have Addressed Lord Bathurst in a letter Directed to the Colonial Department London with regard to have free passage to British America to which we have got no Answer   We have got Letters from Our friends residing there that is John Scott and James Wilson by name that they have made Applications there in Behalf of the Undernamed for a free passage wherein they have Obtained the Grant and Desired that we should apply to his Above named Lordship and let it be known that the Grant was Obtained from the Commiss'is'ary and that there would be no delay of us having every encouragement that is Held Forth by the English Government for the Assistance of Bringing over Settlers there whereas from the Same we have Endeavoured to make preparations for the Voyage which if the above Information is Shown to the Contrary it will be greatly Disadvantage us as we have Endeavoured to make Sale of Our goods and Land in order to enable us for the Passage which we Sir Request that you will find an Answer that will Certify to us whether the like is to be Obtained or not   We are Sir your Obedient Servants,*
>
> *George Argue, John Wilson Sen'r, Moses Wilson, John Wilson Jr., Rob't. Mitchell, Jam's Blair.*

Please direct to George Argue, Clara, Redhills, Cavan, Ireland.[5]

Perhaps Lord Bathurst had been the stumbling block. He had been rumoured to be in favour of such emigration schemes, but it was passing strange that there had been no reply to that first letter.

For the rest, they all had the measure of Lord Dansy by now and even more clamoured to be included. To add more weight to the letter, if that were needed, the above six signatures were affixed to the second letter.

This time a reply was immediate, and it arrived in the person of a Mr. Horace Coolidge who handed George the following letter:

> *Colonial Office, London,*   *Feb 15 1821*
> *Sir:*
> *We have received your letters of Dec 28 and Feb 3 and wish to assure you that your interests had received our Immediate and Favourable attention in that we instructed Lord Dansy to do all that is necessary to Hasten and Encourage your departure from Cavan County to British North America. We have moreover arranged Transport for your group, along with other groups, to leave Ireland at the end of this month, or thereabout, on the Albion, to depart from Belfast, this being arranged for your greater Convenience and Economy*
>
> *By this juncture you should have been informed of all of the above by Lord Dansy or his representative. Your passage monies are to be paid for by Lord Dansy and the Colonial Office.*
>
> *We are aware that this does not leave you much time to make Final Arrangements but we hope that you will be able to expedite your affairs satisfactorily in good time. However the fault for Poor Communication does not lie with our Office. In order to provide all possible assistance, we have entrusted the care of this letter to our trusted servant, Horace Coolidge. He will do everything possible to Assist your Readiness to make the*

---

[5] Public Archives Canada, Microfilm B 881. Colonial Office (C.O.) 384/7 folio 609

31

*journey. Communicate all your circumstances to Mr. Coolidge
and to your local magistrate, Francis Whyte, Esquire.*

*May God Speed your Journey and Give You Peace and
Prosperity in the New World.*

Signed James Walpole for Lord Bathurst.

The letter delivered to Lord Dansy was not couched in
such pleasant terms. The Colonial Office was irate. The amount
Dansy was now expected to contribute to their departure had
risen from one-half to three-fourths.

*You Sir, are being charged with providing from your
own purse three-quarters of the amount of the passage monies,
the rest coming from the Colonial Department. In addition each
man or woman taken from the Poorhouse is to have Five Pounds
settled upon them by Yourself to help with the expense of their
passage, their welfare for their first year in British America to be
borne by our Office. The bill will be submitted to you forthwith.*

Dansy decided to take a tour of the continent and left all
the arrangements in the hands of his bailiff.

Now matters assumed a very different complexion. The
major issues had been settled already: leases had been given up,
freeholds had been sold, and families had been staying with
relatives jammed up in the small quarters. But the joy and the
pain of going now became a certainty and that was all that
mattered.

The issue of what to take with them and what to leave
behind was addressed by Mr. Coolidge, "The transport of goods
is uncertain there. Each family should make do with as few
barrels of stuff as possible. Indeed beyond food stuffs for your
journey and basic clothing, you are encouraged to take the bare
minimum in household goods."

The women did not take kindly to these suggestions. In
each family a council raged about what was essential. Mary
absented herself from these discussions and it was her mother
Anne and George who arranged matters as best they could.
Children could take only what they could carry on their person.
Anne gently pointed out that the little leather Hymn Book of
Songs by John Wesley would fit nicely into a pocket. The
youngest boy, John, decided he would take his very own wooden

32

candlestick holder that was small and had a copper base.[6] Each child could choose and much agony was experienced over the choices. William and Andrew offered to carry something extra for the girls, for after the essential harmonica and whistles, there was nothing more they wished to take from Ireland.

The men were informed that the tools they would need to clear the land would be provided there. That was just as well, as few of the men had an axe or the first notion of how to use one.

The sense of adventure was intense and the men greeted it with much more optimism than the women who were obsessed with the urgency of packing. Barrels, which had been packed several times, were packed several more times and everything was in an uproar.

One morning Moses arrived unexpectedly at the Blair household.

"Things are in a quair auld state over at our place, James. I found out Martha had made no room for my accordion, my music box, you know. I cannot do without my accordion, James. Surely the good Lord does not expect us to be without our music?"

"What did Martha say, Moses?'

"She started muttering something about, 'It's enough to make a saint swear coming out of church,' and I thought I had better clear out for a bit."

James laughed and said, "You are not the only one to consider your instrument essential Moses. Will'am Foster told his wife he could better do without a change of clothing, than do without his fiddle".

"What did she say to that, James?"

"What indeed! She told him she could not do without his changing his clothes and told him to strap the fiddle on his back." James continued to find the situation very amusing.

"It's alright for the likes of you, James. You have a fine voice. The Lord has given you an instrument that's easy to carry. Not so for all of us." It was now Moses who muttered as he took himself off to the Fosters where he expected to find more understanding from Will'am.

---

[6] This candlestick holder is still in possession of an Argue descendant living in Arizona.

The final hurdle to be met was the journey to Belfast, which was a three-day journey by coach. It was the first time these people had ever encountered such a journey and it was greeted with eager anticipation and some apprehension. With 16 families leaving that part of Cavan alone, it was realized that extra vehicles would be needed. Some of the better off farmers loaned their farm carts to them to help transport their possessions. Their offers were gladly taken up. A few planned to travel by public coach. The Argue family could boast of one very ancient carriage owned by cousin Thomas and into this was squeezed George, his wife, his mother-in-law Anne Wilson and his two youngest children, Jane and John. Robert and Anne caught a lift on the cart that took their belongings. The two older sons, William and Andrew, who was barely 13 years, rode alongside the carriage. Their horses were to be sold in Belfast and the funds used to help swell their cache of savings for the start in Upper Canada.

It was of course the journey over the sea that caused the most fear. There was plenty of water in Ireland, but it was the rare person who knew how to swim. No one had needed to, and what good was swimming in the vast ocean?

For George, Mary, and the others, these hours of waiting on the dock for the time to board had provided too much time to reflect. Mary felt a rising panic and shook herself, "I can't think. I won't think, for I can't bear it. There's no turning back, not now and not ever."

CALDWELL

CAVAN 1809-21

Forest's circumstances bore few similarities to those of George Argue other than their common membership in the Methodist Chapel; indeed perhaps he had little in common with the majority of emigrants from Ireland in that time. His story too, begins much further back.

Forest, born in 1780, was the second eldest in a family of five sons and two daughters. His father William owned outright about 400 acres or several Townlands of fertile soil and rolling pastures that had a lake within its boundaries. William liked to congratulate himself that his family had been on the land for nigh on 200 years. William was content in his situation, both in the Parish of Ashfield and within his family, which he commanded in perfect confidence that his word would be obeyed.

The eldest son, William II, was dubbed Willy Too by his younger brother Harold, who also referred to him as Willy Nilly when out of his father's hearing. One suspects that his father secretly feared Harold was right, except for Willy Too's regard for horses. In this field he knew what was worth knowing; in other areas he was useless. Forest, the second son, was tall, thin, gangly and extremely shy. Between the two of them, William felt that neither would make much of a push for matrimony. He placed his hopes in this direction on the next two boys, Ernest and Harold, who were certainly not shy, full of energy and into mischief all day long. Then there were two daughters, Melissa and Louisa, and another son, Samuel.

35

All progressed as smoothly as William had expected until Forest was about 11 years of age when, unknown to his father, he attended a campground meeting held by followers of John Wesley and became converted. It was an event of tremendous significance for a sensitive lad of that age, one he kept secret from his family for many years. It was a poorly kept secret, for his brothers and sisters knew exactly where he went each Wednesday evening. William did not trouble himself over much on the matter; he adopted the attitude that Forest was too young to know his mind yet, and as long as he showed up every Sunday morning at the Ashfield Church of Ireland, William did not know, or want to know, what he did the rest of his time. He expected to be obeyed when he exerted himself to give an order, but on the whole he chose to leave everyday management of the household and the children to his capable wife, Sarah.

It was a different matter for Forest, who despised himself for keeping his conversion a secret. During the following years Forest knew not a moment's real peace. Finally he knew it would never come without making a clean breast of his beliefs to his father, but still he said nothing. He attended chapel every Wednesday and Sunday evening, and if he had been asked a forthright question about his activities, he would have answered truthfully. No one asked. Everyone in the family knew what he was doing and thought that if they ignored this aspect of his nature it would fade as common sense took over. By the time he was in his mid-twenties, more and more areas of his life were compromised. He knew he could not serve both his father and the Lord Jesus and he was beginning to be sorely troubled by the thoughts of the Fires of Hell which he was sure were waiting for such as himself. He had heard the Word and believed, but he was not following. Did not this make him the worst of sinners, worse than those who did not believe? He was in torment day and night. He went out quietly each Wednesday to chapel meetings, sitting in the rear and taking no part, always on the fringe.

Then one night a young miss sat beside him; her name was Mary Smiley and she had come to the meeting with her older brother. She did not say anything either to him or to anyone else, but Forest began to feel happy just to have her there. This was more than strange, for Forest, as he neared thirty, had not a speck of confidence with women, except for his mother and sisters. The next evening Miss Smiley smiled at him and

Forest felt himself actually smiling back. Something strange was coming over him.

Mary Smiley was a rather plain young woman. It was hard to put one's finger on just where she missed being attractive. She looked strong and healthy, a little tall for a woman, and she had large capable hands. Her grey eyes were fringed with dark lashes; her skin was very pale and inclined to go blotchy when she became excited. Perhaps she failed to make the most of her modest looks by her dress and her manner. Her brown or grey garments were plain in the extreme, covering her from neck to wrist and ankle; her feet were shod in good stout boots. The drab colours did nothing at all for her mousy coloured hair, which was at least plentiful, but covered entirely by a plain white cotton cap and a poke bonnet. If Mary had any attractiveness she kept it well hidden, and as she was quite shy, it suited her to do so. Her father was fairly well to do, and she worried not so much about failing to find a husband as having one found for her all too soon. Mary was only fifteen years of age, but because she was tall and the eldest daughter of the family, she appeared much older, and everyone thought of her as a young woman. She was happy enough in her parents' household, and they were happy to keep her there. It was quite unusual for Mary to take the initiative and actually smile at a stranger. One was encouraged to feel that everyone in the chapel was a brother or a sister, but it was mostly the feeling she had that this man was acutely uncomfortable that caused her to attempt to greet him in a spirit of love. That smile sealed her fate had she but known it. To Forest she looked beautiful. He saw only her tentative smile and gentle expression. As for wishing for an attractive woman in bright colours, nothing would have frightened Forest more.

Up to this moment, Forest had approached each chapel meeting with feelings ambivalent in the extreme. He knew he belonged with this group of sober young men and women, but he hated himself for not witnessing to his faith openly. Now that he had been smiled upon by this young woman, he longed for the next meeting, and determined that he would sit by her and speak with her if possible. He overcame his shyness sufficiently to learn her name and who had brought her to the meeting. He had not made more progress than that by the fourth meeting.

Forest knew that his father was hinting that it was time he looked for a wife, and if he could not find one, then one would be found for him. Forest felt that such a pressure was most unfair. Willy Too was three years older, and he was being left alone, but then Willy Too was a bit hard to rouse on any subject other than riding and hunting. William Sr. had no intentions of letting Forest follow Willy Too's example.

One day when Forest was trying to prepare himself for a confrontation with his father about this marriage issue, he waited in his father's study in an agony. He began to pray for help. No formal words, just *Help!* He had brought with him his New Testament that fitted into his pocket and he grasped it unconsciously. Suddenly he felt warmth stealing over him and a strength he had never felt before. It was more a physical thing than spiritual, but it gripped him in amazement. His back straightened, his chin went up and he was sitting this way when his father came in.

His father proceeded to say, "Well I think you know why I have asked to see you, son. I think it is time you were getting married."

"Yes Father, I know, and I am in agreement. I know the young woman I would like to approach, and with your permission I shall do just that. She is the only one for me, I'm sure, and if she will have me I am ready to marry. If she is not willing, then I shall not be willing to marry any other."

William was astounded. He had never heard so many coherent words from Forest before, nor heard him speak with so much purpose. It was not entirely unwelcome. "Er-r, can you tell me a little about this young woman on whom you have set your mind?"

"I can tell you where I met her — at chapel on Wednesday evening. I have been going to chapel for some years now, although I have not spoken of it. I know this cannot please you, but in this matter I can do nothing else."

William waved away these words. "I know all about your leanings to the teaching of John Wesley. I have known for quite a few years now and have been wondering when you were going to own up to your beliefs. I suspected they were so weak that you would abandon them in the first bit of trouble, but that has yet to happen. And so your intended must attend chapel too, eh? Well, I would not have chosen so for you, but better that than no wife at all. Does she come from a good family? What is the name?"

"Her name is Mary Smiley, and I know nothing about her family. They live in County Monaghan, I believe. Her brother brings her to chapel. He seems a pleasant chap but I have not yet spoken to him."

His father's eyebrows shot up. "It seems you have fixed your mind on her before you know anything about her. A poor way of going about choosing one's mate, to be sure. I cannot condone such a match before I know more of the family and her prospects."

Forest said nothing. He felt a different person. He was sure that he was being given strength for this confrontation directly from the Holy Spirit. He did not feel in the slightest afraid. In fact he had never felt so calm in all his life. And two things immediately occurred to him. *"God heard me and helped me. He knows me; He really does love me."* He was overcome with joy. His whole being was warmer than usual, and his face was lit up, but he did not know that. He rose from his chair to excuse himself so that he could be alone. His father looked up in surprise at the thought that his son would attempt to terminate the interview. What he saw on Forest's face surprised him even more. His face almost shone.

Before he could gain control of the situation, William found himself standing and saying, "Well, well, we shall speak of this again, son." And then he was alone to ponder this strange interview.

Forest was never the same after that. He lost his fear of hell's fires. He knew that God had been present with him and, if God was on his side and loved him even when he was nothing but a weak part-time believer, what did he have to fear? Fear was no longer a part of his makeup. Everyone noticed a difference, although no one could say what it was exactly. He was still quiet and not particularly assertive, but those who knew him best, and there were not many, knew that he had changed.

At the next meeting he introduced himself formally to Mary, and asked her if he could approach her father for the purpose of courtship. She was now more flustered than he, but she was privately pleased that a man of such gentleness was willing to seek her out for attention. Forest was still gawky, well above average in height, and thereby inclined to keep his head bent and to shuffle along looking at the ground. Mary herself was considered too tall for a woman of her day, and she was privately pleased to find herself looking up to him. She answered modestly that she would be pleased to further their acquaintance, and was most surprised when Forest showed up at her home the very next afternoon to speak with her father.

William Caldwell was also in for a surprise when Mr. Smiley drove into their yard two days later and asked to see him. His inquiries had not yet been launched and now the father was at the door. Obviously Forest was taking matters into his own hands at an alarming rate. He had him admitted and was pleased to see a man who was well set up, had a horse and buggy of his own, and was prepared to look him straight in the eye.

"Well there's no point in shillyshallying about. Your son has approached me to court my oldest daughter. I don't know your family and you don't know mine and so I thought we had best try to get control of this matter before it goes any further. I have not yet given my consent although I must say your son presented himself well enough."

"Well enough!" humph, humph. "Well I daresay he would. He has been brought up to know how to present himself."

Nothing could be calculated to throw William more than to find the worthiness of his family being examined. He had fancied that all the queries would be on his side. Moreover this man was far too blunt. He had no sense of what was appropriate or he would have accepted a glass of wine and passed the time of day pleasantly before launching into the subject. William sought to regain the role of host now by offering a drink. It was swiftly refused.

"I have taken an oath not to take liquor in any form, but if it pleases you, a cup o' tea would not come amiss."

William pulled the bell to order tea and asked, "Are you a follower of John Wesley then, and is this some ruling of his for his followers?"

"Yes, I and mine are followers of his teachings, but the oath about alcohol is my own idea entirely. I suppose a man can have a few of his own?"

"Oh, aye, aye, that he can." Whatever this man believed, he did not hold with humility. He was as bristly as a porcupine. William was beginning to feel that Mr. Smiley was not quite as confident as he at first appeared. Such a notion served to make him feel a little better.

"Well now, as you say, these two young people are interested in getting shackled. It is up to us, of course, to determine whether they would suit. You, sir, have the advantage of me for you have found me in my home and have met my son, whereas I have not had the pleasure of meeting your daughter." Unspoken words hung in the air.

Mr. Smiley was obliging enough to answer the unspoken question. "I am a merchant, sir. I am the owner of the haberdashery and dry goods store over in Drum in County Monaghan. The business has served well as an income for my family, which is as numerous as yours I believe. My children have not had to serve in the store and have been brought up gently by my good wife. As for myself I am a man of few charms, but I hold myself to be a good businessman. What my father gave me I have tripled in value. My children are accustomed neither to want, nor to riches. I would not want my daughter to wed a man who was either far above or far below her station in life. She is as worthy as any man she would marry. It is my view that such an arrangement leads to a happier union."

"Err, yes, yes, I agree entirely about the value of a common background. As you know we have been on Drumshiel for nigh on two hundred years but — "

William dropped his voice. What was there to say? The man was asking if his daughter, the daughter of a merchant, would be looked upon with favour by our family, a family considered to be gentry, in a small way to be sure, but the difference is there all the same.

He continued valiantly, "I would suggest sir, that our two families might meet. I leave all this sort of thing to my wife, but I think it might be best if we could have you over for tea one day next week. Perhaps our wives can set the day."

"Aye, that might be best. My wife is all in a tizzy about the prospect of losing her eldest. She sets great store on Mary, she does. Her right hand in all matters in the household you see. If she could be at peace about her future that would ease her mind greatly, greatly."

And yours too, no doubt, thought William. By this time the tea had been served and they spent a few moments sipping their tea uncomfortably. William was privately of the opinion that young Mary would have learned few social graces from her father, but on the other hand the marriage settlement might be adequate to help set them up. And Forest seemed determined. The first time, no, the second time, in his nearly thirty years that he was determined about anything, so it had best be looked into.

"Before we come to any terms it is best for our families to meet, but, if all goes well there, and as long as your daughter is of sound limb and mind and we can agree what the marriage settlements will be, I suppose we could consider their courtship. What say you?"

"My daughter is hale and hearty, scarcely sick a day in her life, once she was past two years, and I don't know her constitution before that. Her mother knows about that. She is a sensible lass and by far the best of daughters. I would not be willing to part with her unless I am convinced that she will be well cared for all her days."

William felt that he had just made an uncommonly magnanimous gesture to this oaf and immediately found himself on the defensive. Drat the man. He could not like the sound of him. A pugnacious sort to be sure. He stood up to usher his guest to the door.

"We shall meet as soon as can be arranged, Mr. Smiley. Best to talk no more till then, I'm sure you will agree."

The Smiley household was in a furor. Mary's parents were very conscious of the fact that she was being 'looked over' and were willing to set aside a few scruples about modest dress so that the Caldwells would not snub their daughter. Mary was not so willing. She was very flattered at the interest shown in her by a much older man, one who was well set up in society, but she felt that she was being rushed unreasonably. She was not at all ready to contemplate marriage, and therefore determined to dress as she had always dressed, and not to present herself in any false light. Ribbons and rose coloured muslin were rejected. Finally Mary agreed to a new dress of especially fine quality dove grey sateen. It was a far better material than she had ever had, and the seamstress was instructed to take great care with the fit. As a result Mary's dress revealed a figure of good proportions even if the colour was subdued. Her bonnet was also new, of a matching colour, tied on with a plain white ribbon under her chin. Her hair had been brushed till it crackled but, as it was almost invisible under her bonnet, this effort was mostly wasted.

Mary insisted that her next youngest sister, Elizabeth, who was only 13, go along with her for moral support, as well as her parents. She was not looking forward to the ordeal one little bit, and spent the whole morning muttering prayers and carrying her New Testament about as a talisman. Her only comfort was her firm belief that she would not suit and therefore she would be back home again in a few hours, and she could try to forget this whole dreadful business.

When they arrived on the doorstep in their open carriage with two fine horses on display, Forest was there to greet them. He had eyes only for Mary who was dressed the most plainly of the entire group. Mary's modest style of dress in his father's household pleased Forest immensely. Here was a brave young woman who knew her own mind, and followed it. Nothing could have been better calculated to achieve Forest's admiration.

The tea was as awkward as such an occasion can be. Sarah Caldwell strove valiantly to be polite and keep a conversation going, but most of her attempts were met with nods, half smiles and few words. Surprising everyone, Forest, who was bent on protecting his Mary, came forth with more words than had ever been heard from him on a social occasion before. It didn't help much for he had no skill at all, but it made his intentions clear. When Mr. Smiley rose to say they had best start back, everyone rose in a rush of relief, and could scarcely quit the room fast enough.

The conversation that evening between Sarah and William Caldwell went like this:

William: "It will never do. We cannot ally ourselves with a family who scarcely know their manners for such a simple occasion as this."

Sarah, mildly: "But Forest seems to be determined, does he not?"

William: "Yes, unusually so. I don't quite know what to make of it. If I do not allow the marriage, he would not be able to support a family on his own, and that will be the end of it."

Sarah: "Hmm, yes, I suppose it would. Although I fancy that Mr. Smiley might be prepared to offer Forest a place in his business if they are absolutely determined. He is quite a prosperous man after all."

William turned an unpleasant puce colour: "My son a merchant! Stand up in a store and sell dry goods! Not bloody likely. That will never happen. Surely he has more sense than to even contemplate such an outcome. No one would receive him in society. People might not want to receive us either for that matter."

Sarah was silent. She thought that she had sown a few seeds and now would let them take root. For herself she would have preferred Forest to choose a young miss who was socially more assured, and who could make up for his abominable deficiencies in this area, but she had a strong feeling that this was the girl or no one. One could not dislike her or like her. There was very little one could grasp other than that she was young, plain, shy and appeared healthy. Her skin had a dreadful tendency to go blotchy and almost all afternoon she had been red from her collar up. But Forest had beamed upon her as if she were the most beautiful creature on earth. Her son was lost; she was convinced of it.

By the end of six months Mary had come round to thinking Forest Caldwell was the man for her. Her family liked him very well for no one ever felt the slightest discomfort in his presence. The passing time only increased Forest's eagerness for the state of blessed matrimony but he readily agreed with the Smileys that they should wait until Mary was sixteen.

William Caldwell employed threats, pleas, bullying and every manoeuver he knew, but nothing had been able to dissuade Forest from his intended, and, as Sarah had foreseen, he was prepared to become a merchant if that was what was required. At this blow William backed down with grudging grace and bought Forest the adjoining Townland of Largy/Fort Henry. It was considered best from the Smiley's point of view that the newlyweds have their own home apart from the Caldwells, and Mr. Smiley put up the wherewithal to bring that about. It was an arrangement that suited everyone admirably.

The marriage took place a year later; the year was 1810. The wedding was a modest affair and organized entirely by the bride's parents. William didn't know whether to be relieved or further annoyed. He felt very tempted to go on a trip and absent himself from the whole affair; only the prospect of missing the hunting season kept him at home. His wife took care that he should not hear any discussion of the forthcoming event which she was determined they would all attend with all graciousness possible.

Mary surprised everyone by looking almost beautiful on her wedding day. She had chosen a gown of amber satin which set off her colouring very well, but it was primarily the glow in her eyes and her cheeks that did it. Mary knew that Forest adored her and such confidence put an end to blotchy skin. Everyone was amazed at the composure of this young girl.

Over the years William became quite reconciled to his daughter-in-law as she provided him with three healthy grandsons and one granddaughter; by 1820 another child was on the way. Who would have thought that Forest had it in him?

The wave of emigration that commenced at the end of the Napoleonic Wars had reached a fever pitch by 1820. William paid little heed for he failed to contemplate that anyone in his family, which was well situated compared to many others, might wish to leave Ireland. He reckoned without taking into account a young man's wish for adventure.

Ernest and Harold had been getting themselves in and out of scrapes ever since they were let out of dresses. Now their latest bit of nonsense was that they wanted to see something of the world. If the war had still been on with Napoleon, they would have been content to go to war, but there was no way they were prepared to live out their lives under their father's thumb, suffering his disapproving glares. They hoped to bargain for their freedom, but if not they were prepared to grab it.

The popular route to freedom in that day was emigration and the two favoured destinations were Australia and British North America. For two years they had wrangled back and forth with their father without much success. He threatened to cut them off without a penny if they so much as mentioned emigration to him again. Finally, on a sunny day in June 1820, Ernest simply disappeared. There was no word for several days and then a messenger came with a letter. It was postmarked England. He had made his way across to Liverpool and was waiting now for a ship to take him to Australia. He had sold his horse and it was enough to cover his passage. When he got there he would see what could be done.

William knew he was beaten. Although he had threatened to disinherit Ernest, he now realized he would not see his son again and he wished to give him one last chance to make something of his life. So he sent off his brother Harold with funds to see the both of them to Australia and something extra to help them get started. He justified his capitulation by saying to his tearful wife that it was only a matter of time before Harold would follow him anyway so it was just as well that they went together. He mumbled to himself that they had chosen a penal colony for their lot in life, but possibly amongst thieves and murderers they would appear to be models of rectitude. He could do no more.

At first he missed the two rapscallions; their energy had infected the whole household. But after a few weeks he found that he did not miss them very much. They were determined to make their own way and he was getting to the age where he appreciated a little peace. He no longer had to look at two surly, morose young men at the dinner table. His home was his own once more and if his wife was off her feed, he expected she would get over it or keep it to herself. He would have little trouble from his remaining children. In this happy expectation he was only partly right.

Unknown to William, or even to his wife, Mary, Forest Caldwell was one of those family men who had approached George Argue to ask him to write them after he arrived in British North America. Forest asked George to advise him if it would be feasible for a man such as himself, with four young children, to immigrate to Upper Canada too.

ARGUE

DEPARTURE 1821

It was the first day of the third month of the year 1821. On the deck of the *Albion* stood Captain Andrews, a burly, grey haired man with his brow deeply furrowed. He was not happy about this voyage. Much of what met the Captain's troubled gaze was in no way unusual. Down on the wharf were piles of wooden barrels and boxes. He and his ship's purser were on hand to keep a sharp eye on those, to see that some did not slip away for destinations other than his ship, and also to watch for substitutions. This business of substituting poorer goods than that which he had ordered and paid for was so common as to have become a trade in itself. He thought he had the situation in hand this time but one could never be too sure. A few of his trusted sailors were down there, ostensibly to help load the goods, but their chief purpose was to see what he might miss and to give a signal. The rest of his sailors were safely on board ship. No sense risking disaster with those lads who could not be counted on to stay clear of the watering holes surrounding the piers. It was not his intent to sail with a bunch of half soused or to sail with less than his full crew. Captain Andrews was a very determined man. His chief determination was that no one would get the better of him and this gave him full time occupation. Fortunately for the ship's owners, crew, and passengers, he considered all that touched him to be part of his own interests.

He paid scant attention to the groups of people who huddled together on the wharf beside piles of belongings, waiting for the time to board. He tried to persuade himself that they were not his concern, not yet. The poor beggars did not know what they were getting in for, that much was certain or the wharf would be emptied but for a hardy few. In the back of his mind was what he had learned from his quick glimpse of the passenger list — too many women and children. He didn't like it, not at all. But those matters were not under his control and he sternly reminded himself to concentrate on what he could do something about, namely, getting the food on board to feed these miserable people, for miserable they would shortly be. Of that he had no doubt at all.

The *Albion* was not a vessel an ambitious man would be proud to captain, but one that, under a good captain and the grace of Providence, could do the job. The job was to get these emigrants from Belfast, Ireland to Quebec in British North America, and return to Southampton with a load of timber. From the ship owner's viewpoint, timber was more valuable than passengers, but they hoped to make money going both directions. Captain Andrews reminded himself that his goal was to satisfy the owners so that he might acquire a bigger and better ship before the year was out. To do so, he had to cope with a shipload of passengers, and cope he would, but inwardly he fumed, 'Passengers are naught but a nuisance. Time was when you had enough to do to manage your crew, and look out for the weather. That is precisely what I am going to put first on this voyage too, and no one, least of all a bunch of Irish peasants, is going to interfere.'

That year the *Albion* was one of the earliest ships to leave Irish shores for British North America. They were not the first group of emigrants, not by a few years, but up until this point most people leaving Ireland had first to cross the Irish Sea and set sail from Liverpool or the Clyde. Andrews' first voyage as a first mate had been from Edinburgh. The worst part of it was getting around the top of Scotland and then crossing the Irish Sea. This took three weeks and another week spent in port restoring the ship so that it could set sail again. Andrews was a man of medium to middling faith, if he were to live on land that is. As he had thrown his lot in with the sea, he did not think it wise to make too many pronouncements without acknowledging the power of the Almighty.

The ship's record of its passengers was a rather crude affair, giving only the head of the family or group and the total number of dependents. Two children under 14 counted as one adult. It went on until it totalled 407 passengers. It seemed impossible to get so many people, even if a few were small, into the ship's hold.

It was a modest ship of about 380 tons. About two years after this ship sailed, the British Government enacted the Passenger Act which stipulated that a ship could carry no more than three adult passengers for every four tons of admeasurement or 300 passengers on a ship of 400 tons. By the terms of that Act, the *Albion* was severely overcrowded. The Act also determined how much fresh water was to be carried per passenger and how much foodstuffs. By 1820 all children had to be inoculated against smallpox or they could not board the ship.

Rows of bunk beds, in two levels, had been attached to each side of the hold. More than two levels of bunks were unsafe in case someone was tossed out during a storm. The bunks were five feet in length and a little wider than in the crew's quarters; still this was crowded, but crowding into a bed was far from the worst of it. There were the slops, the bodily excrements from all these worthy people. The stench of so many unwashed bodies added to the accumulated odour of feces and vomit, was going to be a severe trial for everyone. The ship's hold was not a place the captain intended to visit. Imagination was more than enough.

The last of the ship's provisions had been loaded and stored below and the precious barrels of water were lashed to the deck. It was four hours to eventide when the ship was to sail. There was still enough time to give these men who had brought their families to this place a fair warning. He had struggled with his conscience on this point and decided to give the warning. He leaned over the ship's rail and bellowed down a megaphone,

"Ahoy below, let those men who are the leaders for each group now take heed. The ship's company will have told you that we will be taking a most direct route across the North Atlantic and that this voyage will last about four weeks. This we will not do. We are now in early spring; this is the first sailing of the year, and I will not put this ship into the North Atlantic if Providence and I can do otherwise. This is not the time for argument or discussion. What it means to you now is that this voyage may well be summat longer than you planned for, and that those among you who can purchase more provisions for yourselves would do well to do so now while you still have the chance. We sail on the tide at five this evening, and you will be on board by four."

He turned away so as not to encourage questions. He had done his duty by them, which was considerably more than he had been authorized to do by old Coolidge, who represented both the ship owners and the Colonial Office.

Coolidge, whom Captain Andrews regarded as a mincing petty clerk, said, "We've sent out information telling them to expect a four week sail time at the most. If we turn around now and say six weeks or more, half of them may drop out and there simply isn't time to fill up the ship with substitutes. Not but what there aren't plenty to be found. There is a waiting list, but no time left for them to ready themselves."

There was little point in reminding the man that he had warned his employers of the hazards of an early crossing in the North Atlantic, and they had all smarmed nicely back and said, "Ooch man, you're in charge of all that and we put our trust in you. If you need to go south for the safety of the ship, then do it my good man. We're behind you all the way." Then they had gone off and not changed a bloody thing. Their idea of being behind him meant staying well behind on shore, and that suited him just as well. The thought of having one of those *lords* on board was more than a man could stomach.

When safely away from the rail, he looked again to see if any were to take his advice. After what seemed to be a very brief conversation, one man detached himself from the group and headed off. After a few more minutes of wrangling a few others followed him. He made a note of that man, as he was the first to show common sense, the first to follow the advice of one who clearly knew what was ahead.

It was with no small amount of anxiety that George Argue heard the Captain's words. Instead of four weeks on board they now had to think of six, or maybe more. He knew their supplies would not last and what was worse, many in his charge did not have the amount of foodstuffs he had. Each family could only have so many chattels with them and the women were loath to leave everything they held dear behind them. If he brought another barrel of oatcakes and more salt beef and flour, they would have to leave behind a barrel of dishes. He was pretty sure that some of the women would give him a hard time. He almost wished Mary would be one of the protestors, but she had distanced herself from everything that was going on. Did she not

50

know that he was suffering too? Thank God his children were past their first years. And thank God for Anne Wilson too. He could count on her to talk sense when sense was needed.

When he returned with the extra foodstuffs it was clear that some re-packing was necessary. Some of their precious books would have to be left behind; only the Holy Bible would remain. Moses found himself carrying his accordion after all. A woman Mary didn't know rushed to pick up her teapot. Others on the dock scrambled to pick up what they discarded. Anne hoped that her daughter would not have to meet up with that teapot in the New World, gracing another woman's table. They were all down to the basics and, though it may have been wise, it was very hard. They had given up all they had to go to this New World. Mary scarcely seemed to notice.

ARGUE

THE VOYAGE 1821

They were all aboard by four o'clock that afternoon; the gangplanks were raised, and they were separated from Ireland. At five o'clock they were tugged out into the harbour, and when they were out of the way of other vessels, their sails were lifted. To the people straining for a last glimpse of Ireland, the shores were quickly lost as darkness fell. For a few moments there was a strange hush over the crew and passengers. Then a shout from the first mate told the men to get on with their work, and the spell was broken.

Captain Andrews was busy for the first hour, and when he felt he could leave the running of the ship safely in the hands of the first mate, he turned to the loathsome task of sorting out his passengers. By this time most of them had gone below decks where they were told they would spend the voyage. The women were quarrelling over the bunks and the space available to each party. Some voices were getting a bit shrill and the husbands, who had left their wives to themselves to arrange the domestic matters, were by this time even more reluctant to get involved. The Captain, who did not have to live with any of these good women, did not hesitate.

"That will do for now," he roared and a silence fell. "There will be one bunk for a family of four or five adult sized people. More will have to be accommodated if the children are under fourteen. There is not room for comfort. Understand that. You will have to take turns resting on the bunk. You can see as plain as the nose on your face, there will be no luxurious accommodations. As for cooking, you may use the stove here at one end, taking turns. I shall appoint someone to rule over that, if it becomes a problem for you, but I would strongly advise you not to let it become a problem. I do not intend to come down here to sort you out again. If the stove becomes a matter for quarrels, we can solve that by its removal. There is one cabin on the deck which has not yet been spoken for and which can be obtained for 20 pounds. It can hold four adults comfortably but more at your own wish.

"Now for the times when you may go above decks: you can be above when and as the weather allows. You cannot interfere with the work of the crew and I may have to insist that you stay below when or if that occurs. There will be no candles allowed betwixt decks. In the case of bad weather there will be no cooking and no lanterns lit. The portholes and hatches may have to be closed as the weather dictates. We are not our own masters on board ship. We are at the mercy of Nature and the Almighty. I would advise you to acquaint yourselves with your necessities and study good management."

He turned and immediately reached for the ladder to go up to the deck. Then he looked about quickly, spotted George Argue and beckoned him. "Are you the leader of your group?" he asked.

"Aye, I am," George replied.

Then he called out, "Who else is responsible for a group of people?" When six more men had come forward he said to them, "I want you to take charge until this melee is sorted out. If there are any problems, report to me, but I would prefer it if I hear little from you, if you take my meaning." His deep scowl left little doubt as to his meaning.

"And one more thing. Water will be rationed from now. The ration is to be three pints of water per adult per day and that will include what is used for cooking. To ensure that the rule is followed, it will be given out on deck by the crew each morning. I see some of your people already look green and glassy. Such folk will be sick for most of the journey, for we have not had a touch of what is to come. Tell them to eat as much as they can and to endure. That will be all."

They did not see the Captain again for many days. By this time they had learned a few things. There was no need to undress for bed. It was so cold at night that it was best to leave on all the clothes available. Four adults to a bed no longer

53

seemed such a hardship and, in any case, it was the least of one's worries. The chief worry seemed to be the state of your bowels or your stomach. There were some who seemed to be out in their bowels from the beginning, and then there were larger numbers who were keeping nothing on their stomachs.

Two more things conspired against them. The stench from the smell of so many bodies and the excrements and slops thereof, robbed one of description. No wonder even the hearty gagged and heaved themselves up onto the deck, anything for better air. The women were left to tend the sick as well as they could, so there was little fresh air for them. George and the other men became very worried about them and about the future. This was only the fourth day.

The second, and even more grievous issue, was the quality of the food. Those who had brought no food of their own fared the worst. After the first week the water tasted as if it had been in the cask for six months. The biscuits were often mouldy, the good ones on the top of the barrel and poor ones below. It was necessary to eat, but small wonder that their bowels were out of order. The cook, who was a surly fellow, thought that cooking for this group of Irish, was well beneath his status, and the soup, which he served up to them, was mostly poor quality water and foul to taste. Where was the beef they had seen loaded onto the ship?

After a few days at sea Anne noted with great relief that none of her family seemed prone to nausea. To be sure, the food and water were not all that you could wish for, and George had counselled that they needed to keep the bulk of their own rations for emergency supplements. When Mary began to recognize that the situation could become dangerous if they did not look after themselves, she roused herself to insist that her family must accept the food they were offered. There was to be no dissent on that score. Her chief concern was for her youngest boy, John, who had always been the most delicate of her children. Quietly, she slipped the better parts of her food to him. It was not so easy to persuade Anne Wilson to accept the nourishment offered. Anne sought instead to reduce her exertions and to eat less. The chief result of little water and scant rations was constipation, which before long led to biliousness. Each of the family was firmly counselled, 'What cannot be prevented must be endured and your plight is better than that of many others.' The obvious truth of that statement was all around them.

At first, the men who were able to get up on deck, went there, and stayed as long as possible, but after a bit they began to worry about their women. If they were to survive the journey, they needed some relief. A few of the men volunteered to remain below or look after the children on the deck. As often as they could, they carried the most wretched ones to the deck to let them have better air and see if this could improve their disposition. After a bit the crew began to grumble about so many invalids and children under foot. The experiment was sorely limited in order to keep the peace.

At one end of the hold there was a space allocated to a preacher, the Reverend Mr. Tindale, from Scotland. How he and his family came to be on this ship was soon ferreted out. He was to go to Perth in Upper Canada to a military settlement there. So anxious were they to have a preacher in that part that they had prevailed upon him to find the earliest possible passage to British North America. To do so he had come to Ireland and prepared himself to travel with people with whom he expected to find little in common. He dedicated part of each day to writing a journal about his observations. He had plenty of things to impart to any would be emigrants. Would that he had been able to read something of the sort himself, before embarking on this journey.

He recorded,[7]

The first night on board there was a great deal of levity and high spirits. Twenty-two young ones danced and fiddled as if they had not a care in the world. I fear I am in the midst of an ungodly set, which in some respects fears neither God nor man, but praised be, the Lord has blessed me with a better mind. The next day by noon hour there was a different tune. The celebrations of the night before combined with the rolling of the sea brought forth a steady moan from these poor wretches. But those who held themselves to be at the end of their extremity soon learned how relative all things are. We encountered squalls, rain and lightning and great billows and thought that we

---

[7] The following excerpts are based on letters in the Public Archives, written by a Rev. Bell, a Presbyterian minister who came to Perth from Scotland at roughly the same period. The sentiments expressed here are similar but the wording is not exact.

had already endured the worst that could befall us. When water lashed the decks, it poured down the hatches and soon the hold was awash with water. Still some of our members begged not to have the hatches shut for fear we might suffocate and in some respects the water was welcomed for a clean up ensued when the squall was over. We still did not know the full meaning of a sea voyage.

Another day he wrote:

A whale the size of our ship was observed right beside our vessel. What a mercy we are preserved to the present moment.

Eight days out of Belfast they were struck by a savage storm and soon learned all that it might mean. Everyone was sent below immediately; the hatches were battened down, the portholes sealed shut. It was as black as pitch inside and the sounds were fearful indeed. The wind howled and every now and then there was a crash on the deck; everyone cowered, fearful of what it might mean. Was the ship being torn apart? Soon there was enough going on in the hold to keep everyone occupied. Trunks and smaller pieces of luggage began to roll back and forth. Even barrels, which had been lashed down, broke free and became a terrible hazard. One could not see, but only guess where the objects were. Most people tried to keep to their bunks as being the safest place but not everyone could find their place in such a melee.

As suddenly as it started it was over, and everyone breathed prayers of thankfulness. Presently the hatches were opened and they were allowed on deck. There they viewed a scene of total chaos. Passengers, who had been allowed to store a barrel of belongings on the main deck, soon had a full view of everything they owned. Barrels, even those lashed securely, had broken from their moorings and swept down the deck, destroying everything in their path. Heaps of belongings, broken crockery, hats, shoes, basins, cooking utensils, and books had all been cast to the elements. Little could be salvaged. Women ran to and fro trying to gather up what they could, but where could it be stored? When what could be saved had been gathered up, the rest was sent overboard by the crew. One's belongings were now perceived quite differently, as an encumbrance at best and a hazard at worst. Now Anne Wilson could rest in peace about that dratted tea set. It had not been destined for the New World.

There was no ship's surgeon, but the first mate doubled for that duty and was called upon to set a broken arm of one of the women. He offered her a swig of rum, which she promptly refused. As he set about his work she just as promptly swooned, which was the preferred state for setting bones.

Another lesson was not long in coming. The following morning one of the women was trying to melt some tallow in a pot when the whole business caught fire and the flames shot as high as the opening to the hold. The shrieks alerted a passing sailor who leapt down the ladder, grabbed the pot and threw the whole lot into the sea, burning both hands badly in the process. The Captain now forbade the use of the stove by the passengers for the duration of the voyage. For added insurance he removed it from the hold and lashed it to the deck. He was not prepared to allow a passel of witless idiots to burn the whole ship. The cook alone would use the stove and then only when the weather was not too rough. This was a severe deprivation but the episode had so frightened the passengers that it was accepted better than the Captain would have expected. Not that it mattered. His word was the last one.

The preacher was moved to record:

At sea it is easy to discover the natural disposition of your fellow travellers. They soon lay aside all reserve. Some conduct themselves as seriously as the last Sabbath. Some are now saying that there must be some reason why the Almighty saw fit to punish us with such a storm and next a fire. What had been the sins which had brought about these troubles?

Well, when one is looking for sin the harvest is always good. The sailors swear regularly. No one makes a serious attempt to keep the Sabbath; passengers shave, clean their shoes, mend their clothes; the sailors clean the deck and mend the rigging as they see fit on that day. I have spoken to the Captain about this conduct, but he did not seem to be too disturbed about the behaviour of his crew. Even those who claim to have some connection to God have been observed to sin under the conditions we now endure. A man here, who claims that he is a preacher of some sort, was overheard by the First Mate to swear a few days back. He had offered to preach to the crew but when the First Mate reported his language to the Captain, his offer was firmly rejected.

As for the ordinary run of the passengers they are no better than they should be. There is much grumbling and even a few fights have broken out. While one can hardly blame them for complaining about the food and provisions, it is surely typical of that sort of person who will, at the first opportunity blame God and all his workers for the fact that they did not see fit to properly provision themselves in the first place. Now they are dependent upon the bounty of the ship provisions and not liking it one whit. Perhaps after this experience they will be more inclined to think soberly and attend services on the Sabbath.

The Reverend Mr. Tindale had offered to conduct services to crew and passengers together and a goodly number accepted his offer. He delivered a good harangue, exhorting all to examine their consciences and to guide their conduct in a manner befitting the Christians they professed to be.

Let us not so inflame the Almighty that He will leave us to our just deserts in our peril. It should be obvious even to the meanest intelligence that we have failed to do all that is pleasing to Him and we are being chastised by Misfortune. Let us beg His Forgiveness and bend ourselves to Obedience. I have heard language unfit for the ears of women and children and those of us with finer sensibilities. And even if such persons were not present, God is always listening. Take heed and act accordingly.

There was little to give joy or elevate the spirit from that message, but fear that Mr. Tindale was God's spokesman caused many to think it more prudent to walk on a narrow path and there was a visible increase in Sabbath attendance. As for the chapelgoers, they attended the service on the Sunday morning, but in the evening, when Reverend Tindale volunteered his services again, they murmured that they would be having their own service, and they met in their corner of the hold where they prayed and read Scripture as best they could. Some of them felt that Reverend Tindale's sermon was very timely, and if the precepts were followed, they would all have a deal less trouble, but others yearned for some words of encouragement. Everyone felt that they were being put to the test hourly.

For the most part religious differences scarcely mattered, and no one had any energy to spare in that direction. In the Cavan group, Jeremiah Scott and Tim Wiggins seemed to be fitting in well. They were, in the main, quiet living men, and if their beliefs did not coincide with the beliefs of the majority, they took care not to raise such issues or to be underfoot when prayer meetings were being held. Not so easily blended were the last two to join the band of emigrants, James Faulkner and Jock Kennedy. Kennedy was a skilled carpenter and James Faulkner was a blacksmith. When they showed a desire to join up, the reaction from the rest of the group was not quite what George had expected, for these two were Catholics, or at least they ran on the outside of that fold. Kennedy had been heard to swear that religion was something he could do without and Faulkner said nothing, but did not seem to have strong feelings on the subject one way or another. What could one make of a person like that? They had pressed hard to go, and were men full of confidence in their ability to make a go of things wherever they were set down. Indeed, as they had made a go of it in Ireland, and had provided well for their families, they had every right to make such a boast. As far as the original group was concerned, the decision to accept non-chapel members had already been made after Scott and Wiggins had been accepted and future decisions rested on more pragmatic grounds. No one could deny that these two men were skilled tradesmen and that these skills were going to be sorely needed in the new settlements. On these grounds they were accepted with little fuss.

Once Rose Faulkner was on board ship and had seen the place where all were to be accommodated, she revealed a less sanguine disposition than her husband. When the Captain told them of an available cabin for the journey she prevailed upon her husband to establish herself and their three young ones there. Mary Kennedy had no such pull with Jock. He declared in response to her timid pleas that what those prayer-mouthing chapelgoers could do, he and his could do also. The New World would bring them few comforts. Right now was the time to get used to giving up those comforts they had enjoyed.

After a few days in the hold Jock began to hear a different tune, but he kept all the notes of this song to himself. Thoughts he had refused admission before, now besieged him constantly. Mary had never been overly strong and she had shown little spirit for this venture. They had lost four children, their first two to diphtheria and two who were stillborn. Their family consisted of a girl, now eight, who clung to her mother's skirts, and a healthy little boy who was two years old and his father's joy. When Faulkner had urged Jock to have Mary and the children join his wife in the cabin, Jock had refused. His pride would not let him submit so quickly after his claims, even though he had made these claims to no one but his wife who would have been only too happy to forget them.

And so another week passed. The children cried for potatoes but there were no potatoes. It was hard to get them to take what food was available, and yet it was evident that they must have the nourishment. As for the food the cook gave them, it grew steadily worse. The water was hard to manage in stomachs already afflicted with seasickness. The cook seemed determined not to give them any beef until that too was not fit for use.

Many began to feel that if they had known even a ha'p'orth[8] of what they would have to endure on this voyage they would never have embarked. Those who were still desperately ill prayed for deliverance by death. And then there came deliverance of a sort, a deadly calm. Many greeted the calm as an answer to prayer, but it was not a deliverance that suited the Captain at all well.

He kept his worries to himself, however, and he had no need to share them with his crew in any case. When the group leaders approached him to open the portholes he agreed. The men lowered buckets and water for washing was available for the first time since they set sail. Women and men who were able, washed, and those who had been ill the longest were now able to take some nourishment. But they noticed that the water was below the halfway mark and the Captain decreed that it would be rationed more tightly. With each day of calm his gloom deepened until everyone who saw him knew that the Captain was worried.

They were now entering the fourth week and the end of their journey seemed nowhere in sight. The word came down from Captain Andrews, "Ration the water once more."

---

[8] A hae'penny or half penny's worth

The calm continued for two more days, and then the gentlest of breezes crept up. This was not enough to gladden the heart of a seaman, but enough to encourage those who were praying.

Mary Kennedy was one of those who had been ill from the outset of the voyage. Her daughter had clung to her mother's side and now she seemed to be equally afflicted. Jock had become a stone. His son was still in reasonable shape for Jock had kept him at his side up on the deck and out of the putrid air of the hold as much as possible. He got the best of any food that Jock could find. Now, when it looked that Mary would die and his daughter too, he gave up his son to Rose Faulkner to care for, but it was too late for Mary and little Tessa. They died within a few hours of each other.

It was difficult to approach Jock, but inhuman to avoid him. Tindale's offer to provide a service for the burial at sea had been greeted with an oath from Kennedy. Faulkner asked Jock if Captain Andrews could say a few words. Jock, who was nearly beyond caring for his own life, just looked at him mutely. Faulkner took that for assent and went to speak to the Captain about it.

Captain Andrews grunted, "I'd as leave you asked Argue to handle the honours here. He is your leader and a lay deacon I believe. I have my hands full just now, so to speak." Faulkner asked George, who agreed.

It was an intolerable situation. Jock stood apart from everyone, holding his son in his arms, the wind blowing his fair hair across his face. He stared straight out to the horizon, oblivious of what was happening. On the faces of those who stood by the rail was grief for the mother and her child, mixed feelings towards Jock, and an overriding fear for what was to become of them all.

Captain Andrews was only vaguely aware of the ceremony on the deck below. His gaze and all his interest focused upon the hair blowing across Jock's face. He looked to the telltale ribbons and sure enough, they were lifting strongly for the first time in ten days. It had seemed so much longer. His fears of famine aboard this voyage had been very strong, but to say the word aloud was to invite disaster. He felt a tight string around his diaphragm easing and he drew a deep breath.

The sails filled with wind and the ship moved smartly

through the waves. Among the passengers there were sighs of relief and murmurs of thanks, but fear and grief were still too powerful to allow much room for other emotions. The wind continued to grow in strength until it seemed they were riding into another storm. Some of the non-believers sneered at those who had prayed too well, but their sneers were short lived. Presently everyone was gabbling prayers for the survival of the ship.

How was it that so many people had willingly thrust themselves into such a perilous voyage? The answer was they would not have done so if they'd had a more accurate estimate of the dangers. But on the other hand, to place oneself in the hands of fate or of God was not an unusual concept for anyone. Life and death seemed to be very much a matter beyond one's control. If one got sick, one died or got better, not so much in relation to the cures applied, but more so according to success of the prayers. It all depended upon the mysterious Will of God. What the Methodists had going for them, at least those who had experienced a personal conversion, was a sense of God's presence and confidence that life after this one would be with God, and therefore better than the one here on earth. It was, of course, a little harder on those who had no personal faith, and who had to live in the shadow of such confidence. On board ship they were both thrust cheek and jowl fern'st one another, a trying experience for all.

They lay lashed to their bunks, the lanterns out, no sound from within but whimpers and wails. *If God wants to drown us all would He please do so right now. We have suffered enough.* The sounds from without were the roar of the wind, the lashing of the waves against their ship, and the occasional ominous banging. The ship tilted this way and plunged that way, alarming even the most courageous. Few of these travellers had ever contemplated swimming, and those who knew how did not find that fact one bit consoling.

The rocking back and forth threw some of the people right out of their bunks and placed a terrible strain on the fastenings of the bunks to the sides of the ship. Finally a row of bunks on the starboard of the hold broke free, hurling all of the occupants out onto the floor with the bunks crashing down on top of them. The screams were fearsome. In the pitch darkness it was necessary to try to lift the bunks up to remove the ones pinned underneath. It was certain there were broken and bruised limbs but nothing could be done about their condition until the storm was over.

Captain Andrews had weathered worse and felt he and his crew would make it through unless the storm worsened, but he was less certain about those in the hold. None of them were strong enough to take much more of this. Gradually the roughness of the wind settled down to a steady blow, and the ship scudded through the waters at a wonderful rate. Those in the hold gradually came to realize they had come safely through another trial, but they still could not move about safely or help those who had been injured.

One of the leaders went to try and open the hatch, but it was still fastened shut. Banging on the cover made no difference. A few hours later the hatch was opened and George Argue asked to see the Captain to learn something of the condition of the ship, and get some help for the injured in the hold. He made his way carefully for the ship tilted fearfully to one side. Captain Andrews, although he had been on watch for the most part of twenty hours and had not slept for more than that, looked quite chipper, better than he had for a few weeks.

"Well, Argue, it looks as if those prayers are being answered, and not before time. If things keep going at this rate we may see land within a week, and then again we may not. It all depends upon the wind. But you could take a message of hope to your people in the hold. Maybe hope is what they need right now to get them through to the end. I am about to break my fast. Have a sup with me. You look as though you could use it."

George's mouth watered at the sight of the food as he slowly sat down. The dry bread and salt pork tasted fine indeed, but when he thought of the mouldy damp biscuits which was all that was left to some, and of the last fare served to them by the cook — putrid beef cooked in stinking water, rotten Dutch cheese as bitter as soot and bread partly alive — he choked.

Andrews, reading his thoughts clearly, said, "Never mind about feeding yourself. You must keep up your strength for others."

He was quite willing to believe this, but it took all pleasure from the food. He could take but a few mouthfuls for his stomach was now so shrunk and unused to food that he could manage no more.

Andrews asked, "How goes the water?"

"It is very low and what is left is not fit for consumption."

"It will not be cast out. I'll give you some rum to add to the water, and give each person a small portion each day. Guard it well. Come back to me if you run out. And if at the last you have only rum, then you must drink that alone. This is no time to let thy religious scruples hold sway. I'll tell you, Argue, this has been a rum journey. Aye, that's what we call it when the journey is too long, the water is nearly gone, and all that pulls the men through is that tot of rum. If you want your people to pull through, give them a tot of rum too. And don't worry yourself about them getting a liking for it. If they pull through this siege I doubt they'll want to see rum or anything else that will remind them of this voyage for a long time."

The force of this argument was not lost on George who realized that many in the hold were at their extremity. He registered the irony of the Captain thanking them for their prayers and then telling them to forget their folly of abstinence, but such inconsistencies were too trifling to dwell upon.

For the next seven days they experienced fair weather with a steady breeze, and many who had finally gained their sea legs had recovered sufficiently to be thankful for the change in the weather. The only event to take precedence over concern for the weather was the birth of two infants. The Scottish preacher offered the use of his small compartment for the confinements and everyone agreed it was very handsome of him to do so for he looked very poorly himself. Jessie Halliday, whose family was part of the Cavan group and who was only a mite of a person herself, gave birth to a little girl. The babe was small for full term but delivery was easier because of that. The other baby was also a wee girl and both mother and child lay quietly. One hardly knew two more children had been added to the ship's list. The chief concern was getting extra nourishment for the two mothers to enable them to nurse their infants. It looked touch and go. Samuel Halliday endeavoured to give up his ration of water but since there was only enough for survival for each person, the problem had to be solved by appealing to the Captain for extra rations for these two women. He grumbled about those who had no more sense than to bring women who were in a family way on board his ship, but he granted the extra rations.

It was to be another three days before they sighted anything encouraging, and then it was birds, birds so plentiful that they blocked out the sun for a while. They were called stormy petrels, a sailor said, because you could see large flocks of them just before a storm. One man wished he could bring one down and eat it, but the sailors said they had poor fishy taste and were not worth the energy used to fetch one, even if it were possible.

By this time a man from another group had been put to his resting place over the edge of the ship. This time George had been asked to say a few words of blessing as Rev. Tindale was looking very peaked and was not seen scribbling away in his book any more. The strongest were exhausted and ill; those who were poorly from the beginning looked to be at death's door and the little ones were lying limp and quiet.

John McFadden, George Argue's servant boy, crept about, attempting to help others as best he could, but there was little anyone could do. He was fortunate to have a strong stomach and could pretty well handle any bit of food he managed to get. He had known hunger in the past, but nothing compared to this. He had begged to come on this journey, thinking he had nothing to lose in leaving Ireland for he was an orphan, and if he had any kin who cared about him at all, they had never made themselves known. The closest thing he had known of family was the Argues, but now everyone was turned inward and scarcely had a word to say. He felt that no one had a thought for him at all. Never had he felt more frightened or more alone. Even Anne Wilson, who of all the family had taken the most notice of him, now lay on the bunk night and day, not making a sound. Occasionally her lips moved and he guessed she was praying. She looked every day of seventy.

Then one misty morning when the fog lifted a bit, they sighted icebergs. They scarcely knew what that meant, and Argue and Tindale went to speak to the Captain. He was reluctant to tell them that this meant good news. By his reckoning they were close to the shores of Newfoundland. This was not where he would have liked to be for he did not plan to attempt a landing there. But it did mean that they were closer to land and he decided to let them carry that much encouragement to the passengers.

The next day brought more good news: a sailor on the

watch had sighted land. It was now too shrouded in mist for others to see it, but the news was enough. A cry like a raven croaking went up from parched throats. The word spread rapidly to those below, 'land had been sighted'. Hope began to burn more strongly. A message was sent down by the first mate to say that they were not going to attempt a landing here. It was Newfoundland and at this point very treacherous, but the news was good. If the winds held they should sight the coast of Nova Scotia in a day or two at the most and they would make for Halifax to get new supplies and fresh water.

The spurt of hope was dampened to a weak flame. But the leaders of each group went about saying as many words of encouragement as they could muster. They realized that these next few days were crucial.

Two full days later they sailed into the port of Halifax. All those with sufficient strength were lined up against the railing from early morning until they landed at mid-afternoon. The sight was greeted with overwhelming relief and an undercurrent of dismay. The harbour was safe, the boat was relatively steady and the Promised Land was a dreary looking heap of shacks perched in the mud. It was May 21, 1821. They had been on the sea for almost twelve weeks.

The provisions had been inadequate from the beginning. The Captain had ordered the provisions to be increased to allow for a voyage of eight weeks and water for twelve weeks. Unfortunately, despite his precautions, he was cheated, and some of the provisions had not been fit for use. And the passengers, having had no notion of what lay ahead, had not husbanded the bad food and water from the outset, with the result that they lost a portion of what had been provided. It was always in doubt whether the quality of the food contributed to their problems as much as it alleviated them, dysentery and nausea being the chief results of eating the ship's food. It had been the Captain's warning, heeded by a prudent few, which had brought them though. Those better foodstuffs added to the ship's provisions had made the difference between life and death for the majority.

The first thought was to get ashore, but once again the Captain told them that only the sailors would be going ashore at first. They brought fresh water back on deck. Those first drinks were like the honey and nectar they had hoped for in this country. At least it was a land flowing with water. Strengthened and heartened by the water, about five men asked if they could go on shore to buy some provisions. Captain Andrews, having been assured no plague was flourishing in the settlement, gave them permission.

He added a warning, "Don't be gulled by those merchants you meet up with. Examine everything you buy. At this time of year there will be no fresh food except fish. If you bring that back I will see that the cook prepares it for you in a soup. The ship will provide enough fresh water until we reach Quebec. The prices will be above all reason and the goods shoddy; the flour may be wormy, but still usable for all that."

They found it was pretty much as the Captain had said it would be, and they silently thanked him for preparing them. They haggled as best they could but the merchants knew they had the upper hand. These gaunt, grey men were no match for them. Food they must have, and must pay whatever they had to pay. The men were disgusted with what they could bring back, but with good water to mix with the flour at least they could provide some nourishment to strengthen their families.

ARGUE

RIVER TRAVEL 1821

The next few days as they entered the Gulf of St Lawrence, they were rarely out of sight of land and soon were sailing close enough to shore to get a look at the farms. Where were the farms? All they could see was bush, dark green, wet forest right to the edge of the shore. They had never beheld anything like it before. They had heard of the abundance of trees in the New World, but they had never imagined anything like this.

As the river narrowed they saw a school of large white porpoises. They were so big that many people were afraid that everything, from trees to fish, was to be of giant proportions in this country. The sailors teased them for a bit, but then told them that they were white whales or dolphins, but they did not know the name. Sights such as these and good fresh air along with better water and lots of it brought colour back to the cheeks of a few passengers. But most felt that it was far too soon to forget the scare they had all had and were too fearful to speak aloud of good fortune at this stage.

When they landed at Quebec, Captain Andrews sent for the leaders of the various groups. "Your journey is now nearly over and the worst part is behind you. Once you and your belongings are unloaded you can arrange for a ship to take you up river to Montreal. It will cost you a bit but I understand that the fare will be good, and it will help build you up for the last stage of your journey. Now if any of you have young men who are fit and willing, I can offer them the job of unloading here. I think you will do better to have the women and children stay on board until you have made arrangements for them to stay at a hostel or better yet, to board the riverboat. You will find conditions on shore a bit rough. It has been a challenge to arrive on this side of the ocean in one piece and you have done well. Congratulations and best wishes for the next stage." He was heartily glad to have finished this voyage, to rid himself of all passengers and to acquire a hull filled with timber for the return trip.

The young men went forward to get their first job in the New World, bursting with pride and enthusiasm. Nothing would get them down now. Young men who were able-bodied were paid to assist with the unloading; even Andrew Argue, at age 13, proudly joined the elite.

Group leaders were first off after the unloading. At the bottom of the gangplank they waded into mud up to their ankles. Shops lining the shore were high up the bank on drier land. Some of them had a wooden boardwalk in front of them but this was a disconnected affair. Since one had to heave oneself up out of the dirt to walk on it, then let oneself down on the other end, it was scarcely worth the bother. Shops sometimes had wooden floors and sometimes not. In either case the floors were uneven and goods were stacked topsy-turvy. As dismaying as this was to the newcomers it was where business had to be conducted. The sturdiest of the shops, one with a large well-made sign and a verandah at the front, announced itself to be the Montreal-Quebec Shipping Co. The ship that was to take them to Montreal was at the pier. The clerk told them that for an extra consideration they could board the boat in the afternoon and they would sail the next morning. Or they could take a cart or carriage up to Upper Quebec and find a room there for the night. It was all one to the manager of the company.

Some of the men were for staying in Lower Quebec and boarding the next ship straightaway. Others said they thought that their wives would be better pleased to have a night off a boat and opted to go to Upper Town. Surely that would give a better aspect on the town altogether and put everyone in a better frame of mind. From the Cavan group only the Faulkner family chose Upper Town and the rest had to content themselves to hear about the impressive buildings, the glorious view and the better air on the heights.

The next part of the journey put the travellers in better

spirits for the food was good and the passage smooth. The cost was three pounds each, Halifax currency, which all agreed was scandalous, but could do nothing but pay for it. The passengers who had no funds, and who already owed Captain Andrews for some of their board on the *Albion,* had their way paid by the Government. They were expected to repay these monies to the *Albion* and the Government of Upper Canada as soon as they could. Those who had been brought to the point where death seemed kinder than living, were too far gone to pay the slightest heed to this further difficulty. All they hoped for now was burial in the firm soil instead of a permanent resting place at the bottom of the ocean.

Unfortunately, the first impression of Montreal was another letdown. Montreal was a flat muddy shore, with not even a platform on which to stack their boxes and belongings. Several carters came up and cheerfully offered to move their belongings where they wished. A few had to accept their offers of help but when others saw how carelessly the carters handled the boxes and how much they charged for destroying the goods, they looked to the young men of their own group to help them instead. The carters were good-natured, cussed and swore happily, catered to no one and charged an exorbitant price. Happy was the man who could do without the services of such workers who had no sense of what was proper.

By this time it was evident that several people who had been on the ship had been mortally weakened by the voyage. One woman appeared well one day and had declared she was glad to have survived the journey. She had a strong flush to her features. That evening she complained of a terrible headache and clearly she had a very high fever. Her husband was left to tend to her. The next morning he woke to find her dead and their son sickening with a fever too. By the following day the son was also dead. The poor man was not able to give them a decent burial. No one knew what had taken them so quickly but they began to wish they could leave that place very quickly.

Little John McFadden expressed everyone's fears most accurately when he groaned, "This air, it do be damp and cold, and like to give us all a deathly illness."

Whether they would leave or not they had to wait some days before they could arrange transport up the Ottaways River.[9]

River.[9] They spent their waiting days trying to get as far as they could from that wretched waterfront. They climbed up the mountain and learned that Montreal was on an island. They also learned that these inferior houses and shops, which had been established for many years, now represented civilization in British North America. They would not find as much where they were going. They compared prices and learned that a stove which could be had for five pounds in Ireland cost twenty five pounds in Montreal, if indeed it could be had at any price. Flour was twice as much but this was the spring of the year and the price changed weekly. Cloth also was expensive. Now they could clearly see what it was they should have brought with them, but their informants had not seen fit to tell them. The women vowed to have their own sheep and make their own cloth. Cottons were a luxury they would have to do without.

The men were busy with their own preoccupations and were easily persuaded that, along with fishing equipment, they must have a gun in the wilderness to obtain food for the table and for protection. These items were essential, easy to carry and were added to their bundles of belongings. The next matter was to acquire the needed skills.

Transportation from Montreal up the Ottaways River was to be in an open boat called a bateau, much like a barge with a sturdy pole and sail in the middle. Their belongings were piled on haphazardly and the men of their company had to secure them more strongly. It was not the concern of these boatmen or the carters whether their belongings were safe or scattered to the elements. Several people had to leave boxes containing furniture behind them, as there was no room for themselves, their families and these large containers. The carters said they would send them on later to Richmond's Landing, but most said goodbye to them. Now everyone could understand why it was folly to try to take one's treasures to this place. Life itself was precarious; it was folly to think of anything beyond it.

The time was early June and the air off the water was chilling to the bone. The boatmen seemed not to notice it and stood up on the boat with their shirts open at the neck, commenting that spring was here at last when it had looked like

---

[9] Originally it was called the Outaouais River, after the native tribe in that part and later known as the Ottaways River or sometimes the Grand River.

it might not come at all this year. The women huddled together trying to draw heat from one another and when the rains came, they found shelter under tarpaulins. Every mother on board suffered fears for their children who by now were recovering sufficiently to regard this as another adventure. They had lost their fear of the water and were harder to restrain than they had been on the *Albion*. At least there had been a railing on the *Albion* and from that point of view it now seemed to be a comparative bastion of safety. Already the special horrors of that journey were beginning to fade as new ones were thrust upon them.

At places where large rafts of squared timber were coming down river to Montreal, the boatmen hugged close to shore for safety and frequently used oars as well as sail to make their way against the current. At night they pulled over to camp and made fires on the shore for cooking. The boatmen provided the fires and a few large pots and then left them to it to cook what they could. Appetites were strong and burned oatcakes were greeted eagerly. At least the water was good and one day they pulled over while it was still daylight and two of the boatmen went hunting and came back with a deer. It made a tasty stew and the boatmen were glad to share their hunt in return for the women's cooking. Spirits lifted as they began to believe that whatever else might come, they would not starve in this land.

Gigantic flocks of birds winging their way north at times darkened the sky and the men took out their muskets to try to shoot down a few. The boatmen said that they were passenger pigeons and would make a fine dish if you could catch enough of them. There was a contest to see who could bring down a few and to bring them down where they could be retrieved. There was little success in this first endeavour at hunting.

Then came a spate of rough waters where they were told that they all had to disembark and walk on the shore while the boat was being pulled up stream. Four teams of local oxen were hired at this point, where farmers had them waiting at the shore for this purpose. The women and children walked, except for Anne Wilson and Jessie Halliday, who was still too weak to get out and carry her new baby. The men took ropes and pulled along with the oxen, as the current carrying them downstream to Montreal was very strong. Not for the first time, the boatmen told them they had come at the worst time of year. The spring breakup was late this year. At the end of April they could have driven up the river on solid ice, but now they must contend with swollen waters, huge square timber rafts and muddy banks piled with debris deposited by the swiftly flowing waters.

The women looked anxiously for evidence of farm life and a picture of what their future life might be. They saw precious little. Occasionally there was a small log cabin with other smaller cabins around it and nothing but stumps of trees around the cabins. Occasionally they saw small children running about and a woman toiling over an open fire outdoors, then nothing more for a distance, until the same thing all over again. There was nothing like a village unless more than one cabin constituted a village. They comforted themselves that they were going to a Military Settlement and that must be laid out in some system. Surely it would appear better than these poor hovels.

One evening at the end of an especially hard day that saw most of the women walking more than half the time through a downpour of rain, they arrived at a stopping place which boasted of a primitive building the boatmen called a shanty and another building which housed the animals. The shanty doubled as a tavern and a place to sleep. The idea of finding refuge in a tavern was unappealing to some of these men and women who had taken a pledge never to frequent such establishments. The inside of the place was less appealing yet. It had a dirt floor, some crudely made tables and a side room for sleeping which was cold, unheated, filthy and likely home to a few vermin. Despite the roughness of the place the main room was filled with apparently jovial customers who greeted the newcomers with open friendliness and then turned their backs to them.

Once again basic needs determined the decision. Most of them were soaked to the skin after the all-day rain and they needed a place to dry out. The tavern itself was warm enough and any food acceptable. There were too many to sleep in the tavern and the men said they would be happy to use the barns if that were allowed. It was, as long as there was no smoking. There would be no problem with that. Almost all of the women, including Anne Wilson, elected to join their menfolk in the barn, which they found to be cleaner and warmer than the floor of the shanty. Everyone divested themselves of their wet clothing, which they spread out on the piles of hay, and gathered as close as they could to one another. The tavern keeper's wife brought them out a pot of something which passed for soup and told them they could have warm milk from the cows if they could milk them. Since the cows had already been milked earlier that evening this was no mean feat. Cows don't take to being milked twice, and they let down as little as they could.

Still, they were all together, and while scarcely comfortable, this was the best accommodation to be had. They studied contentment and prayed they would soon come to Richmond's Landing which represented to them that most precious objective, the end of the journey.

ARGUE

RICHMOND'S LANDING 1821

Two full days later they arrived. Four of the women and two of the men were ill with severe chest colds. The great dread was that these respiratory infections would become galloping pneumonia. Jessie Halliday and Maude Wilson were the most seriously ill; each with high fevers, they slipped in and out of consciousness. Everyone showed the effects of their journey. Even those who had not suffered seasickness had lost more than a stone[11] and there was little sign of that returning.

In this strange land, with no place to lay their head, help for the invalids came from an unexpected quarter, Isaac Firth's Tavern, which was conveniently nearby. Isaac's wife, Fanny, was an angel to these poor women. She turfed everyone else out of her inn and put the sick women in where she could tend to them better. The first urgency was to find milk for the Halliday baby and, muttering something about a goat, Fanny threw on a coat and said she'd be back soon. In less than an hour she returned with the promise of a steady supply.

Fanny ordered her manservant to fetch her as many pigeons as he could and when he came back with a string of them she made a broth for the invalids. Mary Argue and her sister Lizzie Blair took turns nursing. In Fanny Firth they found a capable, independent, and hospitable woman who gave them what they most needed in this New World: a kernel of hope.

The men were put up in tents by Isaac Firth, but beyond that, their care was left to their kin. Sam Halliday was very ill at

---

[11] A stone is fourteen pounds.

this point and the men did their best to care for him. On the whole they were a very worried group who looked anxiously for John Scott and James Wilson, but they were not to be seen. The ablest attempted to get provisions for the rest of their group while they waited helplessly for James and John to arrive.

Amy Mitchell, the third Wilson sister, volunteered to care for the three little Hallidays, "The two older ones can play with my two young'uns and maybe not ask as much for their Mam. Since I must be with my two, this is the only way I can help."

James Wilson and John Scott arrived the next day. They were almost unrecognizable. They seemed to have grown considerably in bulk, especially about their shoulders. Their hair was long and unkempt, their clothes matted with dirt. In fact, John and James had made every effort they could to make themselves presentable, but it didn't amount to much. Their faces blazed with joy when they saw their kinfolk. They apologized for not being on hand to greet them and explained, "It's the busy time for loggers. We still have to put cut timber onto the river, and we've been hard put to get away, but we worried that you might already have arrived, so we simply left."

"Well, we are right glad to see you to be sure," Archie Scott said, "But what will happen to you now when you have left your jobs just like that?"

"Oh, we are not at all worried about getting a job again. There are too few labourers for an experienced woodsman to be turned away. We won't try for the same lumber camp, but some other outfit is sure to want us. Workers in this country cannot be treated as they are at home, you'll soon find. In this country we are top dog."

James Blair growled, "Few of us feel as good as a stray dog right now. We're nowhere near as hearty as when we left Ireland."

"Well that will all soon change. Soon you will be recovered from that voyage. We saw no point in frightening you about the trip for it only caused us much gloom to think about it at all. I expect that you have sound stomachs for you do not look as far gone as some."

Archie Scott said, "Well, you've not seen all of us yet. Tim Wiggins, Jeremiah Scott and Sam Halliday have come down with trouble on their lungs. And then there is Jock Kennedy. He is not all together ever since he lost his wife and daughter on the trip."

John and James looked at each other and seemed stuck for words and then John offered this lame comment, "Once you are here you will soon forget it."

James Blair said, "You young pups had only yourselves to look to on the ship. You don't know the half we have been through. How long was your voyage?"

"Eleven weeks. And we have heard of trips that lasted more than twelve weeks. The folks who survived were too weak to do much for the first half year they were here. And then it was winter." They seemed loath to add more words to this tale, and were silent for a bit.

Then John said with some energy, "You must not expect comforts here right away. Comfort is something we have not had since leaving home. But we have something much better: independence. There is hard work ahead but in a few more days you will feel ready to grasp it." More silence.

James added, "We are experienced woodsmen now and can show you all that is needful for cutting down the trees and building your cabins." Actually they were much more experienced in cutting down trees than in building a cabin, but at least it was a start. Everyone could see the sense in putting all thought of that voyage as far behind them as possible.

On Saturday Jessie Halliday died. She left her husband with two boys, ages three and five, and the wee girl who had been born on the *Albion*. Samuel, who was still very ill, was scarcely aware of her passing. The baby throve, blissfully unaware that she had lost her mother. The three year old was desolate without his "maw" and clung to Amy's skirts all her waking hours. Families were generally more willing to take on older children who could be of some use as workers but what to do if they were to have three wee orphans on their hands?

Maude Wilson survived the crisis but she was still poorly and the other women took turns looking after her. It was hard to find the old Maude in the new. In Ireland Maude was the unnamed leader of the younger women and, although only a few years older than Mary Argue, appeared destined to become the matriarch when Anne Wilson passed on. A little taller than average in height, she appeared taller yet by her erect bearing and quiet, unflappable manner. Her dark hair showed little gray and waved naturally and neatly into a roll at her nape beneath her pinner; even her hair did her bidding. In her rare moments of repose her hands rested quietly in her lap as she listened to others blather on. Nothing ruffled her calm. In times of ill health people turned to her, for she seemed to have the gift of healing and gave strength as much through her manner of assurance as by any other means.

It was a very different Maude who had slipped into this state of lassitude and no words of exhortation seemed to have much effect. They did not even make her angry. It was as if she scarcely heard them. She neglected her appearance and had to be urged to do up her long tresses and tuck them under her pinner. John Wilson Sr. was concerned for her but felt that caring for his wife in this ailment was out of his domain. He stayed out of the tent as much as possible and left her to the womenfolk.

Anne Wilson proved that she was a woman of extraordinary mettle. Although she remained weak, miraculously she had avoided a serious illness and the mere fact of her survival to this point acted as a source of hope and encouragement to the younger women who felt that if a woman of her age could cope, they durst not give way. Martha, Moses' wife, had turned an invisible corner and was no longer a concern, but she could do little more than care for herself. How these women were to cope with setting up a home in this country was at that moment quite beyond their thoughts. Nearly everyone would have turned again to Ireland had they the strength to face another voyage, which they hadn't.

The women, with no exception, found it very difficult to imagine what their new homes could be like. They had all dreamed of a proper house in this land of plenty, even if it were small. Surely their homes would not be like the shacks at Richmond's Landing. Each day and each encounter with women who had been in the country for some time, caused them to feel that much less certain. Their ideas of fashioning a home in this wilderness were gradually being stripped away. They clung to assurances, 'Oh, Richmond, now there's a real village.' It was reputed to be prosperous and growing and altogether a good place to go, away from the swamps of Richmond's Landing.

It was at this point that George reminded himself to write the letter he had promised Forest Caldwell and a few others. He could well imagine just how anxiously these family

78

men would be waiting for news of Upper Canada and knew he had been putting off this task for he wished to say something encouraging and hardly knew how to go about it. He decided to limit the letter to some advice about the voyage. He now understood the failure of James and John to write letters that were as informative as he wanted. Well he was not going to mince words about the sea voyage. These men should be well prepared for that at least.

He located the paper Forest had pressed upon him, but as no ink was available, he improvised, using bits of charcoal that lay in abundance around the outdoor fires. He whittled to obtain a fine point, but the script would be inelegant at best.

He wrote:

The journey may be longer than predicted. Bring as much food and water as possible; do not rely on the ship's provisions. If you can afford it, get a cabin for your family, Bring only the essentials and nothing breakable. I shall write again soon.

He ended the letter abruptly, and addressed it to Forest, the man he felt was best able to afford the required postage. Then he added another note, asking Forest to share this letter with John Hambly of Redhills, who in turn would pass it on to others. He took the letter to Fanny Firth who provided wax for a seal, placed it in a leather pouch, and assured George that the letter would find its way to Montreal on the next boat going down river.

He knew these men would be hoping for more details about the country and he wished he could find something encouraging to say. He recalled especially Forest's words. 'My friends are encouraging me to go, but they are much younger men than I am. I feel I can trust your views on the matter. Most of all *you'll tell me things a man in my position, a man with four young children, needs to know.* Your opinion would weigh a great deal with me, and my wife too.' With that kind of trust placed upon his shoulders, George promised himself that he would do better in the next letter.

The men now turned their attention to the immediate challenge, namely getting themselves and their families to

Richmond and from there to their homesteads. This journey was to introduce them to the major challenge of the wilderness for many years to come, that of transporting oneself and one's goods from place to place over land.

The Colonial Office, on the advice of the Duke of Wellington, had decided to place military forts at Perth, Richmond and March. The reason behind this decision was the fear that, after the secession of the American colonies forty years earlier, the new United States of America would invade Upper Canada and try to annex this colony. The War of 1812 with the United States, which was only nine years ago, proved that their fears were very real. In order to defend the fledgling and sparsely settled colony they wanted to have a water route between Upper and Lower Canada, one which was safely away from the American border. This route was to be the Ottaways River. The long-term plan was to connect the St. Lawrence and Ottaways Rivers with a series of canals along the Rideau River and Rideau lakes.

The Crown was busy preserving a semblance of these military forts by giving disbanded soldiers generous grants of land around Richmond, March and Perth, and food rations for three years. They hoped that these ex-soldiers would prove useful in defending the country were it to become necessary, and it was far cheaper to give them land than to repatriate them to England and to the dole. The Cavan group aimed to settle close to the Military Settlement at Richmond in the Township of Goulbourne where James Wilson and John Scott had already claimed their locations.

Soldiers of the 99th Regiment had begun blazing the trail from The Landing to Richmond in the summer of 1818. By the summer of 1821 the trail had been widened in places but it was nowhere near ready for a team of animals and a wagon. In the middle of the winter some headway could be made on a sleigh with a team of horses, but travel at all other times of the year was another story. Worst of all was the springtime when the melting snow added water to the swampy ground, swelling the small streams and turning frozen land to mud.

Using what material was at hand to make a road, the soldiers and settlers had lain down logs across the trail, but they had soon disappeared. Not to be deterred for there was no lack of logs, they simply laid down more logs until there was something solid beneath one's feet. These logs were not of a uniform size, nor were they squared off or placed closely together. The danger of losing a farm animal because of serious injury was very real, and horses, oxen and cows were very valuable. Occasionally one of the settlers attempted to use a wagon to transport their belongings but not the people. It was far too dangerous. Scarcely a journey could be completed without the wagon being overturned and all that was in it being cast out. The jerking and jolting as the oxen tried to pull the wagons over the uneven logs was hard on the animals, hard on the goods and downright foolhardy for a passenger. Far safer to walk.

Those who had the strength to travel were itching to get to Richmond where they could apply for their location. Once they had their location ticket they could apply for the Government stores, which were to be allocated to each settler, and could start building their cabin. They were advised to make all the haste they could while the days were long so that everyone could clear enough land and build a home before winter came. In Ireland they had heard about the wonderfully healthy winter climate; they were now informed that winter was very cold, a different cold to any they had yet known.

John Scott and James Wilson offered to lead the first group, which included Archibald Scott, James Blair, John Wilson, Robert Mitchell, Will'am Foster and Jock Kennedy. Jock's son was still being cared for by Mrs. Faulkner and seemed to be quite happy in that family where the older children doted on him. They set out on foot with a few others who were taking their families and belongings with them.

It was strenuous beyond the experience of any of these men from Ireland simply to follow the blazed trail. They carried as much on their backs as they could manage, crossing streams of cold water by means of logs and slogging through the wet places. The route from Richmond's Landing to Richmond first headed west along the Ottaways River to avoid as much as possible of the deep swale which covered much of that area. Then the road turned south and there was no avoiding another extensive swamp later known as the Stony Swamp and one which took a bit of navigating even in winter.

The chief source of their discomfort was the swarms of mosquitoes. These had been bad enough at The Landing but the further away one got from the high land near the river, the

81

thicker the swarms. The mosquitoes were relentless and the men had to put on every stitch of clothing they possessed to prevent further bites. They sweltered and itched every step of the way.

Two days later some soldiers returning to The Landing from Richmond said that they had encountered their men who had sent a message back:

'We're doing fine, but for pity's sake, don't bring your wives and children now. We've had to leave our families behind us, not far from The Landing, and they would have been best off all together on the higher ground.'

The soldiers said that the whole distance from The Landing to Richmond was littered with families who were put up in tents or bark shacks along the way because they could not withstand the trip. The soldiers refrained from adding that they had found the men from Cavan wading thigh deep in a swampy part and had assisted them until they were out onto a higher part.

George and the remaining men, who had hoped, by delaying a few days, to take their families with them, reluctantly decided to follow this advice and to proceed without their women who were not yet strong enough to make the journey. Mary felt that she had to remain behind to look after Maude and assist Amy. She urged George not to expect either Maude or her mother or any of the others to cope with one more challenge.

"They are all used up, George. Don't think on it."

Sam Halliday was to remain at The Landing for he was not yet fit enough for the trek. Perhaps he could be of some use to the womenfolk. In fact he was not much use to anyone, even to himself. His beloved Jessie was gone and he struggled to become the sole parent of three young bairns.

To the group, his illness was a double blow, as they had counted on his carpentry skills in building the cabins. There was another carpenter among them, Jock Kennedy, if they could rely on him. Strange how these two carpenters had been the ones, so far, to lose their wives. Nothing of the sort was said aloud. No one wanted to tempt Providence to notice them and no plans were spoken without adding, 'God willing.'

The women were settled in tents not far from the River. The young boys, settled down to sleep on boughs under the trees, huddled together under blankets. At first it seemed a fine adventure to sleep outdoors. They did not even have to take their clothes off to go to bed, but after a while the adventure palled.

The excessive heat made them want to strip off their clothes and the mosquitoes forced them to cover up again.

The women had enough provision of oats to last them for a time. Cooking was done in a large pot over an outdoor fire. They were left with some fresh deer meat, which they salted and that, along with wild berries, was to make up their diet until the men returned for them. They were not afraid of this place. At least they were not moving. The air was good for they were high up overlooking the river. They were dry and warm, far too warm for people accustomed to a tepid climate, but there was no complaining. If they compared their state to that of Ireland they could feel very sorry for themselves, but when they compared it to their time on the boat they cheered up mightily.

They had Fanny Firth to go to in time of need. She had little to do with religion, but she had her own strong ideas about what constituted neighbourly behaviour, and her status in The Landing was such that no one gainsayed her. If she didn't like you, you could not get into her tavern by any means, and that was power enough.

The second group started for Richmond on a hot day in June. By noon of the first day many of them were wet to their knees, itchy all over, weak and dizzy. John Wilson Sr., who recognized the need for pacing themselves, urged that they find a resting place early that first day or he feared that he would be acting as nursemaid to some of the younger men. They had started out in high spirits and had quickly expended their greatly reduced reserve of strength. Many of them reflected that each time they had entered upon a new phase of this infernal and never ending journey they found that warnings had always been couched in the mildest possible language, never for a moment giving an accurate picture of what they were about to encounter. Nothing in the cool summers of their homeland had prepared them for the sticky heat, the ferocious insect life and the dizziness and exhaustion, which dragged down their every step.

On the second day they tramped along with few words spoken between them. Energy was to be saved for walking. Suddenly Faulkner came abreast of George and huffed, "D'ye not think that the government of this fair country might have wished to make this settlement a trifle more accessible?"

George raised his brow, "I'm not sure that accessibility was as much on their minds as defence."

"Humph", Faulkner snorted. "Well the bogs we have travelled through make it easily defended I suppose, but not easy to take your leave in a hurry. Why don't we just be charitable and agree that they didn't know what they were thinking about, as usual?" There was a faint murmur of assent from the weary men and no more conversation.

Surprising everyone, even themselves, the older men generally held up better than the younger ones in the first few days, but by the end of the journey the tide was turning. The longer the journey lasted, strength of character gave way to strength of physique. The young men were coming into their own.

It had taken the first group seven days to travel the twenty-five miles to Richmond and the second group, which travelled faster without their families and carried less on their backs, made it in four and a half days. Those who had arrived first had to cool their heels until George showed up, for the administrator of the settlement wanted to deal with them as a group and demanded their leader be there.

Lieutenant Colonel Francis Cockburn, the Deputy Quarter-Master-General for Canada, had little to do with the wave of civilian immigrants, which had commenced in 1819, but he had a concept of the sort of village he wanted and ordered it put into effect with all possible speed. Things were not left to develop in a haphazard manner as at The Landing. At the end of 1818 they had 400 families, and by now the numbers had surpassed 900, with more settlers pouring in each day. This looked promising to the new arrivals.

All would-be settlers had to appear before the Land Board to swear their loyalty to the Crown and to the defence of the colony if it should be threatened. They also had to swear that they would use the land for agricultural purposes only, and that they were eighteen years of age. Then they were sent to the Deputy Land Surveyor who gave them a location ticket. Each man of their group was allocated 100 acres, most of them taking land in the township of Goulbourne, in and around that part which later became Stittsville. Kennedy and Faulkner were given 10 acres in the village and 90 acres in the bush, out of recognition that their skills would be needed in the village. This suited both blacksmith and carpenter very well. They had not relished the prospect of isolation in the bush with their fellow travellers, worthy as they were. At the outset however, both Kennedy and Faulkner agreed to go into the bush to assist with the building of the cabins and in return they would receive help clearing their portion and building their homes in the village.

In Ireland they had been promised food basics for six months and the opportunity to purchase agricultural implements at cost. Here they found that some groups of settlers were being given food rations for a year and agricultural tools outright. The Colonial Administration had found that they had to extend the rations at least until the first possible harvest or face starving settlers.

While waiting for the rest of the men to join them, the first group had not been idle. They had assured themselves that the head of each family would receive the essential tools, the first of which was an axe, then a spade, shovel, hoe, scythe, draw knife, hammer, hand saw, two scythe stones, two files, twelve pounds of nails, twelve panes of glass and one pound of putty. In addition each family was to be given one bed tick, one blanket plus a camp kettle and most important, rations for one year. James Blair had looked about and had learned that some were receiving a complete set of carpenter's tools and before they left Richmond he managed to acquire a complete set of carpenter's tools, a crosscut saw, and a grindstone to be shared among their group. They were elated with their acquisitions.

James and John urged the group to make a few expenditures before leaving Richmond, most importantly, at least one team of oxen which they said was better than gold to a logger. The trip out to Richmond had sufficiently impressed all the men with the size of the trees to be removed and so the hard part was not in persuading them to part with their money, but in finding some strong healthy oxen. They found a young soldier who was ready to exchange his location ticket and his oxen for his freedom.

He told John Wilson Sr., 'I'm going to get myself out of this here Godforsaken country and try my luck elsewhere.' The deal was made.

They were able to go part of the way to their holdings by a series of creeks, and then on a blazed trail. A blazed trail was one that had a notch cut in trees at certain intervals. They loaded up the team of oxen and had to carry the balance of their necessities on their backs. Long before they reached their

85

locations they were thoroughly overwhelmed at the task that lay before them. They walked mile after mile with huge towering trees on either side, unable to glimpse the sun. It gave them ample opportunity for contemplation. Arrival meant that you halted in the middle of these impenetrable woods and tried to grasp that this was it. This was your new home, which you had been travelling toward and dreaming of for months. It was not even close to anything they had ever imagined, or ever *could* have imagined! Where to start?

ARGUE

A CLEARING IN THE WOODS 1821

If it had not been for the presence of John Scott and James Wilson, they would have had to turn around and look for someone to direct their labours, but John and James soon had them at work. Their first task was to clear up the small brush then pile it and burn it. They needn't fear a brush fire for the sun could not penetrate the thick canopy and the woods were still damp although it was midsummer. Next they were to cut down the smaller trees. John and James showed them how to cut the smaller trees by cutting a wedge high up in the trunk and a smaller cut below on the opposite side. Despite expertise it was a very dangerous operation until quite a number of the bigger trees had been felled. This was because in such a dense forest there was nowhere for a tree to fall cleanly, and it was more by good luck than anything else that a tall tree found its way to the forest floor. A large tree dangling and leaning on the tops of other trees was a horrible prospect to those who knew the dangers of the forest. Of course, most of the group knew nothing of the dangers, and were willing to set to with a will once they were told what to do. The men with less skill could cut off the branches, saw the tree into lengths, and drag everything but the tree trunks to be burned in a huge fire.

Jock Kennedy and a few of the more imaginative men were soon sickened by the sight of such huge and glorious trees, some more than four feet in diameter, being cut down and most of the tree burned up. The waste and reckless destruction was something they had never contemplated. They had to harden themselves to it and join in the work.

Once the crew was working efficiently, it was incredible how swiftly they cut the trees, burned up the small branches, sawed the logs to the correct length, and using their precious pair of oxen, hauled the larger logs to the centre of the clearing for Jock to direct the building of the first shanty. By now they were using the local language, and were not calling these rude structures a house.

Jock had spent his time in Richmond well. He had examined the style of building, especially the cutting of the timbers at the corners so that they fitted together, and he showed the men how to do it. Then he was faced with making the roof. The roof was to be made of balsam wood, a wood soft enough to have the inside of it scooped out. His first task was to recognize a balsam tree standing in the woods. After the logs were cut into lengths to one half of the roof, a crew was set to work scooping out the centres. When the roof was to be put on, the logs were first laid round side down and hollowed side up. Then a second row of hollowed logs were laid into these with the rounded side uppermost. The result allowed the rain to run off most effectively.

Those first attempts to cut the logs so that they could be fitted together produced many corners where there was more space than fit, but soon experience with the axe began to show and Jock could acknowledge with a nod that James Blair had done a 'daicent job'. It will not go without notice that here in the woods Jock Kennedy was gaining in prestige among the men each day. A man who knew how to do, that was the thing; not a man who dressed well or spoke well, but a man who could do well.

Each night the men lay down under the trees with branches for a bed and branches for a roof. They took turns on the bonfire to keep wild animals away. Especially feared were wolves, which were said to be plentiful in the area. Their food consisted chiefly of oatcakes, fish from the local streams and meat from wild animals of the forest. The opportunity to eat so much game was a luxury at the beginning, but began to pall after a few weeks. Every few days a man had to be sent off on foot to go to Richmond and bring back a bag of oat flour on his back. Occasionally he had to wait overnight for grain to be ground, and he returned the following day. No one chose to travel alone by night through the forest, even on horseback. The fear of wild animals was too strong.

On the first trip, two men went so that they could cut down a tree at intervals along the trail and thereby provide an opportunity to set the bag of flour on the stump when it was time to rest. The next trip could be made alone once the resting places had been assured. This pattern was used for a few years until more convenient means of obtaining a bag of flour could be employed.

At the end of two weeks they had built three shanties and they were beginning to operate a little more smoothly and quickly. It would be nice to say that all went well with the clearing, but unfortunately after three weeks, and just as confidence in their skills was being grasped, there was a tragedy. John Wilson Sr. was struck by a tree that twisted and fell in the wrong direction. He was killed instantly. Standing beside him was Robert Mitchell who was quicker to see what was happening and quicker to move. Still he was struck on the back by an outer branch and was given such a blow that he lay semiconscious and unable to move from the waist down.

The horror of this accident struck a terrible blow to the entire group. It was the first time they had seen a man in full health struck down since they had left their homeland. The loss of John Wilson Sr. was felt by everyone. Several years older than George, John S. was their unofficial leader. More than half the members of the group were related to him in some degree. He was Anne Wilson's youngest brother and therefore uncle to Mary, James, John and Moses Wilson. To everyone in the group he had been as close as a brother. James Wilson, who had felled the tree and shouted the warning too late, was devastated.

The grief they were suffering was evident in every face. Added to this was the immediate problem of his burial without benefit of clergy, and the pressure they were under to continue their work while showing respect for John Sr. George was expected to solve these issues as best he could.

Jock Kennedy volunteered to make a rough coffin from small logs. This was greeted with enormous relief, for a burial in the woods seemed tantamount to offering up his body for the wild animals. Also they needed to have a proper service later when the rest of his family could be present; now with a coffin this could be achieved more easily.

The accident happened toward dusk and all activity ceased except for Jock who spent his time selecting and sawing proper lengths of logs. Using light from the fire, a couple of men started to hack their way into the ground to prepare a shallow grave for John Sr. Each blow of the axe and scrape of the shovel echoed the pain in their hearts.

Robert Mitchell lay on a bed of branches, improvised with more than the usual care, only half conscious, drifting in and out of consciousness and moaning. Every man became urgently aware that this was no adventure but a deadly struggle to survive. How was Mitchell's family to survive? The Wilson family would manage with three sons and many relatives but were they not already grievously struck with John's wife Maude still recovering from her malady.

George agreed to say a few words for his best friend. "What I say at this time is only to be for an interval. We shall mark his grave carefully with a cairn that cannot be moved by the wild animals and shall seek a better resting place for him when his wife and children will be able to attend. We all mark the swiftness of his passing to that better Kingdom and we all can rejoice that he was so well prepared to meet his Maker. May God grant John, our brother, the joy and fullness of a resurrected life and grant to each of us that we may so live that we also will be prepared for the coming of our Judgment Day, which cometh as a thief in the day or in the night. We shall miss him greatly and all we can do now is to bear gladly his burdens. Neither his family, nor the family of Robert Mitchell, my brother-in-law, are to suffer any want in their lives. Their families are to be our families, their needs our responsibility. May the Holy Spirit grant that Robert be returned to full health and strength. And now we will have a silent prayer for John who is gone and for Robert who is with us."

Much later that evening James Blair noted to Moses that he had not heard Robert Mitchell moaning for some time now. They went to look at him and discovered that he was resting quietly. James said, "Now that I look back on it I cannot recall his moaning since George spoke. Do you suppose he was able to hear George's words about our looking after his family?"

"Aye, I think it very likely." They were both quiet for a while. Then Moses added, "Ye ken that we have paid a terrible price for this venture of ours. First Jock's wife and girl, then

90

Jessie Halliday, now John Sr., and mayhap Robert Mitchell too. I know I'd as lief be dead as crippled in this land where a man's strength is all. And there's more that still have not recovered from our journey. It makes a man wonder, it does that."

"Aye," said James, "but when we had made our choice we gave up all that we had; we had no way but ahead. There are some who would not do it again, I know. But life and death is but a chance for all of us each day. Even at home it was so. I have a feeling we'll be right in the end somehow, but when and how that may be I cannot see just now. I know nothing is quite like I thought it would be. I never thought to see a tree the likes of these. I hate them, every one."

Unfortunately for James Wilson, there was virtually no one to comfort him. Over and over he thought, *I brought John Sr. to this. It's my fault. I wanted them here that bad that I did not tell them all I could have. I did not speak of the dangers of this place. If I had, I know many would have stayed by their comfortable fire at home. I can feel it in their thoughts. Even George has naught to say to me.* And he sat away from the fire by himself with his back turned partly to the others.

After a bit, John Scott, who of all of them, had a very good idea of James' thoughts, came over to him and sat down. "Do you want to be by yourself, James? It looks as if you do."

"I am very poor company for myself or anyone else right now, John, and I cannot blame anyone for not wanting to sit with me. But thanks for coming. I feel that I'm a pariah."

"Oh, I think no one knows how they feel. They are all stunned. But I want you to know you did all that I would have done with that tree. No one could have predicted it would fall just the way it should *not* have done. And you warned everyone countless times to always be on the lookout. Your words were not heeded that's all. You and I have seen it ourselves in the bush, more times than I like to think on, but until you see it for yourself you can never quite believe it."

"Aye, I know that, but this was the first time I have been wielding the axe when — ." There was a long pause and James added, "Do you not feel that maybe we did wrong not to tell them more about this country?"

"Aye, maybe, but I was the one to insist we say little or nothing to discourage them from coming." It was generous of John to say so but it wasn't strictly true; both of them had been of the same mind. Their friendship had existed since they were young boys together in Ireland, and now more strands were woven tightly between them.

George for his part was so deep in his own grief that he did not give thought to his brother-in-law's feelings. Had they but known it, their feelings were much the same. George felt that his own determination to come to Upper Canada likely had influenced a few others. Those who had witnessed his humiliation by Dansy might have guessed at his reason, but he had never admitted as much, except to Mary. Despite his firm faith in the Lord and his unswerving efforts to be an obedient follower of Jesus, George was a worrying man. And now he worried, *Was this my scheme or God's scheme?* There was no answer forthcoming. Silence reigned over their camp that night.

CALDWELL

MAKING A DECISION 1821-22

After Ernest and Harold had run off to Australia, William heard no further words of discontent within his family. Willy Too still lived in his parents' household and, as he showed no inclination to matrimony, would likely remain a bachelor. Forest was happily married, if a steady stream of children was a good indication of wedded bliss. Willy Too and Forest managed all three Townlands: Mullaghboy, Drumsheil and Largy/Fort Henry, although to be more accurate, Forest managed them all, except for the horses.

William believed he had a fair assessment of his first and second sons. His eldest son William II gave no trouble at all providing he could be on a horse of the first quality. He was an excellent judge of horseflesh but no one consulted him on any other matter pertaining to the estate.

Forest was steady, sober, able and willing to assume responsibility as shown by his management of the three Townlands. He had shown little resistance to his father's wishes in all his forty-two years — well there was that matter of becoming a Methodist and also his marriage, which William now chose to regard favourably and forget his initial objections. He happily contemplated peace and felicity in his declining years.

Forest had, by age forty-two, become very much his own man, but saw no point in constantly reminding his father of the fact. Forest never missed a day in praying for his father's salvation, but equally he never spoke aloud about it to his father. He knew him well enough to know that his father respected no man's opinion as much as his own, and would only be irritated by any efforts at persuasion from his son. He reasoned that his father was a case strictly for the Holy Spirit. Nothing less powerful would do.

Content in his assessment of his situation, William failed to notice that Forest was preoccupied, even troubled. Mary knew something was wrong, but even Mary had no idea what was going on in Forest's mind. She decided he would tell her when he was ready; meanwhile she did not speak to him of his obvious distraction. Finally, several months after his brothers' startling departure, Forest told Mary what was in his heart.

"Mary, I daresay you have been wondering what's going on, have you not?"

"Aye, Forest. I know something is awry and I have been wondering when you're going to tell me what's troubling you."

"You've noticed what is going on roundabout us."

"Just what do you mean Forest?"

"Our friends are leaving Ireland, or planning to at least."

"Well I know that two of our close friends have gone, but I did not know that more have planned to go too. No, Forest, you have not shared with me this nugget of information. And where are they off to?"

"I thought it best to say naught until I knew more. Morgan and Erskine are hoping to leave next spring. Mayhap they have not made their plans known to all and sundry just yet, but they have been urging me to go too."

"Where are they off to, Forest? Don't tell me we are thinking of going off to Australia after your brothers?" she asked with a hint of alarm in her voice.

"No Mary, rest your mind that there is very little likelihood that I shall follow in their footsteps. Most of the young men, and a few not so young, are planning to go to Upper Canada. I have been hearing of several families going in a group. I must confess I wonder how it would be for us to go too."

"I cannot say aught to that Forest. I have not considered such a thing. I can see now why you've been off in a cloud; you are fair worried and yet, hoping too. What makes you want to do this? It is not as if we need to better ourselves, is it?"

"No Mary, It is not for more comfort that I contemplate leaving Ireland. It's just that with each child I long more and more to be able to provide a safe place for them to bide. I do not think that place is Ireland, much as I love our home and our families. And then too, Erskine and Morgan and all the members of our chapel who are planning to go, want me to be with them. They say they will need me there. I wonder, is this what God wants us to do, or…?

Mary was silent for a moment, then asked, "What do we know of this place called Upper Canada?"

"A good question, Mary. I hope to find out a deal more before I ask you to go off into the unknown. Earlier this year I spoke to George Argue over in Redhills. He's the leader of a group that went from this county to Upper Canada in April. I asked him to write to us and give us his opinion about going to Upper Canada. He promised to write and I think I can trust an older man to tell me what it might be like for a family such as ourselves. What do you say?"

"I am all in favour of finding out as much as we can, Forest. I can't say better than that, can I?"

Forest hoped to hear from George by that summer. He was overly optimistic in this expectation. When the autumn months passed and he still had not heard either from Argue or his friends, he was becoming alarmed.

Mary was torn between two reactions; of course she hoped to hear from Wilam Erskine and his wife Hetty and the others. They were close friends to many who had left Ireland that year, and she could not bear to hear that they had come to some mishap, but she was not yet reconciled to leave Ireland, her home and her family. She did not even have the satisfaction of confiding in her sister or her parents about their plans. Forest felt things were far too uncertain to make plans and he did not want to alarm their families about a nebulous future, a future which could not offer much comfort to her parents or his.

Forest told no one else of his hidden thoughts, not even those friends who had gone to Upper Canada. He worried that word might get back to Ireland before he had made his decision. Forest was comfortably situated on 100 acres free and clear and, with careful husbandry, he could hope to acquire yet more acres. Now that he had opened up the possibility of leaving their home, all its charms seemed ever more endearing. It was only when he went to the marketplace and saw the grim faces of some of his Catholic neighbours or heard of yet another altercation between Catholics and Protestants in a neighbouring county, that Forest was sharply reminded of his reasons for wanting to leave Ireland.

Gradually he learned that many of these same Catholic neighbours were going to Upper Canada too, and he asked himself if his dream of living in a peaceful society were nothing more than a dream. Mary had her own heart-felt misgivings, but felt that the decision was chiefly up to Forest and, seeing how much it was tearing him apart, she chose not to express her fears and add further to his worry.

Early in 1822 Forest finally received a letter from George Argue. It had been written after he arrived at Richmond's Landing. There was no explanation for the seven months it took for the letter to reach Ireland. Forest was yet to learn how mail moved or failed to move from Upper Canada to the Old Country. The letter, which seemed to have been written with charcoal, was short and not entirely encouraging. George wrote chiefly about the voyage, advising Forest to plan on taking a cabin if available and financially possible and to bring all the foodstuffs needed for a long trip. *'Bring as much food and water as you can. Do not rely on the ship's provisions.'* George added that he hoped they all *'possessed strong stomachs for a sea voyage. I shall write again soon.'*

By this time Forest knew that the best time to arrive in Upper Canada was in the early summer, in order to have a home ready for the following winter. This much he had learned in the letters from his friends, but he still did not feel ready to leave in the spring of 1822. Forest shared the letter with Mary and together they decided to wait for the second letter which they hoped would not be as long in coming.

It was as well that they tarried for soon after the first letter arrived Mary felt certain that she was expecting again. The baby would not be due until February of next year.

The announcement of this next child had a surprising effect upon Forest. His ambivalence ended. The baby would arrive in February; he could arrange to leave in April and arrive in Upper Canada as Providence provided. He began to see clearly that he would never be content with himself if he did not make the push and from that time forth he started to move ahead, even before the second letter from Argue arrived. Forest reasoned that it was beyond time that a God-fearing Christian placed a little more faith, in fact all his faith, in the Almighty and put an end to fear and worry. Moreover, he felt God was urging him toward this action. Mayhap God wanted him to add his bit to the building up of the community of faith in this new world, although Forest's innate modesty prevented him from saying this aloud.

Mary tried to persuade him that she was sure she could manage on the voyage while pregnant but Forest would not hear of it. He would not risk her having to deliver a baby at sea with no one to help her if needed.

A few months later he received the second letter from George. It was equally brief and urged him to

Come with all haste. Bring as much sturdy cloth, strong boots, medicines and seeds as you can. Goods are available here but the price is exorbitant. Bring whatever books you value for none are to be had here. It may be your presence and your leadership in chapel that will be most valued here in this country where we have yet to see a church or much sign of civilization, as you know it. Praise God we are all well and able to work for a better future for our families.

George had let him know there would be few graces or comforts in the Canadian wilderness. Mary Argue added a note to Mary Caldwell advising her not to bring anything breakable, but bring seeds for herbal medicines. She then hastened to assure her of a warm welcome when they arrived in Upper Canada. Forest decided that there was little time for leisure in Upper Canada judging by the brevity of the letters. And there was no explanation for the advice to *Come with all haste.*

Forest knew his decision to emigrate would be a terrible blow to his father. The immediate consideration was that he had done most of the estate management, and while he felt that the manager could adequately look after their affairs, he knew inevitably that his father would have more of the care of the farms on his shoulders. Willy Too was little help and Samuel inexperienced. The major blow would be the loss of his grandchildren and the knowledge that he would never see them again in his lifetime. Nevertheless he could no longer postpone this painful interview.

William was poleaxed; the last person he had expected to reveal a partiality for adventure was Forest, and it took some time before he realized adventure formed no part of Forest's motivation. No, William could not understand it. He began to feel that there was little firm ground beneath him after all. Ernest and Harold had at least been open books; Willy Too was a fuddy old bachelor, and Forest too old to direct. All hopes would have to be placed on Samuel, his youngest. Suddenly in a matter of a few months William went from feeling complacent about his good name being well represented in future generations, to wondering about the outcome of his estate in the foreseeable future. What good are offspring if they are on another continent?

Forest hadn't given his father trouble every day of his life, but when he took a notion to do something it was fairly clear he was going to do it, and it was always the big things that he had notions about. William began to wonder why he had ever possessed the idea that he was the master in his own house. Everything was beginning to fall apart. This was a different matter entirely from Ernest and Harold going off to Australia. If things kept going as they were, there might be no Caldwell left on Drumshiel at all. William was anxious, angry and bitter by turns, altogether not a happy man.

ARGUE

THE SHANTY 1821

The following morning they rose at first light to bury John Sr., and marked the place with a small cairn. They then resumed chopping, piling and burning wood, working for the most part in silence, with none of the energy and hope of yesterday morning. This vast forest had become their enemy. They positioned themselves as carefully as they could when a tree was to fall and there were no more serious mishaps, just a few cuts and bruises. With each day they learned more respect for the forest and with more knowledge came more humility.

Robert Mitchell had a slow but nearly full recovery. He regained full consciousness the next day but it was ten long days before he could move his legs. The decision had been made to move him back to Richmond and four men were delegated to carry him out on a bed made of rope, as light and as strong as possible. He was left in Richmond under the care of Mr. Monk, the surgeon who had been attached to the 99th Regiment. As soon as it was established that he would be able to walk again, Mitchell was hard to restrain. But the experience of trying to stand unaided restrained him sufficiently for another week. After that he was on crutches and in a ferment to know how the clearing on his location was going. Reports came back as the men came in for more supplies. His shanty was up. He would have a shelter for his wife and wee ones when they were ready to join him. With this news Mitchell felt some of the ever-present tension leave his body and his recovery proceeded more swiftly.

By the end of September all the men had their shanties erected. None had a floor other than the floor of the forest. The source of heat was not the picturesque fireplace of the pioneer cottage. Many settlers had time only to position the shanty with one wall against a huge hard elm tree and leave a hole in the roof for the smoke to escape. Other shanties left the hole in the centre of the shanty to better heat the small area. Cooking was to be in an iron pot hung over the fire by means of a tripod, fashioned by James Faulkner. Each family hoped that by the following year they would be able to erect a proper fireplace, but that depended upon their finding suitable stones on their lot as well as their having the skill and time required to build it. Quite often all three items were insufficient or none of these requirements were present. Many families had to live for years with the primitive hearth and the hole in the roof. As matches had not yet been made, it was a given that the fire needed to be kept alive always in order to have a live ember to rekindle the fire. At least there was wood in abundance.

Each shanty was 16 by 20 feet, the same size for larger and smaller families alike. The men crafted some roughly made beds and some cabins had a loft as well which could be gained by a ladder. The logs, which formed the inner and outer walls, were of very different sizes, and a great deal of air was visible between the cracks. These were stuffed with moss from the forest, but the moss had a nasty way of drying up and falling out. There was plenty of ventilation.

Each cabin had the allotted twelve panes of glass for two windows and they had made a stout front door, which, if it did not fit too closely, would at least keep out the wild animals. This very primitive dwelling was the very best they could do, but now that the time had come to get their womenfolk, it was hard to know what would be the reaction from their women. Would they be relieved at the sight of their dwelling or would they be horrified?

The men took turns making trips to fetch their families who had been left along the way. By the end of September their entire group had arrived. The arrival of the women differed markedly from that of the men who, up to this point, had arrived in groups and worked in groups. Each family was now in their own shanty, which was not within sight or sound of the next one. From the two small windows they looked out at a small clearing of stumps, then the forest wall. This outlook and these very primitive cabins were their reality at the journey's end.

When Mary and the girls arrived, George wasted no time in sending young Andrew off the next morning to tell each family that there would be a meeting to give thanks at his home that night. They arrived carrying torches through the blazed trails of the woods. The general spirit was of gladness, for this was the first time they had all been together since the men left Richmond's Landing in June.

But they were not all present. Robert Mitchell still could not walk even a quarter of a mile at one go and Sam Halliday, who had nearly taken up residence at the Mitchell home, decided he would bide with Robert as he did not want to face the whole company without Jessie. John Wilson Sr. was not with them and his absence was keenly felt by everyone.

This company of people had left their homes more than seven months ago and most of that time had been spent in peril, severe hardship, uncertainty, and loss of life itself. By now the majority of the men and all of the women knew that the foreseeable future would bring nothing but more hardship, more change, and not the remotest chance of bodily comforts. Their new abodes were the most primitive of shelters, not better than the very poorest hovels in Ireland except that they were more drafty. Those of more sanguine dispositions, and they were mostly the younger unmarried men, glowed with the opportunity of making a new beginning, of seizing their future in both hands, and making their dreams come true.

ARGUE

THE FIRST WINTER 1821-22

One might suppose that settling into a cabin in the woods would be enough to occupy even the most adventurous man, and that putting a floor in the cabin would be considered a first priority. Not so. The men were well aware of the need for cash if they were ever to improve their holdings and acquire desperately needed livestock, both of which were essential to making a go of it in this country. For the first two years they could not expect to get cash by raising enough food to have anything left over for market and perhaps not even enough to sustain themselves over the winter. John Scott and James Wilson were planning to go back to the lumber camps, and although they did their best to discourage others from doing so, many of the younger men wanted to go with them.

The lumber camps were very dangerous places, not only from the hazards of felling trees, but also from getting the logs out of the bush to the water. The business of riding logs on the river, attempting to break up logjams, negotiating rapids, and trying not to lose a whole crib of logs to the river, provided danger at every turn.

Forty men in a shanty often sought to relieve the boredom of the same food and long winter evenings by contests of one sort or another, the most common one being a good fight. It was especially bad if any liquor had been smuggled into the camp; then there was a free-for-all. But even without that, men who felt they had been insulted or slighted to the smallest degree were ready to pick a fight. A favoured way of fighting was to kick out with their heavy boots with the three-quarter inch sharp calks[13] on the bottom. A good place to aim was the stomach. When a man was down, tramp on him. Fighting with men who kicked out wearing such equipment was no joke. It was no holds barred fighting using clubs and feet, axe handles, whatever was handy. Of course, if a rival outfit was encountered that was an occasion for a bigger and better fight. Most loggers were willing to abide by the rules laid out by the camp foreman. When that broke down, there was no law at all in the bush other than the law of survival. If a man died of his wounds, it wasn't called murder or manslaughter; it was an accident. There was no retribution other than what his friends provided. Methodists were not pacifists and being deeply religious did not mean you had to stand back from a fight if it was put to you. Certainly a devout Presbyterian Scot had no such reputation. Even so, experienced men counted themselves lucky to be able to mind their own business and stay healthy.

It was finally decided that if any were to go they must all go together, and be hired on in one gang if possible. So far Upper Canada was not proving itself to be more hospitable or safer than their homeland, but the young men were optimistic and still ready for new adventures. Their health had returned, and there was no stopping them.

The men had a few weeks in which to make the cabins more habitable before they departed. Most of the shanties had a table, benches but no chairs, a shelf or two on the wall and, rarely, a settle, that is, a bench with a back to it. It could be pulled out to make a bed. Beds for the younger people in the family were boughs spread in the corners of the cabin or in the lofts, and one was glad to have other bodies for warmth.

Maude Wilson, her three sons and three daughters, accepted James Wilson's offer to live in his shanty for this first winter when he was away in the bush. He said he would feel better if they took his home as theirs for as long as they needed it and Maude agreed to this plan without any fuss. Their belongings were barely inside the door, when her three grown sons, Orville, 22, Jasper, 19 and Matthew, 15, informed her of their determination to join James Wilson and John Scott in the bush. Maude was not consulted. She and her three daughters, who were now 17, 14 and 12 years, were to attempt to get

---

[13] A calk is a sharp iron spike, designed to prevent slipping.

through this first winter together. It is a wonder that her sons would leave their mother to fend for herself in this entirely overwhelming country, but two factors contributed to their decision.

First, they wanted to go, and quite easily persuaded themselves to regard their mother as she had always been to them: calm, wise, ready for any emergency, the one to whom everyone turned in time of need. Also, Orville told his two younger brothers that if, unaccountably, Mama ran into a little difficulty, she had George Argue about a mile away. Surely he would stop by regularly to see how she was getting on. They happily accepted this reassurance. They laid a great stack of green logs outside the cabin door, added provisions of salted pork and two bags of oats, and took themselves off.

Indeed, outwardly Maude was a little more like her old self; her hair no longer lay about her shoulders, and she now prepared food for her family. It was easy to be reassured that she was once again the mother they had always known. But in place of her old quietness there was now no show of feeling at all. She never mentioned the matter of her three sons going off into the bush to cut down trees after her husband had been killed in such an endeavour, not by so much as a gesture.

George's response to providing support to Maude was to send young John McFadden over to her shanty to assist her with the heavier work. If John were indeed a son of the household he would have felt no degradation in this move, but somehow it made him feel less a part of the Argue family, a sense of belonging that was vital to his wellbeing.

George Argue now persuaded himself that the best plan for him was to go to Richmond's Landing and sell wood. It sounded like a daft proposal to be sure, like selling water in Ireland. Nevertheless, he reasoned that there would be people willing to pay for him to cut the wood and haul it to their door ready for the fireplace. After he had made himself a sleigh of sorts, he harnessed his newly purchased team of horses to it and was away, taking young Andrew with him. Few were surprised at his departure. It would have been harder to imagine George idling in the cabin, whittling wood. There was no point in trying to hold him down. Anne Wilson advised her daughter to save her wind to cool her tea. Not that they expected to have tea.

104

The women and children now had their first taste of being alone in the bush. Unoccupied lots separated the settlers' lots, making the closest shanty often a mile distant or more. In addition, these women had yet to get used to the bitter cold of the winter. Their thin leather boots provided little protection in the deep snow and walking from one clearing to the next meant going on a very rough trail through a stretch of dense forest. Most of the women were too frightened by reports of wolves to consider attempting it by themselves or with their children. Each woman was in her shanty looking out at a small clearing of stumps, then the deep, dark forest.

Later they were to learn that winter could be the best time of the year, the time for visiting when your horse and cutter could sail over the snow and the absence of roads could be forgotten. But that luxury was off into the future, for in addition to the lack of a continuous road through the woods, they had no horse or cutter in their yard. There was no word from any of the men who had left, some as long as two months ago.

Robert Argue was now twelve years old and thought himself to be the man of the household. John, who was not quite seven, was a mere child in Robert's estimation. Robert began to think that it was time he proved that he could take his place alongside his brothers at their work, and this led him to think about cutting down a tree on his own without his brothers being around to order him about. One day he took the axe and went a little distance into the woods so that his mother might not hear the sound of his chopping. The tree he chose to chop down was not a big one, only about ten inches in diameter, but it had a good height. As he chopped, he gained in confidence. He stood there exulting, as his first tree started to bend and slowly topple in exactly the direction he had planned. Then disaster struck. The top of the tree caught in the branches of another tree, and the trunk of his tree, instead of falling off its stump onto the far side, slid backwards toward him. He jumped away a fraction too late. The trunk caught him in the outer thigh and gave him a nasty gash. For a few moments he lay there stunned, but conscious. He gradually realized he had to get himself back to the house for no one knew where he was. He had not been out long and he might freeze to death out here before a search would be made for him. He tried to stand and found that this was very precarious; walking was impossible. He commenced to drag himself and the precious axe back to the clearing. Now he had to concern himself with wolves as well.

In the shanty, Jane, age ten, kept going to the window to look for Robert. "I don't see him Mama. Can I go to look for him?"

Mary was worried, but felt she should not give way to foolish fears. "Not by yourself. I'll not have you out of the clearing by yourself. You have seen how many wild creatures there are about. Your grandmother is still sleeping. I want you to stay here with her and I shall go with Annie. Did you note which direction Robert went?"

"Yes, Mama. You told me to watch, and he went straight through those trees over there."

"Good. We will follow his tracks. Dress as warm as you can, Annie. Put a shawl over your head. It is getting cloudy and colder, and that always seems to bring more snow. We must hasten."

As they went, they called and made as much noise as possible to let Robert and the animals know they were about. Every so often they were quiet to see if they could hear anything. It was not hard to follow the tracks for, although it had begun to snow, the tracks were not yet filled in. They found Robert about a half-mile from the clearing, dragging himself towards them. By half carrying him and supporting him, they got him home. Mary felt a presence with them all the way, but in her fearful state she did not know if this was a benign presence or a dangerous one. She had heard of people being followed by wolves for many miles in the bush before they closed in. She feared that a wolf might have smelled Robert's blood which was still flowing with the exertion he was making.

By the time they made it back to the shanty Anne Wilson was awake and had stirred up the fire to heat water. Jane and John were hovering anxiously at the window. Mary and her mother got Robert onto the bed and tore off what remained of his pant leg. Using water and a clean rag, Mary cleaned the wound as best she could. Anne brought her a strip off her petticoat to bind up the wound more tightly. Beside herself with fear for Robert, and not knowing just what should be done for him, Mary frantically tried to think of remedies which had been used at home. All that would come to her mind were those dreadful times when the remedies had failed, especially the last time.

106

The gash looked deep and nasty. She heated fat and stirred pieces of wild garlic into it to make a poultice. At home she would have used hog's lard and leaves of comfrey or lovage, but her dried leaves were nearly all gone for she had been forever tending cuts and bruises for the men since they had arrived in this country. What could she do but pray, and give him something to drink?

Robert tried to reassure his family that he was not too bad, and not to worry; he would never try anything like this on his own again. He drifted off to sleep. Her mother and the girls made some oat cakes to eat but Mary found it hard to swallow. She insisted on taking the first shift to sit with Robert, and the others went to bed early. Her mother said that she would get up and take the next vigil so that Mary could rest.

Mary knew that rest was the last thing that would come to her. Ever since she had left Cavan, she had been trying to escape her memories of young George and his death. There was no escaping it anymore and she knew she never had escaped, not really. Every day seemed off colour, something amiss. It was like losing a part of herself, a part she would never find again. She bowed her head. Robert's wound seemed so much worse and she had so little to fight an infection if it started.

Mary sat beside Robert on a rather uncomfortable stool. After a while she found it just as comfortable to kneel by the side of the bed and put her head down. Presently, she felt the bed shaking. She felt his forehead and found it very hot, but he was gibbering and shaking as if he were cold. She hastened to put another log on the fire and placed her shawl over him. Presently he was perspiring. She had heard that this was a good sign and put more wood on the fire. But still he was hot and now his lips were cracking. She bathed his face, held water to his lips and a little trickled into his mouth but not much.

Mary felt so much terror in her stomach that it was like pain gripping her. She had little faith in any of her remedies for wounds. What should she do? By this time it was early morning; little John and her mother were still asleep but Jane and Annie were awake and stood by her fearfully as they realized how frightened their mother was.

"Do you want me to go to get some help, Mama?" asked Annie.

"Where would you go and who can help?" Mary asked. "Besides I don't know if it would be safe for you to go out on this day. It is still snowing and you might lose your way."

Annie thought that this was very unlikely for she had gone back and forth several times to their nearest neighbour, Maude Wilson, and the trail was well marked, but she could see that this was not the time to argue with her mother. She was not sure what Aunt Maude knew that Mama and Grandma did not know as well.

Mary and all the other women had brought small chests of remedies, tried and true in their homeland and trusted that they soon would find similar plants in this country to replace their small supplies. But by the time they had arrived at their shanty last fall there had been little opportunity to look for comfrey, lovage, elecamplane or tansy. There is a right time for harvesting each plant, and then the time is past. Going into the woods had been made more difficult by their fears of leaving the clearing, and now they were paying bitterly for that neglect. Mary vowed never again to have a medicine chest as bare as hers was now. The whole study of home remedies seemed uncertain to Mary at best, and the only woman amongst them to have some authority in this was Maude Wilson. But what of Maude now? Was there any point to fetching her?

All that day Robert lay on his pallet, sometimes aware of them, but more often muttering about trees or wolves. It was enough to break your heart to listen to him. John had scarcely made a sound since Robert was brought back injured. He clung mutely to his grandma. Everyone was remembering little George.

Anne Wilson lay on a settle bed on the other side of the fire from Robert. Her lips moved from time to time in prayer and then she seemed to drift away. Mary was concerned about her mother as well as Robert, but could do nothing in that direction, and tried not to think about it.

During the night Robert seemed to worsen. It was difficult to get any water between his lips. Mary and Jane and Annie all kept a vigil, but Mary urged the younger two to pray and pray, and then to sleep if they could. Nothing could make her sleep anyhow so it was not required that they all keep awake.

The next morning Robert seemed much the same. Mary looked at his wound. If any change, it seemed to be redder around the wound and it was very hot. How much longer could he hold out against this infection? Anne Wilson roused herself sufficiently to urge her daughter to let the two girls go and fetch Maude. If nothing else perhaps some neighbour could be asked to find George at The Landing and bring him back.

Off they went, as swift as the wind, eager to be able to take some action. It turned out that Maude did have some new ideas about how to help in the event of a wound. The previous summer up at The Landing, Fanny Firth had brought an old native woman to visit Maude in the hope that she might be able to cure Maude's recurring chest ailment. While the woman had no help for the chest problems, she told her, with Fanny's help, how to bring down a fever, using the bark of the willow boiled up for a drink. Maude had tried it, and while it tasted awful, it had made her feel better for a few hours at least. And she had tried it since, and found it had indeed helped when one was feverish. She sent her eldest daughter and John McFadden out to fetch some bark from a willow near the creek and to take it straight to Argue's shanty. Maude then scrounged about in her bags and brought forth a powder that the old woman had given her to be used on wounds. She could not remember the name of it or how to obtain more. She had not thought much of it at the time. But she had not thrown it out and who knew, if willow bark worked, maybe this would too. So she packed her bags, adding some broth she had just made, and prepared to go back with Jane and Annie.

It was close to an hour before the girls were to return with Aunt Maude; it had seemed an eternity to Mary who had been down on her knees praying. She knew it wasn't right of her to be so afraid. She thought, 'I ought to be more trusting in God's will, but I know I won't be able to bear it if I lose Robert too. I can't bear more losses right now, Lord. If something happens to him, I don't know what will become of us all. I cannot be strong for others anymore if I lose him.' Unfortunately she had no confidence that God was going to grant her plea. She had prayed for the lives of all her children but two of them had died anyway. By the time Maude arrived, Mary was ready to give way and let Maude take over.

Maude asked Anne Wilson to assist her in dressing the wound and sprinkling the powder into it. Then she wrapped it up again in clean rags. Next she added wood to the fire to bring the kettle to a boil. Before it had quite reached the boil, John and Lizzie burst through the door with the bark she wanted. She threw some bark into the kettle and let it steep for a time. After twenty minutes she drew some off and cooled it before holding it to Robert's lips. She managed to get a little down him despite his efforts to reject it, and then she sat down to wait.

Mary had watched her all this time, and had seemed to be comforted by the way Maude had taken over, and how confidently she moved about.

Now Maude turned to her and said, "Mary, I can tell by the look of you that you have neither slept nor eaten for nigh on two nights and two days. Nothing will be served by your getting ill yourself. Your boy is not at the end of his tether yet. I've seen worse recover and I believe these powders will help Robert. You are to sit yourself down and take some broth. Presently you will see Robert's fever coming down I'll warrant, and then you can get some rest. I will sit here myself until you have rested and are ready to take over again. No argument now. It's the least I can do after all that you have done for me and mine."

Mary had no words to say to all of this. Maude had offered the best comfort available short of a guarantee that Robert would be well. She put her head down and was miraculously sound asleep in two minutes. When she woke, she went straight to the bedside where Maude was sitting. She could see that Robert rested more quietly and putting her hand on his forehead she knew that the fever, although still present, was much reduced. She sat down and wept silently.

"There, there, lass don't take on so. He'll do rightly, you'll see."

Mary nodded, "I can cry now because I can dare to believe that. I felt so helpless before you came, Maude. As you know I place no hope whatever in a surgeon, but if the worst had come that Robert had to lose either his leg or his life, there is none here to help even in that extremity. There are times Maude, that I don't know if I can stand it. And I feel terribly guilty saying that to you Maude. You have lost your John and I never hear you complain."

"Well Mary, complaining doesn't represent what I feel. I cannot find the words to say what is in my heart or what is not in it. Sometimes I think my heart is empty and I have no feelings left and that is easier in a way and yet, I miss — I miss —living.

For a long time I have not cared about anything, Mary. Mostly I still don't. But when you were desperate, well that was the first time I felt I might have some life left in me after all."

Mary said nothing; she didn't understand what Maude was going through, but then understanding didn't seem to be very important. There were many things she didn't understand any more. She just nodded as though every word that Maude said made good sense.

Robert recovered slowly. The wound was deep and the powder ran out before all the infection seemed to be gone. Maude and John McFadden trudged through the deep snow each day to watch his recovery, even when it was obvious that he was out of danger. Maude's daughters petitioned for the chance to come too and took turns each day for the outing.

Because they had not sewn up the wound immediately, Robert was going to have a nasty reminder of his accident. He was the better part of two weeks recovering, and since no chair had a back to it other than the settle which was grandma's resting spot, most of this time he lay flat on the cot. When it looked safe for him to try a little weight on the leg, he found that he was very weak. The muscles of the injured leg seemed to have shrunk a bit. However, nothing that they did or failed to do had much effect on the long term. Robert got back the use of his leg, and if the nasty scar gave him respect for the dangers of cutting down trees, so much the better as far as Mary was concerned.

Robert was hobbling around the shanty using a crutch borrowed from the Mitchells, when George and Andrew came in the door. Word had finally reached them at The Landing but it had taken them three more days to reach their Goulbourne home. The horses could not travel all day and all night too and the drifts were deep. This experience taught them that living alone in the bush during the winter served little purpose. Next winter they would all go to The Landing.

ARGUE

THE SECOND SUMMER 1822

In the fall of 1821 there was virtually no harvest. Once the cold weather came they lived off bags of oats provided by the government. T h e following summer they knew they had to do better, for next winter there would be no government rations. This drove them all to work harder than they had ever done before. The men alternated between cutting down more trees and planting seeds for next year's food. The seeding was done around the stumps and the potatoes were put down there as well. Everything sprang up in good heart and then miraculously disappeared overnight. George and his sons worked desperately to throw up fences to keep the animals away. Sometimes these 'fences' were giant tree stumps upended and which proved quite effective when placed close together — no small task. Maude, Mary, Amy, Lizzie and their young ones, grouped together for comfort and courage as they went into the forest to gather food or medicines that could be dried for next winter.

At the end of it all, the harvest was scanty because a fair portion had been lost to wild animals and then, worst of all, they did not know how to store the precious potato very well. Certainly they tried to build a root cellar for they had been told how cold the winters could be, but their first attempts were poor. There were still so many roots in the ground that digging was more like chopping your way into the soil and many of the root cellars were too shallow. As a result much of the precious crop was frozen and had turned to a black mush. Some of the adults silently wept; some merely greeted this setback with grim determination. Young John, then eight years old, was the only one to howl his grief aloud. "Mama, is there never to be any more potatoes?" He voiced everyone's fear.

As the second autumn approached and the men started to get ready to go to the bush, there were a few surprises. Anne Wilson announced, "I'll bide in Goulboune with Amy, or with Eliza. Whatever suits best. I don't fancy the journey and you will have the sleigh well filled without me."

When Mary protested strongly and George urged her as well, she added, "One bit of woods is much the same as another to me now. I'll bide here." And that was that. She always was a woman to know her own mind and follow it, and in a sense it was reassuring to find her unaltered in that respect.

Then another surprise: John McFadden announced that he was off to the woods too and took himself off swiftly before George made other arrangements and before he lost his nerve.

Maude Wilson decided she would not be left behind in the Goulbourne bush and told her sons to procure a place for her at Richmond's Landing, right beside Mary Argue. They were not to take themselves off to the woods until she and her daughters were installed there according to her satisfaction.

Orville, Jasper and Matthew were stunned by her announcement. "Does Mam not care a bit about us anymore?" mourned Matthew. "Doesn't she know we have to go all together and right early too so that we can have a hope of being on the same crew?"

"That's what we planned," said Orville, who being the oldest, knew very well it was now his responsibility to care for his mother, "but it looks as if we'll have to change our plans. I think we should all stick together, don't you?"

Matthew and Jasper nodded. They had no intentions of splitting up, but how they were to manage to fulfill their mam's wishes was just one more unknown.

Clearly, there was a new Maude in the making. Gone was the quiet, reserved woman from Cavan and gone was the numbed, stony woman of the Goulbourne shanty. From the ashes arose an active, energetic woman who neither took instruction from the men nor humbly followed the old ways. Mary felt both proud of her and a little in awe of her. She wished she could be as forthright as Maude now showed herself to be, but she had learned the necessity of achieving her desires in a more

113

circuitous route, that of deferring to the superior wisdom of the men. Such customs were hard to break. Their new circumstances were to exert strong headwinds on yesterday's customs.

The men could protect their women from knowing the worst of what transpired in the logging camps, but not from knowing first-hand the loneliness of spending the winter in an isolated shanty in the forest. The men hoped and prayed that their women, with very little to work with, could make a home in the bush, somehow. The essential ingredients for survival were good health, the support of family, friends and providence. No one could make it alone.

The previous winter George had found virtually no employment at The Landing. There were too few people who settled at The Landing, and those who had, found sufficient time during the winter months to collect their own firewood which lay all around them on the forest floor. But he did learn about the need for haulers to take loads of hay and foodstuffs to the lumber camps. This was called *hauling loading*. James Wilson and John Scott had advised him to get into this line of business as soon as he could, and the idea suited George admirably.

The second winter brought new possibilities for some of the families. If their men worked in the lumber camps, then the women would stay in Goulbourne where often there were at least one or two animals to look after. Archie and a few others planned to haul loading and hoped their wives would join them at The Landing. Archie's wife, Lydia, said she would try it for a bit, but clearly left the door open for a return to Goulbourne with their son Charlie, if things didn't suit. A few eyebrows were raised at this sign of independence, but Archie just nodded as if what she said made perfect sense. The men whose wives were remaining in Goulbourne, planned to bunk together at The Landing. Each family would have to work out whatever was possible.

The Argue family were all ready for their move, and waited impatiently for the weather to clear so that they could make the trek to The Landing. Mary decided to use the time to write to family and friends in Ireland, a task she found difficult and had been putting off. This time she was going to try out the 'ink' she had made using acorn shells, vinegar, salt, and soot.

From Goulbourne, Carleton County, Oct 10 1822

Dear family and friends We are all nicely settled in our shanty here in Goulbourne but the family will move to Richmond's Landing for the winter so that we can be more together than we were last winter and that will be worth a great deal I tell you. George and Andrew will be hauling foodstuffs into the bush camps for the lumbermen. The only flaw right now is that our Mam decided to stay in Goulbourne with Amy and Robert who are looking after the Halliday children. That makes for a large number in one small shanty. But at least they will not be lonely. Sam Halliday will stay in Goulbourne too. We have not given up hope that we may yet persuade Mam to come and join us. Maude Wilson has told her sons to find a place for her to live beside us. Maude's sons plan to work in the bush this winter as do many of our young'uns so it will be good for both of our families to be together. Maude and I have been busy these past weeks and months in Goulbourne trying to find plants that will serve as home remedies for colds and ailments. We have had some success but time will tell if these plants and herbs will serve us well here. We are not sure that they are exactly the same plants we used at home although they often look very like. If you can send us some seeds of feverfew, pennyroyal and chamomile we would be happy indeed to receive them. But do not try to send them unless you find someone who is coming to Carleton County, Upper Canada. A doctor is a rare person in these parts to be sure but as it is not certain what use their remedies are they are not much missed. Your letters are eagerly awaited and read over many times. We pray that your crops do not fail you and we pray the same for ourselves as well. We had a passing crop this past autumn. It was only what could be planted among the stumps. There is a dreaded sweating sickness hereabout called the ague but we have been spared so far. The winter for all its sharp cold is the healthiest time of year in

115

this country. George sends his greetings. We hope to learn of someone returning to Ireland soon so that we can send our letters with him. It costs a fortune to mail even a single sheet, 7 shillings if you please, and we don't wish to burden you with such an expense. Your sister in the Lord, Mary

Mary carefully downplayed the meager harvest. It was normal for the letters, both to and from the Old Country, to dwell in detail on the quality of the harvest and the price of grain. It was the lack of anything hopeful to report that caused Mary to give scant attention to this important matter, but it fooled no one. To downplay the harvest was interpreted as bad news indeed.[14]

---

[14] It was common for letters to be written without paragraphs, empty spaces or punctuation in order to save space and reduce postage costs. The first sheet of paper cost about 7 shillings and the second sheet 21 shillings. At that time, 7 shillings would have been about $14.00 and was usually paid by the receiver.

CALDWELL

WAITING 1822-23

While Mary Argue was penning her letter to her family, Forest and Mary Caldwell were eagerly and fearfully awaiting their next child, after which there could be no more delay.

The Smiley family were every bit as discontented at losing their much loved daughter and son-in-law as were the Caldwells. Mary's father muttered to his wife that if he'd had the slightest notion that Forest was going to take their daughter and grandchildren to another land, he would not have consented to his courtship. Their concerns spread further as they heard of more and more young people who were making plans to leave. There was scarcely a family in all Ireland that did not lose a member or two to emigration.

It was no surprise that their departure was causing unhappiness to both families, but it did not lessen Forest's resolve one whit. He had thought long and hard on the matter. Those closest to them in chapel had already gone and were sending letters urging Forest and Mary to join them. The last letter, written in August 1822, contained a warning. They told Forest that he had better make haste if he were to have any hope of receiving free land in their part of Upper Canada. This was a serious matter indeed. Forest counted on being in close proximity to his friends, a promise that both he and Mary relied on as they imagined their life in a strange land.

The Township of March, Carleton County, Aug 12 1822

To Forest and Mary Caldwell: You cannot imagine how we are missing your presence here with us. Not until we left our homeland did we truly know how much we would miss our brethren. There are seven of us here, our lands fairly close to each other, and for that blessing we must thank our Almighty Father who is looking after us each day. But our Fellowship is not the same without you and Mary. You are too humble to know this Forest but in some way you had the whole Heart and Soul of our Fellowship. Your words were always the most Comforting to anyone who was downcast or in trouble. Without your presence we are foundering spiritually as well as materially. I will not delude you into thinking it is easy here for it is not and my Hetty won't let me say other than what is true. But you are needed. This country is in sore lack of any religion and if we cannot hold fast to our faith we are lost for sure.

The added reason we beg you to come now is that the free lands are disappearing. There is lots of empty land about to be sure, but it has all been allocated to someone or has been placed in reserve by the Crown for the Clergy or what not. In our immediate neighbourhood there are several abandoned places; some have never had an axe taken to them. Some soldiers take one look at the bush and turn their heel. They are no farmers, or woodsmen either. Although the work is hard do not let that daunt you for you will have your friends and neighbours here to take you to our bosoms and to help you raise up a cabin of your own. We will see that you are well looked after and you will find in this country it is better to have friends about you than to have a deep purse. So come to us as soon as you can and we will do all we can to make sure that you never regret your choice. I write for all your friends who will sign below and they join with me in wishing you God Speed. You and Mary will be kept constantly in our prayers, as we know we are in yours.

Hetty wishes me to add that Mary should be sure to bring shoe leather and as much good stout cloth as possible since it is hard to obtain in this country for any price. Bring good seed too and any roots you may want. Seeds can be obtained here but the quality varies greatly. The crossing we pray will be to your liking and will be better if you can come in the summer. Our crossing was not as fearsome as some we have heard of but in the main, those of stout heart pull through. Bring your own provisions. Do not trust to the quality of what will be given to you on the ship. We were glad for every morsel we brought. Fancy things will not be needed here and if you can bear to leave all that behind you will be just as content.

We are your Brothers and Sisters in the Lord,

Wilam Erskine, Thomas & George Morgan, Elias Harper, Jas Melrose, Herb Gourly & John Foster

This letter was not received until after Christmas and fortunately there were only six more weeks to go in the pregnancy. Rarely was a baby more anxiously awaited. It was Forest's task to ensure that they were able to have accommodation on the first sailing. He even went to Belfast to procure what he hoped would be a secure vessel to take his family to the New World. He was advised to take a ship called the Pegasus, which left from Glasgow under the captainship of a Mr. Monroe, a Captain experienced on the North Atlantic, who was well recommended to him on all sides. He had hoped to see the ship and the Captain for himself but both were in Glasgow getting ready for the first sailing. It was the best he could achieve and, having obtained a cabin for his family of eight, he bravely booked the passage. It would be cramped but it was the best he could do. He was advised to be prepared to sail on March 25th, weather permitting.

Whereas the Argue contingent had almost no time to ready themselves for the voyage, Mary felt that she had entirely too much time. She decided to take her silver tea set, but then decided she was being fanciful. When could such an item be required in the wilderness? She offered it to her sister Lizzie who was very happy to receive it and vowed privately that she would get it into the bottom of their food barrel. It would scarcely be a problem if it were stuffed with packets of tea. She confided her plan to Forest who said it was a remarkable idea. He said that anything at all was a good idea as long as it facilitated the packing and took some of the load off his very pregnant wife. Mary countered his endeavours, saying that she had to keep busy or she fretted too much. Never had a pregnancy seemed so long.

Lizzie felt that they both fretted too much and undertook to do much of the packing herself. Pots and pans were essential, sturdy clothes for the children went in, and oh yes, Forest would need a suit for church. Both Lizzie and Mary's mother tried to insert some treats for the children and something fine for Mary to wear. The next day Mary would unpack them. At the last no one knew exactly what had been packed or left out.

Then Forest remembered to tell the women that they could only take two large pieces of luggage in their cabin. Their large family would take up most of the available space. The other barrels would have to be lashed to the deck and *could* arrive safely, weather permitting. If they could manage a few books he would be grateful indeed.

Forest spent most of his days with the farm manager and with his parents. It was a waste of time trying to get his father to heed what he needed to know about the farms. He tried to get Willy Too more involved and Willy pretended to take an interest, but Forest had little confidence in the outcome. Willy agreed with everything Forest recommended, but it was doubtful if he would remember any of it. Forest decided that the best policy was to have the manager present at all meetings and hope that at least he would remember what had been decided. A great deal would depend upon the honesty and intelligence of the manager and since he was going to do the job of two men after

Forest left, Forest decided to give him a raise. Willy Too agreed whole-heartedly with all that Forest recommended. His father William did not care much one way or t'other.

His visits with his mother were both more satisfactory and more painful. It was obvious she was grieving about the loss of her dear grandchildren on whom she doted, but all the while she reassured Forest of the rightness of his plan.

"You must do as you see best for yourself and your family, Forest, and not worry about us. I am sure that Willy Too will take up where you have left off and I feel too that Samuel is eager to learn all he can about how to manage the estate. He really is a very sensible young man, Forest. We are so fortunate in that respect. You might include him in your time with Mr. Hurley."

As usual, his mother had given a helpful direction for the future and Forest spent the next few weeks with Samuel at his side as much as possible, including him in the reasons for every decision to be made about running the farm. The manager would have to keep this up too, in addition to all his other tasks. Fortunately, Mr. Hurley was agreeable to this plan for he could see that Samuel was capable and eager to learn. They would work together.

The baby was due in the third week of February and Sarah Caldwell asked if she could take her four grandchildren from about the first of February until Mary's confinement was over. The children were very familiar with their beloved grandma and her big sprawling house and were very happy with this plan to stay at Grandpa and Grandma's. It entailed bringing the youngest one over to see his Mama briefly every day to relieve his anxiety, but as they lived on adjoining Townlands, it was no trouble for Sarah and the arrangements suited everyone.

The baby did not oblige and was seriously overdue; by the 10th of March there was no hint of action. In desperation in the middle of the night when the house was still and everyone asleep, Mary got up and prowled about, squatting on her haunches. She had heard this would bring on the birth. The first attempt brought no change except that she was mortally tired; she tried again the following night and began to feel the welcome cramps that signalled action at last. The baby girl arrived on March 13th, their last baby to be born in Ireland. Despite all the prior anxiety Mary delivered the baby with as little fuss as she had all her earlier children, for which everyone was greatly relieved. Mary now seemed to be able to give up all the cares and decisions of packing and concentrate on nursing her baby. Her mother, sister and housekeeper, Mrs. Tate, were pleased when she stopped interfering in their superior management of the household and packing and kept to her room.

The obligatory length of confinement for a nursing mother was two weeks in bed, but in twelve days they had to be in Belfast to board the ship. Determined that Forest's careful arrangements would not go awry on her account, Mary was up out of her bed several days before the rest of the household knew aught of it. She walked back and forth in their bedroom when everyone thought she was resting and by the 20th of March declared herself fit to travel. As shocking as this was, everyone was relieved that she 'seemed' well enough. Forest promised a letter as soon as they landed at Quebec, but as they knew by now how unpredictable was the length of time it took for a letter to arrive, the promise provided scant comfort to the family.

The parish priest baptized the infant, Mary Anne, in the Ashfield Church on March 23rd with both families and most of the congregation in attendance. It was a very emotional time for everyone. The long goodbyes had already been said many times over and the final parting came swiftly. Immediately after the baptism, Forest took his family to Belfast to be ready to board the ship. They travelled in the Caldwell's well-sprung carriage which was large enough to hold all the family at a squeeze. Samuel insisted on going on top with the driver to see them off; his attentions were very welcome.

As they stood together on the wharf aware that these were their last moments together, Forest drew Samuel aside and said, "Promise me you'll write and let me know how things are, Samuel."

"I'll do better than that, Forest. I know you are worried about leaving us all, especially Ma and Da. I promise you, I shall look after them all their lives. You are not to worry on that account."

Those final moments on Irish soil nearly overwhelmed Forest. He struggled to keep his composure as he, Mary, and their six children boarded the Pegasus for the New World.

ARGUE

WINTER AT THE LANDING 1822-23

When George took his family to The Landing in the winter of 1822, it wasn't much of a place. It had been a landing point for fur traders who went up the Ottaways River to the interior. It was also the landing point for immigrants — but very few wanted to stay. The high ridge above the river was covered with trees, and then sloped down gradually to a huge swale which stretched from the Rideau River on the east, almost to the Ottaways River on the north and west. Cedars covered the swale and appeared to float on the thick, wet mud, not a very appealing place for the would-be farmer.

Its redeeming feature was standing timber, the source of wealth and industry. Britain wanted white pine for shipbuilding, especially masts and spars, and this was the prize the lumbermen were after. In 1819 they came to The Landing and built a few rough shanties for shelter while they took the trees. By 1822 The Landing had been pretty well stripped of the white pine and the lumbermen had moved further into the vast forested hinterland.

They left behind them a huge mess. There were areas thick with tall trees; other trees stood almost alone, tilting this way and that. When the wind blew it was a dangerous place. The lumbermen also left behind a few shanties they had lived in while they harvested timber. These were usually scattered at a distance from each other, and it was to one of these shanties that George brought his family. As Maude was in the middle of telling her sons exactly where to build her cabin, George intervened and invited Maude and her daughters to stay in their shanty until they learned whether they could remain in this shanty. There was ample space, and Maude was wise enough to know that she and Mary gave each other the support they needed. Rather than protest at length when the invitation was given, she agreed, and insisted only that she not be a guest but an equal in assuming the work in the home.

One can scarcely imagine what Mary and Maude thought of their new dwelling. How much worse it was than their shanties in Goulbourne is not certain. It was filled with heaps of broken branches, which had probably been used as beds, but on the other hand it was considerably larger than the 16 by 20 feet shanties in Goulbourne. This one could house at least 24 men. There was a great amount of debris and cobwebs and the odd worn out piece of clothing, but very little odour. The large gaps between the logs in the walls looked after that.

The fire was centered in the middle of the cabin and the smoke went out through a hole in the roof directly above. Everything was cooked in a pot hung over the fire. Even bread was baked in the same pot. This was similar to the fire in their Goulbourne shanty except for being placed in the middle, and since the shanty was much larger this was a more practical arrangement.

George had been busy between harvest and freeze-up. He had made a bigger and stronger sleigh, to be driven by as fine a pair of draft horses as he could find. Draft horses were not prime animals for clearing land — oxen were best for that — nor were they as fast as George would have liked, but they would be just the thing for pulling a heavy sleigh in the woods.

All was in readiness and George was keen to get going. He wanted to be one of the first to reach the camps and possibly have first crack at the negotiating with the cooks for future deliveries. To do this he had to get across the river as soon as it froze, and load up his sleigh with salt pork, oats, flour and hay from Philemon Wright's village. The first few trips were fraught with danger and Mary implored him to wait until the ice was thick.

"Think of the horses, dear. You can't afford to lose them." And unspoken, 'We can't afford to lose you.'

As impatient as George was to get going, and he was always that, he heard the unspoken words and recognized the sense in her caution. His family did need him. It was a matter of survival in the wilderness, and so he cooled his heels until he heard from more than one source that the crossing was safe. Off he went the next morning just as the day was breaking.

He did not know when he would be back, but he assured Mary, "We'll be fine, fine, Mary, Andrew and me together. Bide thee well now."

Andrew was fifteen and having had one winter of bush experience, felt he was already a man, fit for any occasion. Robert was no longer limping but he had been told very strongly that there were many tasks that he could do for his mother and Maude at the home front. His father left him a list containing many necessary and some not so necessary, tasks to keep Robert occupied.

The youth was fairly downcast as he thought that he was not trusted to do anything more than be a mother's helper. He felt that his accident last winter had made his father less inclined to believe he was grown up and trustworthy. George was astute enough to see this and took him for a walk a few days before his departure.

"It may not be just what you wish for right now, Robert. I can see that you are eager to go to the bush with your brother too, and it won't be long before you do. But just this winter here at The Landing I cannot rest easy unless you are about. I am placing great reliance upon you to know when you need to step up and take charge. Please don't let me down."

Robert thought there was very little likelihood of his being in charge with his mother and Aunt Maude about. When George went on to ask what Robert would do if a complete stranger showed up at the door, Robert was further surprised. In the first place it was very unlikely that a complete stranger would show up without someone else having seen this person already. There were very few people about and everyone was noted. If by some miracle one did appear you would welcome him or her, both for the diversion and as the neighbourly thing to do.

Robert said, "I'd tell them to come in, Da."

"Aye", George said, "that'd be the very thing. I was sure I could trust your sense, Robert."

The confidence his father was placing in him lessened the sting of his staying back at The Landing, but only by a little. He could see the sense of a having a man around the home, although he was determined that he would teach John how to be

125

a man, and that right early. Next winter he would be fourteen, and then it would be his turn to go into the bush.

The first trip out was a fairly quick one. George was away only two nights and came back triumphant with success. The bags of flour, oats and salt pork sold for a good price. This was somewhat of an accomplishment because the margin between what you paid at the store and what you sold it for was quite unpredictable. In the fall, when the stores were full of provisions, the haggling over price was less severe. He found that he had changed from a year ago. He was now more comfortable in bargaining with the storekeepers and in expecting a welcome at the camp. Life looked altogether more hopeful, and as he looked sideways at his son Andrew he saw optimism and fearlessness in his face. On this account too, George was happy that he had not revealed his own trepidation about his entirely new venture as a salesman of sorts.

When George returned home late at night on the third day Robert was waiting outside the shanty to greet them. He looked in much better fettle than when they had left.

"What news, Robert? Is all well here?"

"Oh aye," Robert said carelessly, and then added with evident satisfaction, "Some strangers did show up while you were gone, Da. I invited them in just as you said would be the right thing."

"Who was that then? Who are these strangers?"

"They were come to see you, Da. They had a message for you from Forest Caldwell."

"Well that is a surprise, Robert. Go on, go on. Out wi' it."

"I think Mam wants to tell you herself, but it is something about his coming, I know that much."

George and Andrew received a robust welcome which included hot stew from the ever ready pot. Mary and Maude, who knew of Forest Caldwell by name only and that he had seen George before they left Ireland, told George that three men, Wilam Erskine, John Foster and Thomas Morgan, had come down from March Township expressly to tell them that Forest and Mary Caldwell were coming to Richmond's Landing next spring, on the first sailing vessel they can get.

126

"Well", George mused, "it has taken him a longish kind of time to get here. I began to wonder if he received the letters I sent. There were only two."

"George, it turned out that he did not get a letter at all until last summer and then two letters close together. It was too late in the year to start, and that was just as well for just after your letter arrived, which urged them to come as soon as they could, they discovered that Mary was pregnant again. They plan to come after she safely delivers the child."

Maude added, "These men came to tell you that it must have been your letter which urged him to come that settled Forest's mind in favour of leaving Ireland, and they came to thank you in person. They were overjoyed and that's a fact."

George appreciated that both Robert and Mary had the pleasure of imparting news to him and that this out of the way occurrence had given those at home a lift in their spirits. He noted ruefully that his life of action was much easier to take than the long days of inaction and no society for the womenfolk. He was impressed that Robert had managed the situation very tactfully, surprising for a 13-year-old boy.

George's first task was to stock his own home well before he and Andrew left for the next trip. He was already full of plans for future trips but had not shared his plans with Mary yet. Very soon he planned to go further into the bush where the higher price he received for the extra distance would be considerable. He needed to take more hay for the camps and for his own horses as well. He was beginning to think about two sleighs and another team of horses. He had a lighter step these days.

He took Robert aside and asked him how the time had gone. Robert replied, "Apart from these men coming, nothing happened at all. I got that pile of wood you said we needed; Jane came and helped bring it back. On the way home we came across a stray dog. I wonder what you think of our having a guard dog, Da? Would that make your mind feel more at ease?"

George could well follow the trend of his thought, and chose not to put a damper on his hopes just yet. So he replied that he would think on it. "Of course you would have to be sure that it was not just any stray dog but one that really could be a guard dog. You will have to train the dog, and judge if he can be trusted."

That was encouragement enough for Robert; he felt he had made a little progress. A dog might help him get his freedom a bit sooner, and in the meantime he would be out of the house with the dog. He would make sure of that.

After seeing that Mary and Maude had coped when he was away, George made a point of not asking just how they had coped. He was not ready to hear of problems for which he had no ready answer. The chief trouble seemed to be keeping heat in the shanty with a hole in the roof and holes in the walls. It was evident that they had been busy gathering bark and twigs and moss to try to fill up the cracks in the walls but something more lasting was woefully needed.

To George's mind, the immediate need was to find out who owned the land he was squatting on. He did not want to go on adding buildings and fireplaces and other improvements on someone else's property, only to be kicked off it as soon as the improvements were done. It was no easy task to learn who owned what, but he learned that virtually all the land belonged either to Crown Reserves, Clergy Reserves or, most often, to an absentee landlord. He hated the sound of that. He wanted to be far away from *Landlords*. But really there was little help for it.

He recalled meeting a man last winter who owned land here at The Landing, or at least had been allocated to the land. Two hundred acres it was, and not too far from the river. His name was John Honey, an unusual name he'd thought at the time.

There were very few people remaining at The Landing by the time George tried to get information about Honey. Every able-bodied man was off to the woods, and even those no longer able to cut and haul trees tried to get work in the camp kitchens. He decided his best bet was to ask Philemon Wright, the 'stonewall of information', if he knew aught of Honey.

Wright was a Yankee who had come from Massachusetts in 1800; the first white man to attempt a settlement on the Ottaways River. He'd had the foresight, born of pioneer experience in the Americas, to bring with him a whole passel of experienced people, including many of his close kin and their families. He brought men to cut back the forest and build log cabins and fledgling industries of the kind they were going to need almost immediately. He situated his community close to the Chaudiere Falls on the north side of the river, across from The Landing. The falls were to be the source of power for a gristmill, a sawmill, a tannery, and so on. He also brought the families of many of these men who wished to come and paid for their transport, promising them return passage to Massachusetts if they wished to go back after a year was up. For those workers who did choose to return he kept his word, paying their wage and their transport as promised. As he had hoped, a number chose to remain and form the nucleus of a nearly self-sufficient village called Wrightsville. Wright became the first lumberman on the Ottaways River in 1809 when he and his son Tiberius made a raft of square cut timber and, with a crew, took it down river to Quebec.

Philemon was an extremely handsome man who still had a plentiful head of hair brushed back from a high forehead. He conveyed an affable manner to one and all and bore his tall slender frame easily as if he were to the manor born. Perhaps it was in part due to his family background that Wright came by his manner. The Wright families in Massachusetts were descendants of the earliest pilgrims to come to New England's shores in the early 1600's.

George and his friend Archie Scott knew nothing of Philemon other than the fact that he had established a thriving pioneer village on the north shore of the Ottaways River and that he was the person on whom the whole enterprise seemed to depend. Whatever the truth of legend growing up around him, by the time George met him, he was sixty-two years of age and had earned his leisure. He no longer ran the store or any of the particular enterprises, but delegated, allowing others to work independently while remaining accessible for help and advice.

George and Archie were a little diffident as they tramped through the snow to where Philemon stood watching a horse and sleigh approach the shoreline below. Philemon turned as they drew near and greeted them warmly. As he shook hands with George and Archie, he gestured for them to follow him out of the wind while they talked.

"I think I have seen both of you over at the store a couple of times recently, loading up for trips to the bush."

"Aye, that you have," George replied. "With all that you have to do, and considering all the people coming and going, I am surprised you would notice two people such as ourselves."

"Well Mr. Argue, do you mind if I call you by your first name? It may surprise you to know that I made note of you last year when you came over to get some provisions. You and your friends seem to be the kind of settler needed on the south shore of the river. Although I am not sure if indeed that is your intent."

"No," answered Archie to the implied question, "we are both located at some distance from The Landing, in the township of Goulbourne. But at present we feel the need to find a place where we can bide while we make a living off the lumber trade. As you guessed, we are in the business of hauling loading into the bush each winter and are looking for some place at The Landing where we can establish our families."

George added, "That's what we have come to ask your advice about. Someone, now I forget his name, said we could do no better than to talk with John Honey, and he might give us some direction. Do you know how we might contact him?"

"Hmm, I can give you some help in that way I guess, but the first thing I have to tell you is that he is not hereabouts at this time of year. He has a place here, but he usually spends most of the winter months in Montreal where his father, brothers and sisters live."

This was the sort of reply George feared. It meant further delay. He asked, "Is there any means of contacting this man Honey?"

Wright replied, "Well there's always someone heading to Montreal. This time of year it's an easy trip. If you give me a letter I can see that the next traveller gets the letter to him. In the meantime, can I help you out?"

"Aye, you might at that. I aim to find out just who owns the land where I am hoping to set my family up for the next few years. We have occupied a shanty not far from the Point, and of course I would like to know if we could buy that bit of land or even rent it for a few years. But I don't know who owns it and thought maybe Honey could advise me. And my friend and neighbor here is in the same need. I speak for both of us."

Archie nodded vigorously.

"I daresay he could, for it sounds to me as if you may be on the very piece of land Honey just sold. He had two hundred acres there but he sold them last year to a former worker of mine, Nicholas Sparks, a fellow countryman of yours, I believe."

George was downcast at this news, and Wright, seeing this, decided to give him a piece of advice, "In your shoes I would not be too discouraged. I know Sparks is a man who hopes to make a good profit on his investment and thinks he can do so by renting the land for a few years, hoping to gain from improvements on the property while he is waiting for the land to increase in value. He may be very happy to listen to your proposition."

He could see that George still looked pretty unhappy and guessed what bothered him was that he needed know if he could trust this man Sparks, countryman or not.

Wright added, "Still I think you cannot do better than to contact John Burrows, and I think he'll get back to you about this matter. He is always going back and forth from Montreal to The Landing. He has a reputation as an honest man, a surveyor to boot, so there is no one who has a better grasp of property boundaries than he has."

George said, "Have I got the right man? I thought his name is John Honey."

"Aye," Wright said, "the one and the same. Sometimes he goes by one name and sometimes the other. Confusing to be sure but I think you will find him to be a sound man for all that. He has managed to convince our Governor, Lord Dalhousie, of his abilities and has been doing some survey work for him in these parts. Can't have a better recommendation than that, can you?"

"Is this the same man who is reputed to be a Methodist?" George asked.

"The very one," said Philemon. "Personally I think that is a good recommendation, coming as I do from a Dissenting family."

Now both George and Archie were nodding. With this encouragement George set about writing the letter to give to Wright on the spot. He stated his situation clearly:

I the undersigned have recently come from Goulbourne where we are located on a 100 acre lot. We, that is, my wife, two daughters and two young sons, as well as myself and two older sons who are out in the bush, plan to live at The Landing each winter for the foreseeable future to try to Make a Living with the lumber trade. We Haul Loading up to the lumber camps and on

131

these trips I am away for a few days at a time. We have Settled ourselves in a large shanty left behind by the lumbermen, but we cannot like putting forth Energy and Expenditure on Improving this dwelling unless we can buy or lease the land and thereby come to some Agreement with the present owner. Mr. Wright has recommended that I contact you as you are Well Qualified to Advise us in this matter.

If you can give us any Direction in this matter we shall be most indebted to you for your assistance. I have heard that you are a follower of John Wesley and as I too am of that persuasion you cannot have a better recommendation

I am your brother in the Lord, George Argue

At this he folded the single sheet of paper, addressed it as Wright directed and started to wonder how he should handle the matter of postage. George felt perhaps it was a poor idea to expect Honey to pay for a letter when George was the one needing assistance. He decided to pay the postage, as this was a very important matter to him. Archie supported this decision all the way.

It was difficult to wait for a return letter from Honey, especially since the womenfolk were very cold in the shanty, which was too large to heat from one fire, especially when most of the heat escaped through a hole in the roof. Everyone wore all their clothing each day and night and the winter was not yet firmly underway. George thought that a stove and stove pipe through the hole in the roof would go a long way toward greater contentment in his household, but there was no way he could contemplate such an extravagance unless they were to have security in their dwelling place as well as security of employment.

To George's amazement a letter came back within a week. The letter said that Honey planned to make a quick trip to The Landing the following week and would be sure to meet with George when he was in town.

His letter concluded:

The issue of Land Ownership is such that it Cannot be dealt with in a letter.

Yours in the Lord, John Burrows Honey

With this encouragement, George and Andrew were off on their next trip. This one went well too, and with two successful trips behind him, George resolved to get another sleigh and another team of horses as soon as he could. The stove and stovepipe receded further into the future.

ARGUE

HAULING LOADING 1822

With this new notion of running two sleighs to the bush growing stronger in his mind, George thought he would see if William felt like joining up with him in the venture. He had only a very rough idea which camp might be William's. He thought to ask the cook at the next camp if he knew his son.

The cook had no notion whatsoever. "There would have to be something very outstanding about your son altogether for me to notice him."

George was hard put to think of anything out of the way about William. He was tall, thin, inclined to be serious, almost taciturn, fair hair plastered straight back from his forehead. None of these characteristics brought his image to the cook's mind. The cook thought perhaps George better try the next camp. There was another one just three miles further north. George decided there might be enough light left in the day to try for it, so he and Andrew unloaded as fast as they could and set off.

As the light was almost gone from the day, they spotted smoke in the woods ahead and following a well-marked trail, they arrived just as the men were coming back to camp after their day's work. There was little talk between them, just a single-minded intent: get food, warmth and rest. George decided to stay out of their way and not to approach them at this time. Andrew remained very still at his side.

Suddenly Andrew jumped up and hallooed, "Will, Will, it's us, your Da and me." The man Andrew thought was William looked up and about, puzzled. He could not see very far but he thought he recognized a voice. He must be imagining things. His shoulders drooped; he looked exhausted.

Andrew leapt out of the sleigh and streaked over to William who was amazed, but there was no doubting that they were a welcome sight. Now a dilemma arose. William was desperate for his grub as he called it, and if he tarried too long it would be all gone. But there were a load of questions he had for his father, and George had as many questions for him. William thought that the best thing to do was to try and arrange a spot for his father and Andrew to stay for the night and try to scrounge a meal for all of them.

George said "A place to sleep out of the cold would be welcome indeed, but don't try for food, lad. I don't want to be seen taking a portion that someone who has been out in the woods all day might think belonged to him. We have our own provisions, but aye, a hot cup o'tay would be very welcome, indeed it would."

Andrew's face revealed a longing for hot food as well as the thrill of eating at a proper camp meal, but he held back. He knew his older brother well enough to know something was amiss here, and he knew there was no point in coming right to the point. They would hear what was afoot when Will was ready to speak and not a moment sooner.

William took last place in the lineup for the food and said he would ask the cook if there would be anything left over. He was not optimistic but they would likely get something hot to drink, for sure. George and Andrew stayed by the door.

At first no one noticed them at all. Everyone was bent to the serious business of eating as much and as fast as possible. By the time William had a plate heaped with a brown mass, some of the men were finished eating and now were looking to see if more food was being offered.

The cook called out, "No leftovers tonight, boys. We have some guests."

Guests were all well and good but better liked if they brought their own food. Or better yet if they brought some home brew.

One man hollered, "Hey, Argee. Is that there yer auld man and a young'un too? D'ye think they might be much good out in the woods now? Maybe ye're going to teach them." He made a big guffaw.

135

William flushed darkly under the grime on his face and said, "Nay, but they might be bringing loading up this way one day. I know naught the now."

These were a lot of words for William to get out at one time. George sensed a lack of comfort for his son here at this camp. Most of the men turned their backs to this scene but the same man who spoke before continued to stare at William, and then said to the man at his side,

"It don't seem to me that his sort will be bringing what we need, now do it?" The man replied with little more than a shrug. There was something unpleasant in the man's speech, but just what was the problem was hard to put your finger on.

George made a point of conspicuously rejecting the offer of food, and giving thanks for the mug of something hot. William took his family to the very last table, and proceeded to eat his food in silence.

When he finished he said, "Don't worry too much about staying the night, Da. I'm pretty sure I can rig up a place for you to stay on the floor beside my bunk. You can have the cot, Da. Andrew and I will have the floor. There are enough blankets, and you can bring in what's in the sleigh as well. I'll check with the boss man and make sure that's okay." And off he went to the front table where the man who had spoken earlier was still sitting. He spoke with another huge fellow who nodded as if in agreement and William came back and said it was settled. They could stay the night.

"But there is something important, Da. You mind as how John MacFadden wanted to try his hand at working in the bush. The thing is Da, he's right here in this camp."

This came as a big surprise to George. They had worried about John for he had not seemed strong enough to manage this sort of job, but he had been determined, and they had not heard from him for a long time.

"Where is he, Will? We don't see him."

"He's here in what passes for a sick bed. That amounts to a cot at the back of the kitchen. He does not get any care, but at least he is warm and he does not have to go out in the bush. He must be in a despert state to be sure, or they would have him off that cot in jig time. Maybe you can ask to see him."

"I'll be sure to do that, William. I'd like to get him out of here, if we can."

George wanted to step outside to speak privately with William about the other matter on his mind, but when he attempted to do so, several other men followed them outdoors and stood by them. Maybe it was only the wish to talk with someone new to the camp, to learn if they really were going to haul loading into the bush; it was hard to say. Some drifted away but two men asked George on the side if there were any chance he might bring some home brew on his next trip.

"I shouldn't think so," George replied. "You know well I'd lose the chance to ever bring a load again if I brought as much as one bottle of liquor to any camp. I have to walk the line to keep the work."

The men knew this well enough, and started to explain to him just how it might be done safely, when William said to them rather brusquely, "There's no point in asking Da to do that kind of work. He is a teetotaler, or as good as."

These two men seemed prepared to take the disappointment in their stride, but as they turned away one said to Will. "That is pretty much what everyone here thinks of you too Will, especially Abe. You had best keep away from him if you can. He is a man who likes his liquor overmuch, and gets in a rare old humour when he's had none for weeks at a time. No one can look sideways at him then, certainly not a teetotaler.

"Thanks, Dougall. I'll take your advice and try to keep my distance."

When the two men moved out of earshot George wasted no time, "Will, I came here to put a proposition to you, and maybe now is the right time. Andrew and I have made a few good trips to three camps with loads of foodstuffs and hay. With one sleigh we cannot carry as much as we could sell. I'm giving serious thought to driving two sleighs and getting another team. But I'd need to have another man with me. Andrew is ready to do all he can, but I'd not like to have him in charge of a whole load of goods all on his own. We would have to go in tandem. What do you think of coming in with me and having your own sleigh? The distances are longer than they were last year, and I can see that being the case even more so in the future. That means more sleighs are needed. What think you?"

"If you had asked me last week I'd have said nay. The work here pays well and I feel I am getting stronger and can hold up my end of the work. There are a few men I don't care to work with but most of the men are well enough."

"What say you now?"

"Well you saw the lay of the land," said Will. "Somehow, and I know not how, Big Abe has singled me out as someone he does not like the sight of. That is not a good spot to be in. I've had more than one warning to stay out of his way. But it seems he takes every opportunity to single me out. It goes against the grain, but I can see that unless I remove myself I am going to have to fight this big lout, and quite frankly, I don't think the odds favour me. I could hold my own perhaps for a while if the man fought with some degree of honour, but that's not the case. I have heard it said that he is under a warning."

"What sort of warning do you mean?"

"Something about his being fired, and not taken on at any more gangs if he disables one more man. The man who tried to warn me of this had to break off, and would say no more for he did not want anyone to hear him speaking about Big Abe. I could go with you early in the morning, but I would have to go without a weeks' wage. In fact, I might not get a wage for all the work I've put in so far. That would be a big penalty."

"Yes, it would. But you would still be able-bodied, able to find some other work. Let us sleep on it and pray on it, and make the decision at first light."

Unnoticed by either George or William was the change in Andrew's demeanour. His eyes were as wide open as they could get and his step was quicker and lighter as if he wished he could hietail it out of this spot, which now looked more menacing than interesting. Morning could not come fast enough for him.

Morning brought more surprises. First, George asked the cook if he could see John MacFadden, and was given a flat no. George was clearly taken aback and the cook added,

"I don't mind for myself if you see him, but I'm told that no one gets to see these men if they come down sick. We don't aim to make being sick at all pleasant for them. Dad-blamed fool for coming into the woods. This is no place for a weak'un, as he be." With that announcement, he spat out a wad of wet tobacco, wiped his mouth with the back of his hand and turned to his work.

The second surprise came before George got out the door. Big Abe came up to him with a proposition, "You're heading back to town today, right?"

"Aye", said George. "We're about to set off and hope to be down to The Landing by early afternoon."

Abe asked, "Can you take me with you? I don't think I can bide here another week without trouble to meself and others. What I need is a bit o'time away and then I'll find my way back."

"We-ell," George said slowly as he began to see the wisdom in exchanging William for Big Abe, "if you can arrange it with your boss I see no problem with that. When can you let me know?"

"I can let you know right now," said Abe "and I'll let my boss know in a few minutes. I'm ready to go when you're ready."

With that he took off in the direction of the small hut off to the side of the bigger shanty. This was the boss' quarters, William had told him.

Will came up and said, "I heard that, Da. I'll bide here till the next trip. By that time I hope to arrange with the boss to quit without losing all my wages."

George rubbed his head and said, "Well of all things, I never would have come up with this solution. Truly, God has great imagination. I think after Abe has spent a few days at Firth's Tavern he'll be ready to work for a few more weeks. And since I have been the one to save him, so to speak, maybe he will give you a greater berth when he comes back."

"For a little while that may be so, Da, but I have decided to take you up on your offer anyway. The woods have many kinds of danger, but when the danger comes from those who work with you and live with you, those are the kind of dangers I can do without."

Andrew, of course, had nothing to say to all this. He was not looking forward to having Big Abe in the sleigh behind him, and he volunteered to stay in the back of the sled himself. Big Abe said not one word in the five-hour journey until they approached the Point and then said, "You can let me off here. Much obliged." He jumped off and was gone.

George decided that the best entry to getting Mary to accept the outlay for another sleigh and team of horses was the prospect of having William out of the bush and working with him. Otherwise, with the womenfolk living in extreme hardship, it was a bit of a stretch for George to make plans to buy another sleigh and a team of horses. He had planned to broach this idea that very evening as they all huddled around the fire, trying to get as much warmth as they could, but something held him back. What if William had to give up all his wages? He might think this was too big a penalty. George decided he had better wait until things looked more certain for William.

George had other news to impart: "I was able to find John, Mary. He was at William's camp."

"How was he?"

"He is not well and is being kept on a cot in their kitchen. The odd thing was, I was not allowed to see him."

"How is he being cared for?"

"I doubt he gets any care at all. And no visitors allowed."

"That sounds awful George. I don't like to think of John in a place like that. Can you please see him somehow on your next trip?"

"I intend to Mary. I don't think a lumber camp is any place for John or any sick person."

ARGUE

JOHN BURROWS HONEY 1822

As promised, John Burrows Honey arrived the following week. Honey was a tallish, spare man, with a heavy shock of brown hair, fine features, hazel eyes and a ruddy complexion, a man very much in the prime of his life and one who seemed pleased to make the acquaintance of another Methodist. It was Honey who found George for he had the advantage of knowing where to look for him. As Honey approached, George realized he had seen this young man the previous winter at The Landing, and he went forward quickly to introduce himself.

George held out his hand, "I am guessing you may be John Honey?"

"Aye, and a pleasure it is to meet you Mr. Argue. Your letter told me that you are a man after my own heart, a professing Methodist, that is. Am I right in this?"

George was pleased by such a forthright statement at the very outset of their acquaintance and nodded. There were very few men who openly declared themselves to belong to the Methodist faith or to that of any of the dissenting churches. The religion of advancement was most definitely the Church of England, and the majority claimed themselves to be Anglican, on paper at least. This common faith drew these two men together, but still prudence reigned. George had his family and their future to consider and Honey had an equal interest in his own future.

"I understand you are wanting to learn where and how you can establish yourself up here at The Landing. Do I have the right of it?"

At this point Archie Scott joined George and was introduced to Honey. George replied, "Aye, that you do. Archie and I and a few friends had hoped to be able to buy a few pieces of land, not much, just enough for a shanty with a bit of land. It seems to me that most of the land here is unoccupied but I am not able to learn just who owns what. Or even where one property starts and another one ends. I understand from Mr. Wright that you are the man who will know."

John Honey ran his hand through his hair, and made it stand up even further. "You are not alone in confusion on this score. The land has been surveyed of course, but there is one thing you already know about the challenges of surveying here in the bush. That is, you will know if you have been out in the bush. In your letter you say that you have land in Goulbourne. It is very hard to achieve a straight line. Do you know how the survey must proceed when there is only thick forest?"

George confessed that he had wondered about this more than once, but did not like to admit that he was worried that the survey was not to be trusted.

"Well, just last year," Honey said, "I got my surveyor's ticket. I took a look around me and decided that was an obvious need, and frankly I could not see myself making a living as a farmer, so I decided to find another route. An older man told me that Stegman, the man who surveyed these parts about twenty years back, went out into the wilderness with one other man, an axe, two lanterns, a few candles and lots of string. One man stood still with his lantern held on high and the end of the string. The other man took the other light and the ball of string and went into the bush as straight as he could go. When the anchorman could not see the moving light he hollered out. The second man then backtracked until his light was visible once again. He was told to stay put, and the string travelled forward and was fastened to that trunk. Whenever or wherever possible, a stake was put into the ground. They cut markers on trees, of course, as best they could all along the way. But can you imagine what mayhem was done to that survey as trees were cut down, or stakes disappeared? And mind you, these trees were not saplings. Some of them were four feet across." He paused and shook his head.

"After listening to that story I wondered what I was about, getting myself into such a haphazard profession. And then I was told that this was not the hardest part of the job."

142

"How so?"

"The worst part was the fear of getting lost. You might think that you have a good enough trail to follow all the way back to the starting point, but the fact was that the trees were so tall and thick that you had little idea of the time of day unless your stomach told you. It was always pretty dark in the woods, but total nightfall could come on very suddenly, and you did not want to be trying to find your way back then."

Neither of them mentioned the fear of running out of fuel in your lantern. If their wits were about them it would not happen. One could always light a stick from the lantern before that happened, but not all sticks would light readily or hold the flame. One needed your wits about you at all times.

George nodded as he envisioned the scene, and said that for himself he would not want to go far into the dense woods day or night. "Can you imagine ever finding your way out?"

Honey replied, "The only ones who can find their way out of the woods are the natives. We don't know how they do it. They must be born with some sense we have lost. Unfortunately, there are not very many natives who stay in these parts, and you would be lucky indeed to find one when you needed to. Myself, I intend to stay out of the wilderness unless I can count on a guide.

"But that is a long digression," he added. "You need to know how you can find a place to settle down right here? Have I got that right?"

"Aye," said George, "we have several other families who would like to be able to live in a shanty here during the winter so that travelling to the lumber camps will be somewhat easier. Do you have any suggestions?"

"The first thing to realize is that all this abandoned land is owned by someone. And if you cannot put a name to the owner, it is likely Crown Land or Clergy Reserve Land."

George and Archie grimaced. No need for words on this topic.

Honey continued, "The absentee landlords are people who were given the land or bought it for a shilling an acre, or even less. And they are waiting and hoping the value will go up and they will make a profit with no effort on their part. Much like myself, I suppose. A large number of these owners are the sons of United Empire Loyalists (UEL) who also got free land. Some of them are getting impatient while they wait for the value

143

of the land to go up. In some parts it is worth less now than when they first got it, for valuable timber has been stripped off and the owners did not get a hae'penny for it. Some of these timber men are like pirates or wolves. They grab what they can get and, with the owner far away, they are gone before he can do aught about it or know who is responsible."

George and Archie looked at each other silently.

"But," said Honey, "all is not lost. As you may have been told, I used to own this land we stand on and when I learned that it was not fit for farming I decided to sell it and move on to do other things. The owner now is Nicholas Sparks and he is a man who wants to make the land pay. If I read him rightly, I think he will be happy to rent the land to you."

"What do you know of this man?" George asked. "Is he likely to want to break a lease after we have put our back to improving the land, fixing the shanty and so on?"

"I don't know him all that well. He used to work for Philemon Wright whom I believe you know. And he is your countryman, not mine. Maybe you can get a better handle on him by asking Mr. Wright." After a pause he added, "Maybe the best course is to get him to sign a contract with you. Do you have any idea how long you may be needing the place?"

"No," said George. "That's the bad thing about it. I have a hunch that it may be quite a few years before we can clear enough land and harvest enough food to get us through the winter months. And getting it to market to sell it is another story altogether. Until we can get produce to market, or until I can no longer haul loading, we would be better off earning some cash. The thing I fear is needing to depend on the local store to get us through the winter or until the next crop comes in."

Archie heaved a sigh, "I fear we may be dependent on the good charity of this Sparks fellow to extend our lease. We would feel a deal happier with a man whom we know personally but that is the way it is for all of us in this country, is it not? Can you introduce us to Sparks?

"I can that," said Honey. "I'll meet you here tomorrow morning at the same time, if that suits, and I expect I can bring Sparks with me, or if not, I'll know what his intent may be."

"Tomorrow morning it is then," said George, "and we will bring a few other friends, if they are free to come. In the meantime I shall be asking my friends to pray for a good outcome to this venture. Either that or we try somewhere else." And with that John Burrows Honey shook hands once more and took himself off.

George thought, 'I didn't manage to find out why he uses two surnames. He seems a straightforward person. Strange that. Well, I expect we'll see more of each other.'

That evening there was an important gathering at George's shanty. The Scotts, the Fosters, George's brother-in-law, James Blair, Archie Magee and Archie's father-in-law, Thomas Buck, all showed up. Each man set down a block of wood and used it as a stool. Maude Wilson was there to represent both her sons and herself. Although they all had serious matters on their minds, they were happy to have the occasion of gathering together. Too often they were too worn out at the end of a day to think of anything but their bed.

George explained the possibilities and asked each man if he would like to sign a lease, and if so, for how many years? Each of them had been trying to sort out how long he was going to need the extra cash made from working at the timber trade, but few had a ready answer.

"We think we are going to be coming and going from this spot for a good few years, maybe five years at least, before we can go back to the farm year round," said John Foster as he nodded to include his brother Will. "If we have a spot we can call our own for that time, maybe we can persuade the womenfolk to come to The Landing too. We all need our wives here, and they would be happier too if we are all together. That's what we want."

There was some argument back and forth about the length of time needed before they could sustain themselves out in Goulbourne. Those with a more optimistic disposition thought that three years was surely the outside of enough. George finally said that he had decided that he would ask for five years at least. When he went back to Goulbourne he wanted to take with him some livestock and the skill to build a proper fireplace in the shanty.

It was hard to find anyone who did not want as much as that and so they decided they would all ask for three to five years, and perhaps their petition, since it included at least six families and maybe more, might be regarded favourably. They

145

asked George and Archie to speak for them, and to arrange things as best they could.

The rest of the short evening passed enjoyably in one another's company, and in sharing their hopes and ambitions for the year ahead. Will Foster brought out his violin and if the pieces he chose to play were closer to a lament than aught else, they still were welcomed. Any music from home, would be tinged with sadness, no matter how gay the lilt.

There was a silence after Will stopped playing. Then Thomas Buck, trying to change the tenor of their thoughts, said, "I hope Jacob might get work over at Wrightsville. It would be a good place to work. If he can get taken on in that village he can learn a trade first hand, any trade, blacksmithing, tanning leather. Whatever he learns will help us all back home." Goulbourne was emphasized now as 'back home'. "We'll have to do what Wright was smart enough to do at the outset and learn to do all these things ourselves and not be beholden to the store. I don't want to tread that road."

There was no argument with this assessment and not much appetite for further chat. They parted that night with prayers and wished George and Archie, "God be with you", at the meeting with this Sparks fellow.

ARGUE

MEETING NICHOLAS SPARKS 1822

The following morning Archie and George went off to their meeting with Sparks bright and early, but they were not there before Sparks. Sparks was a short man; his abundantly curly, reddish hair stuck out in all directions. He struck George as being very energetic and bright, but George was uncertain just what to make of him.

Sparks took the lead in the conversation, and he went straight to business. "I hear you wish to rent some land hereabouts?"

Archie replied, "That's true, if we can find something that suits."

"Well," said Sparks, "I am ready to rent you a lot or two, or as many as your group wants for that matter, if we can come to a price."

George began to feel that the bargaining was proceeding at the speed of a waterfall, and wanted to step back a bit. He said, "We need to think of more than price for this year. We need to think how this land will suit us for a few years, perhaps five at least, and for as many as six families."

Sparks rubbed the back of his neck, which appeared to have seen a great deal of weather. "Well," he said, "I find it hard to see that far into the future. For the time being could we just talk of year to year? I can give it to you for a very reasonable rate, but I could not go beyond two years at this point."

Archie put in, "We have looked the land over, what there is of it, and can see it is of no use for farming, just a thin bit of soil over bed rock, right? Wouldn't grow a hill of beans would it?"

Sparks confessed, "I was a bit of a fool over this land. I bought it sight unseen, and now when I see what a barren looking spot it is and that there is confounded little soil, I don't know what to make of it. I may sell it, if and when I can. I cannot do anything for a few years yet as it seems to take a quair long time to get clear title to anything in this country."

George began to think a little better of this young man for his honesty on this crucial point. He said, "We may be squatting in one of the shanties at the east end of your property right now, but we can move out at any time that suits you. You see, we have some land in Goulbourne and we intend to go there each summer, and that's where we'll farm, but we need a place here each winter as I'm in the business of hauling loading to the camps."

Sparks nodded vigorously. "A right good business that is, and more power to youse. Thing is, you see, I cannot look after the property for you when you're away, even if you rent it for a whole year at a time. Last summer I saw that the lumbermen who threw these shanties up still think they have right of way and stay in them in the summer just as they please. Fortunately, many of them please to go to Montreal where there are more taverns and it's more of a town altogether. And I say good riddance. They seem to operate by their own laws or no law at all so we are happier when they are in the bush or away."

"So", said Archie, who sensed that George was pulling back, "even if we were willing to rent for two years at a time, we have little security of keeping the shanty for ourselves?"

"There you have it," said Sparks. "This is a wide-open spot. I cannae think of a good word for it, but it may be a long time before we see anything like a town or even a village here, I'm thinking."

"We appreciate your time and your honesty on these matters," said George. "Perhaps if we look for a shanty a little further away from Isaac Firth's Tavern we may not have so many uninvited visitors. We'll look a bit more, and let you know our intent."

"Aye," Sparks said, "I could see that you both are God fearing men. Methodists are youse? I would not want to be leading fellow countrymen astray by only half-truths. So I wish

148

youse well. God be with you." And with a handshake he was on his way.

"Not a man to waste any time, is he?" said Archie, "but not a bad man for all that. At least I think he was pretty straight with us."

"Yes" said George, "he's all right, but we don't want a short-term lease. We'll try to find another shanty not too far off, one we can fix up a bit, and not regret our labour." He looked around, "I thought we would see John Honey here this morning, but he didn't show. We might as well spend the rest of the morning looking further afield for another shanty."

As they turned away, they saw John Honey waiting for them further to the west. He waved and came forward. When they met up, Honey admitted he had been waiting for them to finish their business with Sparks before he spoke to them.

"Why is that?" asked George. "Are you not on good terms?"

"Oh, that's not it. I told him you wanted to see him and I came over with him, and then I thought it well to stand back while you conducted your business." He stroked his jaw a few times and said, "There is a bit of discomfort though. I think Sparks is not too happy with the land he bought. He did not look at it beforehand so he has no real cause for complaint, but still, he's not happy. It is a poor strip of land to be sure and if he had asked, I would have told him as much, but in the long run, if this place ever amounts to anything, it may not be too bad. The legal details of the purchase are not all wrapped up and I prefer to steer clear of him until that is finished." He paused, "Where are you off to now?" Honey asked.

Archie explained that they were going to keep on looking until they found a shanty a little further away from the charms of Isaac Firth's Tavern up at the Point.

Honey recommended they go a bit west, where the land improved slightly and they were still far enough away from the swampy part. "I'll go along with you for a bit, if you like."

They were happy with this suggestion and presently Honey pointed to a shanty with a lean-to, one that had another log cabin of sorts not too many yards off. On the whole this looked like a better prospect for the beginning of an area where several families could live together until they were able to add another shanty or two.

149

Honey said, "I'll try to find out who holds the title to this bit of land. Maybe it's the Fraser family; they have sewn up much of the land in these parts."

After George had made another trip to the bush, Honey was able to tell him that, not only was Fraser the owner, but that he was glad to rent any and all of the shanties on his land to them for only two shillings a year. He was even prepared to sign an agreement for five years to this effect, but after the first three years the rent might go up a bit. He could not go beyond this.

George and Archie were ready to sign agreements forthwith and were confident the others in their group would agree too. Honey added that Fraser had asked him to obtain their signatures on rental papers, "If that is satisfactory to you and your group."

This was good enough for both Archie and George who decided that they would get as many friends as possible to attend a meeting at their place that evening for the signing. Honey was warmly invited to take a meal with them and to attend a chapel meeting afterward, if he so wished. Honey agreed readily to both invitations, and the beginning of a warm friendship was established.

After that it only remained to move their few belongings. Robert spoke up and said that he could handle the whole business with nothing more than a good sleigh. He relished the prospect of being in charge of the operation while the older men were away to the bush. He was becoming reconciled to his role as the man of the household, especially after Andrew had given him an account of what went on at William's camp.

ARGUE

WILLIAM'S CHOICE 1822

George and Andrew were in high spirits as they set out on their next trip to the camps. George had not yet talked with Mary about his hope that William would be on the sleigh with them when they returned. If it turned out not to be, then he felt Mary would be very disappointed, as would he, but he thought he was better able to handle a disappointment right now.

They took as large a load as possible and saved some of the food and hay for William's camp which they reached just as the sun went down. As before, they saw men walking to the big bunkhouse for their supper as they drew up. One very large man detached himself from the group and approached them directly. George was glad to see it was not Big Abe, but at the same time this man did not look too friendly either.

The man wasted no time on niceties. "You be Will'am Argee's father, I ken?"

George nodded "I am and you are…?"

"I'm the boss here and I don't like what happened the last time you came to this here camp. You took away with you one of our strongest workers and you gave Will'am ideas he could go walking too."

"I know that Big Abe went down with me but I told him I would take him if it was okay with you. When he returned and hopped on the sleigh I assumed…"

"Well you ASSUMED wrong. I don't let any man go off just because he don't like it here. If I let one more man go, the whole camp will take off. And my job will be finished too. I told Will'am if he plans to go walking, he will have to fight me first, and I shall thrash him until he won't be good for anything for a week, if then. He won't be going anywhere, not until spring breakup. Have you got that straight?"

It was very clear and very disappointing. George nodded.

"I see you brought more supplies. Supplies are always welcome, but in this case I think you had best take them somewhere else and not show your nose at this camp again as long as William is here. Nothing against you, mind, but if it unsettles the crew, I can't have it."

"It seems I have made a rather big mistake Mr... ?

"MacLennan's the name and aye, you have. Don't you think to ask before you go off into the bush? We have our own laws here and no one can come and go as they please."

George said, "You'll not see me again this year." And with that he turned the sleigh about to head back down to the previous camp, knowing he would have at least three miles to go in the dark before he could reach it. Andrew nudged him, "Ask about John, Da."

George thought it was poor timing to ask just now, but it was now or not at all. He called back to MacLennan, "I heard from my son that John MacFadden is here but not well. Can you tell me aught about him?"

"So ye know that one too, do you? Well I can tell you he's nay use here and likely won't ever be. If you want to take him, you're welcome to him."

With that, George got down from the sleigh and the two men went toward the cook's quarters at the back of the kitchen. There on a cot, almost on the ground, was John. He looked a shadow of his former self. George tried to hide his shock at the change in young John and said as happily as he could, "We've come to take you home John. Would you like that?"

Behind him MacLennan muttered, "Don't matter if he do or don't. He's going." And louder, "Ye can take his blanket with you. That's all I can give you." With that, MacLennan picked up John as if he weighed no more than a plucked chicken and marched out to the sleigh.

Andrew wrapped John up tenderly with the buffalo robe and then got down beside him and murmured in John's ear, "You're going home now, John. Hold on."

As they started up MacLennan called out, "Hae ye got twa' lanterns to put on your sleigh fore and aft?"

"That I have," said George.

"Good man", said MacLennan. "Hold up a minute and I'll check and make sure you have enough fuel to get you back to the next camp. It'll take you more than an hour at top speed to get there and these horses look like they could do with a rest."

"Yes they could use their feed right enough, but I think they can make it. I'll let them stop and have a taste of snow and hay and then we'll be off."

Now that MacLennan had made his point he seemed prepared to be as cordial as the circumstances would allow. "When you get there, tell McMurtry, that's the boss there, that I sent you and hope he'll put you up for the night." After a pause he added, "And dinnae fash yerself about Will'am. He has some friends here now and he will make it through. He's a hanged sight more able to handle an axe now than when he got here. I'll let him know that I seen you and that John has gone back with you. Cheery'bye."

"Thanks and good night to you, Mr. MacLennan."

From MacLennan's point of view the whole transaction worked in his favour although he kept the particulars to himself. He had been looking for a way to get rid of Big Abe without loss of face to himself. That man was as vicious as a bobcat and altogether too powerful in a fight. MacLennan needed always to win hands down in any contest with his men, and although he was a big man, well able to hold his own in most fights, he had not liked his chances with big Abe who was a dirty fighter and a man desperate for his drink. So he had turned his back as Abe took off, and was sure that he had seen the last of him. Experienced men knew they could not go and come back as they pleased. So now Abe was gone, young John MacFadden was gone and Will'am was staying. A guid night's work.

George was bitterly disappointed and very glad he had said nothing to Mary about the possibility of William's coming home. Not a word was said for quite a few miles and it seemed that perhaps John had fallen asleep.

Finally Andrew blurted out, "I don't think I'll sign up to go into the bush. I thought William could be home for Christmas at least. It seems like he is in prison there. And John is so sick. I don't like it at all."

153

"I feel pretty much the same way you do, Andrew. I hope next year William can come with us at this job. But right now we had better bend our thoughts and our prayers to getting back to the last camp before they have shut down for the night. I think they may not be at all partial to being woken up after they've shut down. And we'll say a prayer for young John too while we're at it."

"We could manage on the sleigh Da if we both got into this buffalo robe. And cover ourselves up with hay too."

"It's good to see a way through, Andrew, but I'll feel a deal better to get the horses into shelter and out of the woods. A great deal better." Neither of them mentioned the threat from wild animals or the likelihood of running out of coal oil in the lanterns, but it was in their thoughts.

They pulled into the camp about an hour later, and were able to see a few lights flickering. Considering the lateness of the hour, they were greeted hospitably enough. After they tended to their horses, McMurtry got them a hot drink, which they shared thankfully before they bunked down.

In the morning the rest of their load was left with the cook who was glad to get it, and they set off for home.

"Of course we won't mention anything about this to your Mam, Andrew."

"Of course not, Da. You don't think me as daft as all that do you?"

"No Andrew, I don't think that at all, but even though it may be hard, you had best not say anything to Robert either, just now. He might forget and let something slip or tell the girls. I think it better to say nothing at all until William is safely out of the bush. Right?"

"Right, Da. I can hold my whist. It will be just between you and me. I'm glad we were able to get John at least."

"Aye, me too, Andrew. Me too."

The women greeted them eagerly. When they saw John, they were first pleased and then shocked. Maude set about right away to get him warm drinks and more blankets. She did not like the look of him at all. It was hard to know just what had happened to the young fellow. Maude placed him close to the fire and shooed everyone away while she undressed him and examined him head to foot. There were no obvious marks on his body except a few old scrapes and bruises in odd places, but he

154

was dreadfully thin. He lay still and said not a word. Maude did not think that malnutrition was the whole story, but John would have all the benefit that food, drink, warmth and care of family could provide. It was to be the caring that mattered most.

ARGUE

A CHANGE OF HEART 1822

The following morning, as soon as George departed for the camps, Mary grabbed a heavy shawl and, without saying a word to Maude or her girls, left the shanty abruptly. An overwhelming sadness came over her as she saw George drive out of sight. He had been so eager to get on the river and away; she envied his enthusiasm and something more than that: she envied him leaving and going into the woods. She needed time to think what this was all about and she needed to do that alone. It did not seem to Mary that there was much she could do toward making a home out of this shanty and once again she had more leisure than she wanted.

Mary was not naturally prone to melancholy, but after little George died she'd had an empty place within and she began to wonder if she would ever feel whole again. She had always thought that strong believers in the hereafter would not suffer prolonged grief at the loss of a loved one, but George was the happiest of all her children, and she missed his laughter and little eager face so much. She could not imagine him happier in heaven than he had been in his own home.

She leaned against a tree trunk and looked out at the scene before her. A skim of snow partially covered the tree stumps and some of the grey mud. It was an improvement over two weeks ago. But when she closed her eyes she saw the deep green of her backyard in Ireland, the white sheets on the clothesline, a string of geese wandering over the grass, and she heard the sound of a child's laughter. Abruptly she opened her eyes and turned sharply. Something had to be done, Something, and she had to do it herself. Neither George nor Maude, nor anyone else could take her out of this … this morass. The only times she felt any cheer was when she was busy preparing food for the family, whenever they were around. With William away perhaps until springtime, and George and Andrew away for several days together, there was altogether too much in between time.

Maude seemed to have found her salvation in preparing medicinal herbs, sorting and drying them on racks over the fire, taking care to keep them away from precipitation coming down from the hole in the roof. It was largely upon the women's shoulders to care for the sick and injured, for few had much faith in medical doctors whose reputations were at low ebb. Doctors had done little good and much harm in the preceding century by bloodletting, purges, cupping and blistering, and now they added amputation to their meager battery of skills. Nothing much was then known about cleanliness, and the resulting infections were disastrous. Women who had some skill in healing were much sought after; they in turn had to rely on the herbs they grew or gathered, and on the strength of the body to heal itself. Maude put herself into this endeavour wholeheartedly.

Mary scarcely knew how to use her time. Meals were primitive, cleaning entirely unnecessary. Moreover, Maude had taken over the care of John completely; she was not needed there either. In Ireland she had never had much leisure. She spun yarn and got it ready for the loom, sewed clothes, pickled and preserved; the list was endless. Here she had a house which could not be cleaned, no wool, no food to prepare other than bread, salt pork and beans and, on rare occasions, some game. What to do?

Well, could she not spin yarn here too? Why had she become someone who scraped food out of a single pot and never lifted her eyes to other possibilities? George was always saying that they could not afford to get into debt with the store. He wanted to pay cash for everything and she had not minded too much. The list of needs was so long that she had not known where to start and, God's truth, she had not cared. Now she began to see that the spinning wheel could be and must be her salvation. She clapped her hands together and turned abruptly to go back to the shanty to broach the subject with Maude only to see Maude standing at the door of the shanty, watching her.

"Maude, Maude, you'll never guess what I am thinking and yes, planning what I should be doing."

"Perhaps not, but I want to hear it. If it can bring so much pleasure to you I am ready to embrace it, even unheard."

"Here it is. We should get my spinning wheel from Goulbourne, buy a bag of wool and start spinning. If I don't make some headway on yarn and then on weaving we shall all be threadbare 'ere long."

"You'll have no argument from me about that, Mary. I have been wondering when we were going to start and the sooner the better I'm thinking. The price of wool is not as low now as it was a few months ago but we know that the price will keep on going up until the next shearing in the spring."

"Right you are, Maude, as usual. I thought you might not be interested since you are so busy with herbs and looking after John and such."

"Mary, we may require fewer medicines if we have enough warm clothing to keep out the chill. How many layers that would take is unknown to me. I am never warm. Myself, I think we need to wear fur as the natives do.

"As for John, he demands nothing. It is time and love he's needing, I think. So I'm ready for spinning, and I'm thinking we cannot start too soon. I shall have George fetch me a few bundles too. We can teach our girls how to go about it as well. That spinning wheel will be kept going. We may need more than one."

Mary was delighted to find a partner with so much enthusiasm. "Yes, Maude, we may, and if we can make a trip to Goulbourne I don't see why we cannot get your wheel too."

When they went back to the shanty, they found Jane and Annie huddled together near the fire, looking very serious indeed. Maude's three daughters were standing by, the oldest one, Lizzie, looking every bit as serious as Jane and Annie, but the younger two, Sarah and Essie, appeared to have set their mouths hard against being glum and worried, at least until they knew what it was they were supposed to worry about.

"Girls," said Mary, "we've got a proposition for you. We're going to spin." They gaped at her. "Yes, you heard me, spin. And all of you can join in and help, especially in dying the yarn once it is spun. We cannot have the wool made up as it is into a cloth that anyone would be prepared to wear. It would be

158

dirty white to start and not long before it would be the colour of mud. Come to think of it, that's not such a bad colour. It would save a lot of washing."

Jane and Annie were visibly pleased, both with the prospect of a project and even more so with the change in their mother's demeanour. She had actually attempted a joke. They had come to dread these periods when Mama withdrew into herself, and nothing seemed to cheer her up. Please God, this was going to turn the corner at last.

Maude's three daughters were drawn quickly into the planning, and from the gust of joy from Essie and Sarah, one knew they had been more worried than they wished to admit. Questions flew back and forth. What colours were wanted? Where could they find berries at this time of year? It was a fascinating topic for the young women. The morning sped by.

John lay quietly by the fire.

ARGUE

ANOTHER BEGINNING 1822-23

It was hard to wait until George returned from the trip
and when he did they had a plan to set before him. He quickly
saw that there was to be no period of rest between trips this time.
Mary had a long list of needs that must be addressed
immediately. Wonderfully enough he made no objection to
buying wool from Wright's store. Indeed he saw this as a
necessary step, both for Mary's wellbeing and for the wellbeing
of all concerned. A trip to the store was planned for early the
next morning and a list made of necessities.

George was delighted to see Mary with that familiar
determined tilt to her chin as she laid out her plans, plans which
he intended to aid and abet. He smiled and rubbed his cheek as
he mulled over what this might mean. It was so needful to have a
full partner in this new land, one who could be strong with you.
He had begun to wonder if he was ever going to get Mary, his
Mary, back again by his side. For once he was ready to set aside
his rule, 'Never be in debt to the store'. The next day he
discovered that he had enough cash to pay for a few bags of
wool without borrowing, but he would have to delay getting
another team of horses. Mary was worth any number of horses
and George could be seen moving about with a small smile on
his lips for no reason at all and even breaking forth into a lively
song now and then. Maude and the girls scarcely knew who
looked better, Mary or George.

A few friends stopped by that evening and the plans
were shared all round. James Blair and Archie Scott were on
hand as usual; Archie had been back to Goulbourne to visit all

the neighbours, and he was of a mind to suggest that Robert Mitchell be asked if he could fix the loom they had brought over, but which had received a few hard knocks on the way.

"He'll have to put it all together, and I'm thinking he'll find he has to replace a few parts. By this time he has had so much practice with carpentry that he can almost call himself a carpenter, deed'n he can. It will give him a real lift to be able to set us all up in this way."

He turned to Mary and Maude, "If we can get the loom going I know Neelin and Garland will use all the yarn you can give them. They're master weavers mind, and it'll be a great boon to us all." Mary and Maude looked at each other and said not a word. They both were determined that they were going to learn to weave and that right soon, as soon as a loom was ready.

To celebrate the occasion Mary and Maude served warm scones and precious berry preserves The tea wasn't recognizable as such but it was a hot drink; they were all together and hope was in the air. Hallelujah!

The following Saturday, when they drove into Robert and Amy Mitchell's yard there was a great reunion, all the better for it being a surprise.

"We had not thought to see you 'til spring", exclaimed Amy. Everyone talked over the top of one another for the next five minutes.

Anne Wilson said very little but her deep pleasure was so very evident no words were needed. When George came in last, carrying John MacFadden, she broke her silence and clapped her hands. As for John, he showed more emotion than he had since he left the lumber camp. George propped him up in a cot near the fire beside Anne where she could tend to him.

When George asked Robert if he thought he could reconstruct a working loom, Robert rather shyly took him to the back corner of the shanty, and showed him some carvings. They were pieces of what would become a new loom. The ground was littered with a pile of shavings and his wife proudly said, "And those shavings are the result of what he has done this morning alone."

"You see, George, I've had too much time and not enough to do since the ground froze up. It was our Mam, Anne, who suggested that putting the loom back together was something I could do and I thought it a good way to pass the winter. I had some good pieces of dry wood I'd put aside, so I was pretty keen to get going at it. I knew there were some broken parts of the loom over at your shanty and a few more over at James Blair's place. Not a good idea to have them scattered 'bout like that so I went over and helped myself, and now I think I am getting somewhere. At least I have a few pieces I think might be passable.

Amy called out across the room, "Our girls have been busy gathering leaves and berries, Mam's idea there too, but we don't have near enough, just a start."

"The hitch is, George, I'm neither a weaver nor a real carpenter. I won't be able to put it all together, but Sam knows what I'm doing and is keen to help. I'm pretty sure I'm going to have lots of help."

"Of course you'll have lots of help. Sam Halliday will be the very man to help you. I daresay he would like to be involved all the way. Once the story's out I'm sure you may get more help than you want. Our people are wanting to get back to what they used to do in the auld country and weaving was a big thing in Cavan."

There was a good feeling in this shanty, a feeling of completeness, which surprised George. Maybe Anne's presence had something to do with it. As afternoon passed and the day darkened, a great many plans had been laid. Amy sent the youngsters out in the afternoon under Andrew and Robert's supervision to bring back heaps of fresh branches for bedding. While they were outdoors, the conversation shifted. Anne bent over John and said a few words; John nodded silently. She then took Mary aside and told her that John would bide with her for the rest of the winter. Mary agreed slowly, but pointed out that the cabin was already very crowded.

"Aye, that it is, but I think that John may be better here for all that. And maybe next year, who knows? That will be in the Lord's hands."

Mary nodded and then said, "I notice there has been an expansion to the shanty, that lean-to at the back."

Anne said, "Oh that is Sam Halliday's doing. He has his own place of course but he spends more time here in order to spend the evening with his children, and for the company too. The extra room gets well used."

162

Amy took George aside and told him that Thomas Wilson from Huntley way had been over to see her, and was surprised to learn that the family was away to The Landing.

"He asked me, 'Are you expecting the family at Christmas?' and I told him, 'Aye, that we are'. The thing is, George, I'm thinking he's intending to ask to marry your Annie. I noticed them paying special attention to each other last fall before you went to The Landing. I am surprised he did not know she was to go too. What do you and Mary say to this? Did I do rightly to tell him Annie would be here come Christmas? I thought I had better advise you of what's in the wind."

George raised his brows but was quick to reassure Amy, "You did rightly Amy. Mary and I shall talk this over. The lass is twenty years, but that may not be too young I'm thinking, and Thomas is old enough, ten years or more her senior and a steady man. We shall see him here at Christmas then and thanks for preparing us."

The fact was, George was loath to let Annie go. She reminded him of her mother when they were courting, and he knew he was going to miss her very much.

The young ones burst in with branches from which they had shaken all the snow and, using all the blankets and furs available, they made up beds. Everyone made an early bedtime as George declared his intention to be gone before first light. No surprise there, George could never wait to get going.

In the morning the parting was just as sorrowful as the greeting had been joyous, but it did set the women to wondering why they might not have these gatherings more often in the winter when the roads were passable and the possibility of seeing one another the chief antidote to almost any problem they might have. While they wrapped up oatcakes for the travellers, they had time for a few words. A nod to one another as they went out into the dark morning sealed a plan for another visit as soon as possible; that hope made their hearts a bit lighter.

When they met again at Christmas, there was a large gathering in the Mitchell cabin. John MacFadden was on his feet and while still thin and weak, he was markedly improved. Bundles of yarn lay beside large bags of wool and most wonderful of all, behold a loom, ready for use!

Midst exclamations of delight Robert insisted, "It has been a group effort. Every day someone showed up to assist with the carving and best of all, Garland and Neelin came over to look over the project."

Sam Halliday interrupted, "They made drawings of a loom and came back from time to time to ensure that when this great labour was done, we, but I think they meant 'they' would have a first class loom."

Every man in the room was proud to bursting with their accomplishment, especially as none but Sam Halliday had professed much skill with carpentry before this time. The talk moved to where the loom should be set up.

"Garland and Neelin want to take the loom back with them to their shanties and of course they are expert weavers, but these men are getting on..."

George raised his eyebrows and thought, Reggie Garland and Gregg Neelin are only a few years older than I am and they were the best of the weavers in Cavan. Aloud he said, "Gregg and Reggie are the best. All the more reason for them to be teaching others their skill. I am pretty sure Mary and Maude are keen on learning and mayhap others too."

A few brows were raised at the thought of women being trained in what was surely a man's field. But not many were prepared to raise their voices to object. Maude Wilson was not a woman they cared to redirect.

Thomas Wilson had joined the group too but he was not involved in the planning at all. He feared his own plans were to be thwarted by all this talk of looms and sheep. Sheep and wool were vital of course, but...

"Mr. Argue, could I have a wee word with you over here out of the way?"

George had not noticed Thomas in the crowd at all and was taken a little by surprise. "I think I know what you wish to talk about; it's marriage you are thinking about, right?"

"Aye. D'you mind when I spoke with you four years ago now? I said I wanted to wed Annie, but you said she was too young, and I said I would wait. Well Mr. Argue, I have waited four long years. They seem very long to me. Surely, she is old enough now." He looked a bit anxious, but equally determined to make his case.

George struck his brow. "Yes William, you did ask and I think Annie will be a fortunate girl to have you for her husband. I must admit the time has gone so quick I've scarce had time to think about it. Mary and I are agreed you can wed, but how and when? There's no preacher nearby most of the time."

"Yes sir, we know about that but you know many are getting married just by stating their intention to marry in front of family and friends, and then, when the preacher is by, we can make it all legal-like."

"I cannot say I am happy about that way of going on, but I know, I know, it is how it is done here in the woods. Let me see if I can arrange a preacher to come by this summer. Can you hold till then? It will be easier for us to get Annie ready and have a proper wedding. I think she would like that best."

Thomas, who had been hoping for an immediate wedding in front of kith and kin, looked downhearted, but Annie, who overheard some and guessed the rest, looked a little relieved. She wanted to marry Thomas and was pleased this wonderful man wished her for his bride, but what was the rush? Thomas went to her side and stayed there for the rest of the evening, frustrated and determined in equal measure. He was not going to leave without a firm date, preacher or no preacher.

George went back to the discussion; they were talking now about buying sheep...

James Wilson declared, "The best time to get them is right now. We can fetch them home on a sleigh and house them right in our own shanties." These precious animals were not to be housed in any outdoor lean-to. They would live with the family. One wondered which shanty would be honoured by the presence of the stinky ram.

It was decided that they would draw lots for the ram and when the cabin was chosen they would build a very sturdy addition to the end of the shanty for the ram. Ewes were one thing, but a ram in lust was something else again. His Majesty, as he came to be known, must be well protected from wolves, but the family must be protected from the ram.

Archie Magee, who was at The Landing during the winter, leaned forward, "You can use my shanty for a barn for the animals this first winter. They cannot do much to a shanty that cannot be fixed and since my place is pretty central, you can arrange some means of feeding them till springtime. And as soon as we all get back in the spring we shall build new barns. What d' you say to that?"

"We're beholden to you Archie. That will be a big relief to all of us. We'll take turns on looking after him, never fear," said Sam. "Now we need to fix on how much cash each of us can put into the pot and who can go and fetch these critters."

George suggested, "Since you will be looking after them and providing the feed too, those of us who are away at The Landing had better try to put in a little extra cash, to even things up." This was agreed to with a degree of relief as a few of the more silent men had been wondering where the cash was coming from for all these excellent plans.

James Wilson and John Scott agreed to fetch the ewes and ram. Moses Wilson said, "I and my oldest would like to go too. We'll take our own sleigh, of course, and it will make for a fine outing. Safer to take two sleighs don't ye think?"

When evening came most of the neighbours spread out to sleep at home or at neighbouring shanties, but promised to return the following day. Thomas Wilson started out for Huntley the next day with as firm a date as he could obtain: the first weekend in July, 1823.

Robert Mitchell and Sam Halliday took George Argue and Archie Scott aside and told them how much it meant to have them back with the group again. "We came to this country all as one large family and when half our group, and you the leaders of our group, went away for at least half the year, we felt adrift and even a bit hopeless in this very strange land. We have brought our womenfolk to very harsh circumstances and while they don't complain out loud, we can hear every word they are thinking. Women don't take very kindly to not being able to make a meal for the family, and to watch their children grow up in such rough ways with no education."

George and Archie could do little more than nod and acknowledge that to split the group up as they had done, was a high price to pay for their attempt to earn cash, and while they made no outward commitment about how often they could make visits during the winter, they privately decided to make as many as possible.

They reassured them, "We'll be back each spring, have no doubt. Goulbourne is our home now too and we only wish to be able to stay here the year round. But when that will be so, we cannot know just now."

Few of them realized how much they had all suffered some degree of depression. The gloom of the forest and dark canopy of the huge trees cut off whatever light was available. The ugly view of nothing but stumps between the cabin and the wall of trees was all that many felt they would ever see in this land. But most of all, there was a sense of hopelessness at the immensity of the task before them, without even the prospect of a good meal or the company of friends to look forward to. All these things had taken a huge toll on their spirits.

When they gathered the next morning, there were a few moments of silence that no one seemed ready to break. Then John Wilson stood up, cleared his throat and said,

"I did a bit of thinking last night and I realized a change had come over me after our meeting yesterday. I know we don't like to give way to our feelings but I can say that I have been down ever since we came to this country. I know John Sr.'s death had much to do with it. I thought that was reason enough, but I know now it was not the whole story. When we set out to come to Upper Canada, I think we expected the world would open up for us. There would be opportunity in every direction. Instead I felt that everything was shutting down. Upper Canada was just the opposite of what I had dreamed. Well, after yesterday I began to feel hope again, that same hope I had in Ireland. I can see my way forward now. And I think maybe a few of us feel the same. That's all I have to say."

There was another silence, this time broken by James Blair who said gruffly, "And you've said a great deal, John. I could hear John Sr. speaking just now. You have got the same stuff in you, that you have. I think we have here a new beginning."

Murmurs of assent arose; Anne Wilson regarded her youngest son with pride while Maude looked on with tears in her eyes and a hard knot in her throat.

They looked around at one another and nodded. Each man and woman felt the importance of this meeting, and realized they were setting a pattern for their future. If they could make their own cloth and sell it to the local store, they could overcome other obstacles too. There was a gristmill at Richmond but why not have their own mill nearer home? If they could not find waterpower, they would grind their own grain as had been done in biblical times. If the government would not build a road for them, they would have to work out their own salvation. Just how was still uncertain, but this was no time for doubting. It was time to believe in themselves again. They set about making plans.

Before long the conversation veered to what was uppermost on everyone's mind: *food*. Few people manage to think so little of food that it does not matter what they eat, and these hard working men, women and children thought of food a great deal. Ever since their arrival they had been living on oatmeal, and the first addition to that staple was salt pork. Each family had bought a pig or two for it was an easy animal to raise. It almost fed itself by rummaging around on the forest floor. It loosened up the soil, fertilized it and was smart enough to keep out of the way of predators during the day. Each settler had built a small shed to protect it from the wild animals at night.

If possible, families had two sows, one to eat and one to keep until she had a litter and raised them to independence. With so many of the men leaving for the bush, it was a challenge to find one who would volunteer to keep the boar, but this too was a necessity, and Sam Halliday had stepped up to do his duty. It was the task of the other families to get their sows to his sire, and a difficult task it was too. However, there was lots of labour, and hunger made them drive the not-too-cooperative animal through the forest to the Hallidays for an overnight stay, or more if it seemed needed. The women were not too experienced at knowing just when the sow was in heat, as she usually seemed contented if she had enough to eat, so Samuel and Robert had to lend their more experienced eyes to this task. After the first trip the sow seemed to know what was ahead and required more restraint than direction.

Pigs are said to be intelligent creatures but no one had any sentiment about them whatsoever. They may be smart but they are not cuddly, and after all, they had a pretty carefree life until the day of reckoning. On that day the children were sent out to visit their neighbours or gather berries under the supervision of their older sisters. The men and older boys were called upon to do the nasty work of killing, shaving the pig with a well-sharpened straight razor and cutting it up into pieces. It was a community event and the women invited as many neighbours as possible for a meal of fresh meat. Each family repeated this routine when they had an animal to be slaughtered. Fresh meat for the whole community for a day or two at the most and the rest went into a barrel of brine.

Sam Halliday built a smokehouse, and took as many pieces as he could at one time. The result was wonderful bacon. Many neighbours had willingly walked a few miles for a plate of bacon and oatmeal cakes. Nevertheless, a diet of pork and oatmeal can be arranged in only so many different guises, and by the end of the winter of 1822-23, everyone was heartily sick of every version. Their challenge was to do something about it.

ARGUE

LETTERS HOME 1823

Maude and Mary now found that winters at The Landing passed more swiftly as they were busily employed spinning yarn. They also found another occupation, that of letter writing. It came about quite accidentally when one day a young woman, who stayed at The Landing while her husband was away in the bush, approached Maude and introduced herself diffidently.

"I be Mabel Longford, Ma'am, come from Newcastle and I seed as how ye was writin' somethin' down t'other day. Would ye be willin' to help me send a note to my folks? I've not heard from them nor they from me but the once since I come here and that be so long now."

Maude hesitated, "Mabel, you know we shall have to wait until we find a person leaving for the Old Country?"

"Oh aye," said Mabel as she handed Maude a small sheet of paper.

"What is it you wish to say, Mabel?"

Oh, I jest wish to say that I be well and that my Albert is away to the bush and earnin' good money or at least he be gettin' food ivery day and the promise of some money at the end of the season. Tell them we have enough to eat and that I wish with all me 'art they could be here with us. Tell them we would welcome them an' look after them an' care for them. I don't like this country as well as Albert does

170

but he tells me not to fret an' I will soon think 'tis
the best place on earth. [15]

Then she paused and went on with some anguish,

All I wish for is to be able to have a cup of
tea with ye. If ye can come we would be that happy
to see you. It is a good place for the young an'
strong but, although ye are getting on Maw, I can
look after you as long as I'm able. If I be still alive
by next spring I will look after you. Tell Molly that
she would find many men out here that wish to marry
her. There are no spinsters here, men are that needy
of a wife.

"Are you sure you want me to put that in about your still
being alive next spring, Mabel?"
"Oh aye, sure, we can never say what we will do in too
strong a way. 'Tis temptin' Providence. And anyways, how can
ye ever know in this country? If'n I gets sick, I'm as like as not to
die."
Gradually a few others came to have some help with
their letter writing. One was a young orphan boy of fifteen who
asked to send a letter to his Aunt Foster. His message was very
brief.

Dear Aunt Foster,
I wish we might see one another once more
before we die but if not join with me in writing, it
seems the only satisfaction we can have here.

He could think of no more to add. He did not want to tell
her what life was like for him here for she would only be
unhappy to hear it. He said that several times he had been hired
to work and after he had worked a whole week a quarrel was
picked with him and he was turned off without his wages. At
least while he was at work he could eat but he had not yet saved

---

[15] The letters in this chapter, with the exception of Mary Argue's letter, were
found in the Public Archives, the spelling and language unaltered.

up money at all. "Mostly," he said, "folks are not paid with money but are paid in promises."

And so the letter was added to the other letters and the long wait for a reply commenced.

One other young woman called Lucy did not hold back her gloomy story. She had come over on a boat with her brother, Martin, his wife, Lilith, and their four children.

Dear Mam and Father,
I hope this letter finds you in better spirits than we are here.

We have had some very bad times. The children were very ill by the time they reached Quebec, especially Harriet who had a hooping cough. Then at Montreal, which was a terrible place, we were put onto open boats and were exposed to the dreadful weather all the way to King's Town. Harriet kept getting worse. On July 1st Harriet died and Lilith was very bad. On July 3 Lilith died. The doctor said it was the scarlet fever that took her. The other children are well so far, but this is a sickly country. One can go to bed at night well and harty and may not be able to rise in the morning alive. Many people are plagued with the ague, which is a very bad thing. I am sorry to have to write you such bad news but I have waited long enough to tell you as I hoped things would get some better somehow.

I am well at the moment and am busy looking after my brother's children so I can have no thought for myself. I would not ask anyone to come to this country and if I could be at home I would be. But I have no hope for that in this lifetime. Write to me when you can. I hope you are getting enough to eat at home. At least here we have enough to eat but it be hard for Martin to support us all. Often he is not well paid for his labours. He is paid with a bag of flour, maybe mouldy but it is all that can be had. If I had the time I could be hired out as a servant and no reference needed.

Your affectionate daughter, Lucy

For some letters there was no reply ever and after a bit, the rumour spread that if you wanted your letter to reach your folks back home, you had best not say what's wrong with this country. The letters are read and only good reports are wanted about Upper Canada. So you have to say how happy you are when your heart is breaking for home. But the reason for no reply may as easily have been the excessive cost of the mail.

Some people wished to give advice about how to manage the voyage, but the majority wished to forget all about it. A man by the name of Amos Corsbie approached Mary for the paper and pen to write as he was short of the means and was quite desperate to convince his brother to come with all possible speed.

December 30 1822
Dear Douglas,
I write to you from Richmond's Landing, U.C., where we are staying for the winter. The cold and the loneliness proved too much for Millie out in the bush and so we are here for a bit. It is every bit as cold here but there are a few more people about and this suits better. You must not think the weather bad. It is brisk and clear and very enjoyable if one has good stout clothing. We hope this letter finds you all in good health. We are well enough. I think if a man can maintain himself through the first year in this country, he may live very well afterwards. You may hear that a man and his family with only 200 pounds sterling will be in for a hard time of it in this country. Do not let that discourage you. If that man is blessed with some strong sons it is better than a fine purse. Labour is expensive and very independent, not at all reliable. In this respect you are well away for you have all the help you will need in your family.
Have all your agreements in writing and bring several copies. Keep your circumstances private on the ship. People are always inquiring about what means you have and what you are going to do when you land. The main thing to bring with you is as much money as you can muster. Don't bring much other than cooking pots and Millie says that your wife should bring as much sturdy cloth and strong muslin as possible, for it is hard to come by in this country except at top price. You will be sick on the water but you must not mind that. Lie in bed and eat as much as

you can. Some epsom salts will not be amiss. It will soon be over. Do not undress the children at night. It will be too cold. Wear only old clothes on the ship. Bring shoe leather if you can but do not let anything hinder your coming. Don't believe anything the French tell you when you land in Quebec. They hate the English and wish to see the back of us. A collar maker and a blacksmith stayed two days in Quebec and returned to England. I met with a good deal of trouble at first but I expect I shall soon be rewarded for my exertions. We look forward to the day when we are united again. Your brother, Amos

Mary then wrote a letter to her brother Gideon and told George that he must take all these letters to Wrightsville at his next crossing.

April 10 1823
From The Landing
Dear Gideon and Agnes and all our friends;
By the time you get this letter you will know that Maude and her girls are with us and we are all very happy together. Maude and I busy ourselves trying to learn as much as possible of the healing herbs and plants in this country. Maude puts herself into this wholeheartedly. You would hardly know her for she is not a quiet person any more and everyone takes note of her. She has no idea of all the notice that is taken of her. She has received two proposals of marriage but didn't think of them for a moment. She says that she now has only herself to consider and is enjoying this state of freedom so much that she will not change it for any amount of security or other social advantage. We also are back to spinning and are teaching our girls how to take it up too. Not before time as the clothes we brought are getting well worn. This project has been a good one for all and we have made several trips to Goulbourne so that we are not getting out of touch with our friends. They too are at the spinning and the men have rebuilt the loom. We are very excited about the cloth we plan to make and perhaps trade at the local store. We were happy to hear that the Forest Cauldwell and family are on their way to this country. We are looking for them each day. and hope they arrive before we leave The Landing for Goulbourne. The summer months will be fearfully busy so it may be next winter before we have time for visiting. John McFadden has come back

to live with our family. He was very poorly but under Mam's care he is coming along now. A word about Jock Kennedy, whose wife and daughter died on the crossing. We saw him in Richmond last summer and he has landed on his feet rightly. He has married a lively Scots Presbyterian lass called Moira Bissett and now has his son with him again and a newborn girl as well. Rose Faulkner arranged the whole thing or so I've heard. Moira's Presbyterian parents were not overjoyed at the match but the arrival of the wee baby has mended things somewhat. George sends his greetings and prayers for everyone.

Your sister in the Lord, Mary

CALDWELL

ARRIVAL 1823

From the moment Forest and his family set foot upon the ship and the gangplanks were drawn up, they were able to turn their thoughts from the distress of leaving loved ones behind and gird up their loins for the voyage, about which they had some trepidation, for reports of other voyages had not included one favourable comment. Their welfare would be their own concern, and then there was always the weather, which was everyone's concern and under no one's control. On the plus side, they had brought enough provisions to last eight weeks and they had their own cabin. Surely they could make it through.

The children were delighted with the cabin, which seemed as small as a doll's house. Forest took the oldest two boys out on the deck while Mary nursed the baby and nine-year-old Margaret, assisting her mother as best she could, felt she was playing house for real. James and John, aged five and two, were already regretting that they had not gone out on the deck with their brothers. This was to become the pattern for many days to come. If the winds held the boat steady, Forest took all five children with him, young John on his shoulders, James and Samuel on each hand, and Margaret, holding her brother William's hand. Then Mary could have a few moments of blessed peace. But far more often he took three children at a time and in this way he was outdoors in all weather possible. Forest and the entire family proved to have good constitutions for a sea voyage. This was an enormous blessing, one for which they could scarcely be properly thankful as they had no other experience.

They had only one or two days of calm and just one storm during which they learned what the North Atlantic might become. Mary, having nothing to do other than nurse the baby and maintain the peace amongst the six children, declared a sea voyage provided the best rest she'd had for years, just the thing for a nursing mother.

Good weather and steady winds brought the Pegasus to the shores of North America in little more than four weeks and they docked at Quebec 29th day of April 1823.

Forest went to thank the Captain for a good voyage, and said, "It was much better than we had been led to expect."

Captain Monroe replied, "It was the best voyage I have experienced at this time of year, in fact at any time, in any year, on the North Atlantic. We have made record time and no severe weather. E'en those in the hold have done well." He shook his head and added, "I would nay have believed it possible. It beats all I ever heard of, it does that. I'm sure we made a record."

Forest said he was happy to put that into the letters he had already written to their families, ready to post in Quebec. Captain Monroe said, "I'll look after that for you. This ship turns right around for Southampton. I can put your letters in the mail there. It'll be a sight faster than mailing them here, I can guarantee that."

All in all, the Caldwell family arrived in British North America in better shape than when they left Ireland. Getting to their friends in Upper Canada was another matter. The ice was still solid on the river from Montreal to Richmond's Landing and they and their belongings were pulled up the river by the team of oxen they had purchased. The family walked much of the way behind the sleigh.[16] It took four more weeks before they reached The Landing.

They were disappointed to find it such a barren place, with nowhere near as much population as Montreal, which now bustled by comparison. Prices everywhere were exorbitant, compared to home. Forest decided that they had best remain at The Landing until their friends could come and escort them to March Township. With assistance from Isaac Firth, he sent a

---

[16] The winters must have been considerably colder and more long lasting for the river to be still frozen for this mode of transportation to be possible during May, as the family story claims.

message to Erskine to let them know they had arrived and would wait for them to come to The Landing to fetch them. There was a message for them from George and Mary Argue which said:

We waited as long as we could to welcome you to this country, but we had to leave for Goulbourne in mid-May in order to get ground ready for seeding. We hope to see you in the fall.

They had a few days to look about them at The Landing. One look at a typical log cabin let them know that it would be quite a come down for them. Mary, who by this time was a very mature 28-year-old matron, didn't complain, but she was appalled. She had not contemplated a dwelling without a floor but that was the case for the most part. One could sometimes see clear through between the logs to the outside of the cabin. She could only wonder what this would be like in the middle of the winter. It seemed to be unpleasantly drafty in early June. Where was the fireplace or chimney? Women were cooking outdoors and she did not wish to inquire too closely into their reasons for that as she hoped it was not the usual way.

The accommodations were not their worst blow. The word was out that Colonel Burke was not allowing any more settlers in the Military Townships. They were too late. Forest waited anxiously for his friends, trying to ignore the weight of despondency that gripped him.

Four days after their arrival his friends arrived en masse. Not one, but five friends greeted him as he left the door of the hostel. What a welcome he received. Mary came forth at the hubbub with all their children in train and they had a wonderful reunion. Finally Wilam Erskine, who appeared to be assuming the role of leader, broached the subject that was most on Forest's mind.

"I can see by your look that you have heard that Colonel Burke is not locating any more settlers on Crown Lands."

"Aye", said Forest, "that I have."

"Well don't upset yourself too much on that account. There is lots of land left vacant roundabout. We've been thinking on it and have come to the same mind on the subject and here it is. You are to set yourselves down on a piece of that there vacant land and make it yours. That's what you are to do. Once you

178

have done the work of clearing it and building a house and show yourself to be the very kind of settler that they be wanting in these parts, well then, we are right certain that they will grant you the land. And there you'll be, right as a trivet on your own one hundred acres free and clear."

"You mean I have just to put in my labour and hope that someone does not snatch it back from me. Such a risky venture is one I cannot relish overmuch."

Tom Morgan broke in, "Well on that point, Forest, we are not all of the same mind. There are some of us that think that you might speak to Colonel Burke and see what he himself would advise. You might feel a deal easier in your mind if you have some assurance from someone higher up that your labours will be honoured, as we are sure they will be."

"Have you got a certain hundred acres in mind then? And why are ye so certain sure that the first man will not come back and claim his own once they have been cleared for him?"

Wilam answered, "Who, Maxwell? Ha! We have seen the last of him, you can be very sure. Indeed, none of us ever saw the first of him. We heard tell that he arrived one day on a fine horse, took one look at his bush and said, 'If this is the kind of free gift the Government has for the likes of me they can keep it. Sure an' I don't have the money to lay out for anyone to help me clear the land and I'll need more help than I can get from an axe and government rations to clear a wee patch of ground. I'm away and they can keep their dad-blasted free land for the likes of some other eejit.' And he was off and away."

"Aye", George Morgan added. "And he's not the only one to scorn the offer of free land. At the back of his lot there is another empty 100-acre lot being held in the name of an Irishman called Armstrong. Apparently he fainted at the thought of so much work and he's left the country too. You'll find there is lots of land around to choose from. Just take your pick and we'll help you clear the land. By now we know a thing or two about the bush which is a heap sight more than we knowed two years ago."

Forest replied, "Mary and I will think on it. Perhaps we could all go to some quiet spot to give thanks to God for our safe reunion and to have guidance about what we are to do."

It was not hard to find such a spot in the bush right at hand and if their heartfelt concentration was a little rattled by the drone of the first mosquitoes of the year, this was something they were to get used to very shortly.

The course Forest favoured was to approach Colonel Burke directly. However that privilege was not to be. Colonel Burke was at Richmond and they did not know when to expect him. In truth they did not expect him at all and suggested that Forest speak with Sergeant McFee, one of Colonel Burke's assistants. He was reported to be at The Landing; perhaps he could be found and his advice sought.

A few hours later Forest had tracked down Sergeant McFee. Forest approached him and made him aware of his dilemma in as few words as possible. McFee asked for the ex-soldiers' names, nodded as if what he heard made sense to him, asked a few questions of his own to assure himself that it seemed unlikely that either Maxwell or Armstrong were to show their faces in the country again, and then he nodded his approval.

"Mind you", he added, "I'm not giving you any guarantee, and I'll say as much if asked. But it seems only right an' proper that the Government would be happy if some of these here abandoned lands gets put to use. An' maybe they'll lift this here ban on settlers afore long. Myself I think they will. So do your best, and if asked who told ye to do so, forget my name an' just say you were given such advice from all sides. Which 'tis true enough. Guid day to you sir."

CALDWELL

HIS FIRST YEAR 1823

Forest's debut in the primal forest frequently brought him to his knees. His neighbours were as good as their word in helping him get started. They brought a second team of oxen and did not quit clearing land and hauling logs until they saw him housed in a shanty of the usual 16 by 20 feet.

Moses Wilson, one of Forest's neighbours, advised him, "It's small for your family to be sure, but anything bigger will only be harder to keep warm in the cold winter. In that season you'll be happy to keep to the same bed or two at the most. But that is a ways off yet. The next thing we need to do is build a lean-to for your oxen. A couple of pigs and a cow are wonderful things to have here to be sure, and the sooner you're set up the better you'll be."

Since Forest did not come under the umbrella of settlers on free land he received no food rations for the first year. He found the price of a bag of oats right through the roof and he realized that seeing his family fed for the first winter would put a big hole in his reserves. The prospect of the harvest for the fall of 1823 looked to be indifferent to downright poor in spots and the prices would reflect that reality. It was imperative to clear the land as fast as he could so that he might have a better harvest next year.

Forest was a farmer and he had some notion how to go about things in his own country. It did him little good here. His first, second and third tasks were clearing the land. Considering that he was not a robust man and that his best helpers were his oldest son, William, 12, and daughter, Margaret, 10, what he accomplished was truly a miracle. Each day he could scarcely drag himself into the house. When he sat down he was too exhausted to have much of an appetite and when he was finished eating he could hardly get off the bench to go and lie on the cot. One would think that the first two weeks would be the worst, and then his body would get used to the abuse and not speak back at him so strongly. Not so. As his muscles got attuned to the actions of swinging an axe, he simply swung the axe for more hours of each day, sometimes refusing to quit until total darkness. Actually it hurt more to stop than to keep on going. Each morning he did not think his limbs would obey his mind and crank themselves into action but each day he rolled himself onto the floor and allowed Mary to help him straighten up and get going one more time.

Mary worried about him day and night as she saw him hobbling about, but she said little. Her own tasks seemed endless and her days were even longer than her husband's. Taking the little ones with her at all times, she scavenged the woods for greens that were edible and found many things that seemed similar to plants in Ireland. Her first effort at nettle soup tasted wonderful as their bodies needed the nourishment so badly it went down like nectar. The food was always plain, needing to be cooked in a pot over the fire or in a heavy black iron skillet. But Mary soon found that nothing was turned down and burnt food was eaten as well as that which was undercooked. Everything tasted good.

Despite Lizzie's efforts to squeeze extra tea into their provisions, they soon used up their tea, a great deprivation to both Forest and Mary. Upon the advice of Hetty, Mary sent the children out to pull dandelions. They competed with one another about who could make the biggest pile. The next task was to scrub the roots of the dandelions until they were absolutely clean; the children with the smallest piles no longer felt downcast about their smaller piles. Together they made a big bonfire and threw the roots in to roast them. When the fire cooled down they retrieved the roots and pounded them into a powder. This whole procedure took several days, and the children felt very accomplished that they could provide this powder that was to be their 'tea'.

Mary and Forest found that it was not a difficult task to get the children at their chores. It readily became the norm for everyone but the baby to have a job and then another job. They worked in teams and the little ones aped the older ones. They begged to take on new jobs, just to show their mother how capable they were and she observed them gaining in confidence and independence every day.

Wilam Erskine came by one day and presented them with the luxury of a homemade chair with a back to it and Tom Morgan had made shelves. The silver tea service now found a resting place and as the precious barrels were emptied, they were put into use storing whatever food could be gathered from the forest. They unpacked the largest barrel and put it at the door where it was used for keeping ashes from the fires. From the ashes, they would obtain lye for soap making. The list of tasks was never ending.

That first year they dried the fruits they found in the forest and Mary welcomed the absence of sugar which made jam and jelly-making impossible. Then Hetty Erskine brought over a jar of maple syrup and Mattie Morgan brought two cakes of maple sugar. Hetty said, "We bring these to you, Mary, for you to know there are resources in this country. Once you learn how to collect maple sap next spring you will always have a supply of sweetening for your cooking. The natives have been using this maple molasses instead of salt to flavour their food. We will teach you how to do all this come April next. And yes, there really is such a thing as a sugar tree."

Her friends kept telling her of things which were to be done before the cold weather came and Mary forced herself to stay on her feet after they had all gone to bed in order to make candles for the winter. This was a job best done when the little ones were safely asleep for the large vat of hot fat was a terrible danger when little ones were racing around and a babe clutching at her skirts. There were times when she felt that her arms could not be raised one more time as she dipped the racks of strings up and down and up and down to form the candles. In the old country one had a maid to help with this task or one could buy them in the village. Here every man and woman must do for themselves or do without. Her eldest daughter, Margaret, learned all there was to learn about being a little mother and a helper to her Ma, and she was a great help, but there was always so much to do.

Each night seemed to be less than a moment long; one could never recall going to sleep, and gradually it was hard to believe one had slept, for the weariness reached over from day to day. They truly thanked God for the commandment to rest on the seventh day.

On that precious day their friends and neighbours, who were all from Counties Cavan and Monaghan, gathered in each other's homes turnabout and held a worship service. They felt that they, more than many others, had much to be thankful for: their nearness to one another and for each day and week that passed without a dreaded illness. During the week they saw little of each other for each man and woman was hard at work about their own affairs and after hours of toil had no energy to spare for visiting.

One Sunday late in September, after their worship service was over, Moses Wilson asked Forest if he was giving any thought to getting some animals for the next year. Forest replied, "I've been meaning to ask you how I can go about this. I see that all of you have managed quite a number of animals amongst you. I've been wondering if I can buy some of the offspring of your sheep or cows."

"Well, that you could do, to be sure," said Moses, and Thomas Morgan nodded his assent, "but there may be a way for you to get a few more animals brought up the river for you. Fortunately we are not too far from the river here and Mr. Pinhey has proven very happy to assist any of us to get animals brought up from Montreal. The thing is, you must be ready to receive them. And you are not the now."

Forest nodded glumly, "I cannot see my way clear to getting a barn up before it gets too cold. You have told me it will freeze the hind end off humans and livestock alike by November and it will take more time than that to see another log building on this place."

"Well now," Morgan said, "don't be too sure about that, Forest. You have a pile of logs there and if a crew of us get started tomorrow, we should have a barn up in a day or two at the most."

Forest protested, "I'm too much indebted to all of you already. You got together, cleared land and put up our home, and I love you all for it, but I cannot keep on taking and taking and not giving back. You can see that can't you?"

"Forest, Forest," came a chorus of dissent, "you must give up that way of thinking. We are all indebted to one another here and we all have to lend a hand where we can. Our whole community is growing bit by bit you see, but after you and your family came, we began to feel more whole, as though you have brought good to us all. We begged you to come did we not? We pledged you our support, did we not? Well, there you are now. This is the support we meant. You cannot wish for your family to go a whole year on nothing more than oatmeal, can you?"

In the background Mary prayed that Forest would please see the way to accepting their help. She herself did not see how they could go on without it. And Forest glancing back at his wife, saw her standing there with her eyes closed and her hands clasped tightly. He willed her to look at him and she opened her eyes and beseeched him wordlessly.

"Right then. We'll go at it. When can we start?"

"Tomorrow looks like a good day. Let's get to it," said Thomas Morgan, "and ladies, mayhap you can find us summat to eat come noon and nighttime? We'll be here just after sun up, Forest, and that means we start from home before light. Step lively now."

It did not take long to clear the cabin and get everyone to bed. Only Mary stayed awake to wonder how on earth she was going to feed all these men. And how many were there going to be? Forest noticed her restlessness and admonished his wife, "Close your eyes Mary. There is nay much you can do between now and morning to make things come about. The women told me on their way out that they will come along too and help with the food. I think they are really looking forward to this hurrah. This barn-building seems to be a regular occurrence here. We have been too busy this first summer to do our part, but after this, things are going to be different. The next time anyone needs a hand with a big job, you and I will be there too, you'll see. All you need to dream about is what animals you most want and how many." And with these words of wisdom they both dropped into a deep sleep.

It seemed to be no time at all before Mary heard their children stirring. She flew out of bed and went to the fire, which Forest had already brought back to life. A pot of porridge, already partly cooked, hung over the fire, but Forest himself was gone. The oldest boy William, said, "Da has gone out to find the best spot to put the barn. He said he'd be back soon, Ma."

It was still dark when Forest returned and consulted Mary. He made a startling proposition. "Mary, I think with your consent we'll add the barn right to the back of our house."

186

Mary raised her brows in amazement. "Why Forest, won't the smell be more than we'll like?"

"Yes it may be so Mary, but the warmth at the back of this drafty shack will be pleasing indeed. And by this time next year or as soon as we can, I'll build us a better house and this shanty and the lean-to will be our barn. What do you think of that?"

Forest was very pleased with this plan and Mary tried to be, even though she wondered if the goals were being set too high. Mary had constantly felt overwhelmed ever since she landed in Upper Canada and knew she had little idea whether the plan was realistic or not. In lieu of any better intelligence on the subject it was easier to agree and let things take their course. She couldn't see that she had much choice.

Later in the day when she saw a doorway being cut into the back of their shanty to lead directly into the barn, she almost wailed aloud. Forest, who had a fair idea of how Mary might view this new step, had sent William into the shanty to reassure his mother. William, who now considered himself grown up, told her, "Da has been told this is a good plan, Ma. We won't have to go outdoors in the cold weather to feed the animals."

"I thought we were told that winter is the best time of year around here. Do you mean to say we are not expected to go out the door because of the cold weather all winter?"

"I don't know, Ma. Da will tell you what he thinks."

Forest had been told many tales of how high the snow might drift and was ready to follow the advice of his more seasoned friends concerning this matter. But when they came to their meal at noon hour he hastened to assure Mary that a door was going to be put into the doorway. "A right sturdy door it will be Mary, have no fear that the animals will take over entirely." He gave William a meaningful look and a wink. Although William was not at all sure he understood what his father meant by that wink, he was enormously pleased to be in on the secret.

The women who had come over to help Mary prepare the meals consoled her with a word about how much better things were going to be next year.

Hetty said, "You won't believe how much better you will feel when you have some milk from a cow and eggs from the hens. The barn may become your favourite part of the house, Mary. I know our boys wanted to sleep in the barn. They said it was much warmer than the house. I didn't know what to think. My expectations have taken a quair twist since I came to this country. It has been a rare old loosening up, I can tell you, Mary." The look they shared showed complete understanding.

As promised, the barn was raised in two days. Now that the outside was finished and the roof secured, Forest, with William's help and advice from Moses Wilson, put his energies to the door and to a few partitions. He needed room for a pig or two and determined that these creatures would be placed in a separate pen furthest from the house. Next to them would be a cow and his team of oxen, then his two horses and, God willing, a dozen hens. Altogether the barn was a little bigger than the shanty, and if Forest could manage it, it would be filled before the snow flew.

Forest and Wilam Erskine made a trip to Pinhey's establishment the very next day. "No time to waste, Forest. I hope he's home. He does a fair amount of going about. But he's a good man, always willing to help out a neighbour when he can. He's a cut above us, of course, a very wealthy man, but he says he wants to see us all thrive, and even offers to lend us money to help us get started with our livestock."

Seeing Forest frown at this, Erskine added hastily, "Not that you will have the need for that perhaps, but a few of us welcomed the help. And the interest he charged was next to nothing. He said that he would like to have the offer of our help when he came round to enlarging his buildings and we could pay off the interest that way. But what was even better was that he told us in advance just how much it would cost to borrow 10 Pounds and there would be no changes to that later on. So far he has been as good as his word. It is a big help to know there is man in these parts who is both honest and wealthy and stands ready to help his neighbour. It is not so everywhere I assure you. In fact I could say he is the only one to earn this reputation hereabouts."

This was a long speech for Wilam and they went the rest of the way mainly in silence, holding to the trail along the riverbank where the walking was much easier.

Pinhey was home but just about ready to take his boat down river to The Landing. From there he was aiming to go to Montreal aboard a craft Philemon Wright ran to Montreal every second day. There was scant time to meet this man who had been so highly praised by Wilam, but for all his rush to get into the boat, Forest found him to be very approachable on the issue of bringing back some livestock with him. He promised to fetch hens and cows at the very least and perhaps a pig, although he did not care much for this animal.

"Very necessary though, very necessary. I'll see what I can do. And I shall likely make another trip next month so perhaps the next trip will see you with all the animals you can manage."

To Forest's surprise there was no chat about financing this order, so he added hastily, "I believe I have sufficient funds to pay outright for them Mr. Pinhey, and I'm much obliged to you, I'm sure."

"Fine, fine, we shall work out the details when I return. You won't know what you are getting 'til I do. I can see you are well enough set up, and I don't fear to help out a neighbour. Must be off now." And with that he got into the sloop, and ordered his clerk to cast off.

Forest turned to Wilam, who was looking very pleased with this transaction. "I hardly know what to make of him, Wilam. Is he always so trusting with someone he does not know at all?"

"I cannot say about that but then I would not be surprised if he does know something about you. He makes it his business to know about the whole community here and we are not so many that this is beyond his knowledge. He is one smart businessman, Forest; don't ever think he's not. And I daresay he can see you are an educated man. That would be in your favour; Pinhey's a great man for education I'm thinking."

Forest went home to Mary somewhat bemused by this brief encounter. The only reassurance he could give her was that Mr. Pinhey would see what he could get in Montreal, "and he didn't ask for a penny up front — an amazing man, Mary and not too old either. I doubt he's even reached forty years yet and he seems to be a gentleman of leisure already. Wilam thinks the world and all of him, that's for sure."

"Wilam knows better than we do, Forest. I am grateful for Mr. Pinhey's help and Wilam's too. We have come a long way since last Sunday, have we not? But where would we be without the help of our neighbours?"

"Mary, I think we both know now that without our friends we could not have managed at all. Even a much younger man than I am needs help with labour and he either must have very deep pockets or good friends. We have those friends, and I predict in the long run, good friends will win out over deep pockets, as our friends told us in their letters."

Mary nodded, and Forest could see by her bearing that she was somehow lighter, and held herself less tightly. She immediately confirmed her happier outlook. "I feel so much better about the winter now. It will be our first winter, but I am not as fearful now that we see some prospect of better food. Praise be."

For a week there was no word from Mr. Pinhey. Forest became a little restive. He walked over to Wilam's place to discuss how he should handle it. "Should I go over the Pinhey's and find out if he is back yet. What do you advise?"

"I expect he'll get word to you when he returns. In the meantime he has room to house your animals for a day or two. Don't fret."

"I shall have to offer him something for all his trouble, but I don't have the first notion of what that should be. Do you?"

"I'd just ask him when the time comes."

Two days later Mr. Pinhey sent word with one of his workers that he had two pigs, one cow, and a dozen hens, and when would Mr. Caldwell like to fetch them?

Forest set out the next morning with four of his friends. Wilam had a cart with huge wheels that would help them get over the rough terrain; he hoped the hens were well crated and could travel that way. The cow and the pigs could walk, of course, but they made sure to take sturdy ropes for the three animals in case they were obstreperous creatures, determined to have their own way.

It was an all day excursion but they arrived home safely. All but one of the hens looked lively and if that one did not spruce up fairly quickly the family looked forward to a rare treat. Forest told Mary that the price was less than he had been prepared to pay and Mr. Pinhey would take nothing for his trouble.

"He claimed I did him a favour as he also ordered some animals for his own use, but that was all one trip could manage in a boat. It was a bit of a squeeze and he was glad the cow was docile or they might have had to leave her at The Landing and make another trip. The pigs he stuffed with food and ale from Firth's Tavern and they slept all the way back. He said it would be easier to get more animals after the river froze for the larger animals could walk the distance and the smaller ones could go in the sleigh. It may be easier in one way but it's a long walk in the winter to drive a cow from Montreal to The Landing.

I have no wish to repeat that trip. I think we'll settle for the animals we have until next spring."

The first winter finally came, and Mary began to understand that this was a time for rejoicing. Nothing more than the daily round of washing, cooking and baking could be attempted. As for cleaning, there was little to clean other than their long table and it was constantly in use. Now she had a moment to try to teach the little ones their letters, and listen to the older ones read from the Bible. Forest could teach them their numbers and try to ensure that they did not grow up to be as raw and wild as the creatures of the forest around them.

Until now there had been neither time nor strength for letter writing. Mary's last letter to her parents was sent from The Landing and then it was only a hasty thing to let them know they had arrived safely and all was well. They would be worried about such a long silence and now she could finally give them some reassuring news.

The children enjoyed every moment of their new life. Every day was a new adventure and they longed to be outdoors in the snow rather than sitting at the table working on sums and letters. Their slates were wiped for the last time at noon hour, and their afternoons were devoted to chores and exercise. Little Mary Ann, still under one year, insisted it was her job to feed the hens. Her brother John carried the bucket and she tottered alongside and scattered grain to the hens, which ranged freely in the barn. The older ones were sent out to bring in the wood, to make sure the cow had some hay and to shovel a pathway from the cabin to the woodshed. They loved every bit of it, and the younger ones tagged along. When they were done they rolled in the snow, threw it at each other and squealed and struggled until, wet and tired, they came indoors ready for a supper of bread and soup and early bed.

This picture was taken in the 1840's or 1850's, which explains the large area that is cleared.

CALDWELL

LETTERS TO DRUMSHIEL 1823

November 14, 1823
Dear Mother and Father:
It is with great pleasure that I can sit down and write you a letter about our life in this new country. I shall admit that at first I was quite overwhelmed at the huge task before me. Our friends and neighbours soon made it plain that they would help us in every circumstance. We lived in a tent until enough trees were cut down to build a rough shanty. I was amazed to see what a crew of experienced workers could do in a short time. While this is not the home I plan to have for the duration, it will protect and shield us from the weather and the animals which abound here and I expect that with God's help and that of our friends we shall be quite comfortable in this home for a year or two.

Before winter commenced we were able to obtain a couple of pigs, a cow, some hens and two oxen for our barn, which once again was erected with the help of our friends. The eggs and milk have added much needed variety to our diet and pleased Mary very much. It pleased all of us of course but for some time we were too busy to pay much heed to our diet.

In addition to our own dear neighbours there are some unusual settlers in this area. One is a very wealthy Englishman who has chosen to make his home here in the wilds of Canada. He is a retired merchant, although a young man. It is my impression that he intends to establish a house and estate of some significance. For all that, he is not a man to stand on ceremony and he has been quite helpful to many of his neighbours. He is the person who transported livestock up the

River for us and others too. There are also several former naval and army officers who were given two hundred acres each when they were discharged from the Militia. I do not know how much we shall have in common with these families, but we are content with those friends we now have.

Thanks to your generosity as we left Ireland, we have had sufficient funds to buy the livestock and to hire a local mason to install a proper fireplace in our shanty and still have a reserve for emergencies. Many of the first homes do not have a proper fireplace, but a few of our neighbours came along to watch the building of our fireplace, which was made from stones off our own land, and they are now attempting to imitate his work. I am not sure that the mason welcomed all these onlookers but there was little he could do about it. It is his livelihood he wishes to protect of course, but I am quite assured that he need not worry overmuch on that score. A mason here can charge pretty well whatever he likes as masons are in demand. In fact that is pretty much the case for any skilled worker.

There seems to be a good deal of limestone on this land, very much as in some parts of Ireland. We were encouraged to make piles of the stones and of the smaller branches from the trees we cut down. Now we are in the process of making huge bonfires of the branches, hurling the stones into the fire and after they have cooled, pounding the stones into powder. We mix the limestone powder with sand and water and use this mixture to fill the cracks between the logs. It is wonderful how helpful the children are at nearly all parts of this work. They especially like throwing branches onto the bonfire and they try to make sure the fire does not go out day or night. They assume far more responsibility here for their little jobs than I think would have been possible at home. They are conscious of how much their work is worth for they feel the shanty warmer now after the spaces between the logs were filled with limestone. Even now in the winter months, once the bonfire is started, the children keep dragging branches to it and keep it going for days at a time. Of course we keep the embers alive in the fireplace too, as there is no convenient way to have a fire but to keep it going.

We don't yet know the quality of the soil on our acreage. And of more concern is that the Militia has not yet allocated the land to us in writing. The Militia was in charge of allocating lots to settlers, but it appears that this work has been taken from the

Militia and given to some other branch of the government. With the whole matter in transition it is very hard to establish our right to the land we are living on and working every day to improve. Your prayers in this matter would be greatly appreciated, as I cannot feel comfortable about anything until it is clearly written in the Land Book that we are allocated to these 100 acres.

In my next letter I shall be sure to tell you more about how this country is governed. Thus far I have seen no sign of governance at all but I have not had the time or strength to pay heed to anything beyond my own affairs. You will find a separate letter to Mary's kin under this cover. Thank you for all that you have done to help us settle in this new land. Your help has gone a long way. And your prayers are much appreciated. If God has guided us to come to this country, as we believe He has, then we are sure He will see us right in the end. We are all healthy, Thanks be to God.

Your loving son and daughter, Forest and Mary.

Shortly after he had posted his letter to his parents, Forest received a letter from Samuel.

Dear Forest and Mary, Drumshiel, August 30 1823

The farms are progressing well. I think I need to learn more about bookkeeping. Mother tells me that I can learn what I need from Mr. Smiley in this respect. But I shall have to take care how I go about it. I do not intend to give offence to Mr. Hurley for he has gone over every step of the farm decisions with me and I trust him. Still I need to be my own man, as you were so fond of telling me. On the whole I enjoy the added responsibility and I look forward to every day.

I do not want to give you any needless worry about our father but I am beginning to see him decline. I promised to keep you informed and am telling you this as part of that promise. I suppose this is natural enough given his advanced years. He has just passed the 70-year milestone. Mayhap if his spirits were to realize a boost, he might do well for many years yet. Write him and give him all the good news you can, especially about what sort of education his grandchildren will receive and so on. You know him well enough to know just what he would like to hear.

Wish me well Forest and do not worry about Ma and Da. I will keep my promise to look after them all their days.
Your brother in the Lord, Samuel

Forest reacted to Samuel's letter with shock and chagrin. He could not help but believe that the decline in his father's health was due in large part to his decision to leave Ireland. He sought immediately to write the most encouraging letter he could about his circumstances here in Upper Canada.

Dear Mother and Father,   December 2, 1823, U C
It is my pleasure to write to you again as this time of year is the most leisurely for us. There is very little to do but the daily chores, after which I take the opportunity to teach our youngest children their letters and numbers. I know you have a concern that they may grow up with an inferior education. I plan to do all I can to educate them myself to that level that will make you proud of them. Toward this end I spend tutoring time with them every day. The older children would benefit from more books; it was unfortunate that we could not bring more with us on the voyage. The younger children are not disadvantaged in this respect for they have the Bible for reading practice.

Father, you asked me in your last letter to tell you something about our neighbours and the society in which we find ourselves. As for neighbours we have quite a variety. The earliest settlers in this township are retired members of the military, some of them quite high in the instep and not likely to trouble themselves with settlers whom they consider below their social equal. Their chief concern is to live as much like aristocracy as possible. But on the other hand there is also a settlement of Irish Catholics brought over by Peter Robinson. As far as can be seen, they are law-abiding men and women and are adapting to the challenges of this new country as well as anyone can.

Up to this point we have no church building but Mr. Pinhey, whom I have mentioned before, is planning to build a handsome stone church on his land, to which one and all are welcome to attend. We shall avail ourselves of this opportunity of worship but also continue to have chapel meetings in our homes. There are Methodist preachers who travel on horseback over a vast area, so that they seldom attend our hearths. They

197

are expected to maintain themselves and their families as the settlers do not provide for them. How they can run a farm at the same time as preach the Gospel over a large area is unknown to me. Theirs is a harsh existence to be sure and it is only their love of spreading the Gospel that keeps them at their task. Most of these young circuit riders die in their prime from the rigours of their calling. They often ride from one settlement to another at the end of a long day, an adventure few of us would choose because of the danger from wolves. Of course they are welcomed into our homes and share the meal we have, but the weather is often unkind to the man who spends long hours in the saddle becoming soaked and chilled. Pneumonia too often claims the lives of these brave disciples of Christ. I look forward to the time when we can provide a better living for them.

Most settlers are absorbed in furthering their ability to provide for their family and are not interested in political matters. Of course this suits the ruling class very well and they are willing to leave the poorer settler to his own devices. The taxes are very low. We are only expected to fulfill our settlement duties which consist of making a road at the front of our property. There is no jail in this township or the next. The chief hazard to a farmer seems to arise from indebtedness and should that happen, one can languish in jail until the debt is paid. Most people who are indebted simply leave the country, many of them going to the United States.

Mr. Pinhey, whom I consider a leader in this community and very honourable and helpful to all those in need, is of the opinion that the task of ruling the country ought to rest with those of the landowning class, much as in England. He fears that the poorer settler is not well enough educated to have good judgment about affairs of state and his poverty would make him open to corruption. He and others of the military class are prone to underestimate the intelligence and ability of the poorer settler. You can see that attitudes here are similar to those in Ireland. I grant the overall level of education of many settlers is limited but most are far from illiterate. The barrier to further education is the lack of books. Most of us had no space in our luggage for a library and have only the Holy Bible as our guide for conduct. While we lack knowledge of world affairs and even the affairs of this country, I hold that an education in moral values is a good foundation for a public leader and fits him to represent the people of his constituency to those who wield power.

Forest had difficulty in reassuring his father that this country was developing just as William would like. He always started out with good intentions and somehow veered dangerously into criticizing the ruling group. He congratulated his restraint in forbearing to mention that the Vicars of Christ in the Church of England are very well provided for by the government. He decided he had done all he could and turned the letter over to Mary to give stories about the children that would gladden his mother's heart.

He had minimized the extent of his daily labour in order to convince his father that his grandchildren's education was not being neglected. He felt that he had better redouble his efforts in tutoring them in order not to make a liar of himself.

That night when the children were presumably asleep Forest shared with Mary the struggle he'd had with the letter.

"Why Forest, you did admirably. You comforted your father and told only the truth. Why are you upset with yourself for managing to provide comfort to your parents in their old age?"

"I did not tell him what I really think about the way the government of the country may be heading. It seems as if I have lied, by omission at least, and was cowardly, that's why."

"Well Forest, you tried to tell him what is happening in the country without making it harder for him to accept your choice in coming here and bringing all his grandchildren here as well. I consider that is a kindness you owe to your father and you are not to reproach yourself for it. If you had done the opposite it would only have soothed your pride and caused your father anguish. I'm glad you swallowed your pride, as you always do. That is why I love you."

"And I told you all about it, knowing you would do as you always have and make me feel better about my choices. Thank you, dear heart."

CALDWELL

NEWS FROM DRUMSHIEL 1824

Forest waited eagerly for another letter from his father. Considering the length of time that letters usually took to go to Ireland and back, he was surprised to hear again in late April from his father.

Drumshiel, Cavan, March 10 1824
Dear Forest,
The letters are moving more swiftly it seems. As you requested I am sending a shipment of books to you on the next boat from Ireland. I am pleased to hear that you are taking charge of your children's learning yourself and not leaving it up to the public school. They will not learn how to be gentlemen from that source.
I am sending this letter with a friend who hopes to sail to New York. Ships leave France for New York even in the winter months and I hope the letter will reach you 'ere long. Your last letter made me feel a little more hopeful about your future out there in the bush.
Your mother sends her love. I am feeling my age. Give my love to Mary and my namesake William and the other children.
Your loving father William Caldwell

Forest was relieved that his last letter seemed to please his father. For the foreseeable future he would have little time for correspondence. Once again he was out all the hours God provided to clear as much land as he could. The thought of being put off this land was always at the back of his mind.

Four months later Forest learned that his father had died shortly after writing his last letter to Forest.

Drumshiel, May 1824
Dear Forest and Mary,
It pains me to tell you that your father died quite suddenly in March. He had just written a letter to you and organized the shipment of books he wanted you to have when he suffered a stroke. I am able to tell you that your father did not suffer long. After the first stroke he was quite lucid in his mind, but helpless in his body. Thanks be to God, he had another stroke and was gone, as he would have wished. Your letters greatly relieved his mind about your circumstances there in what he liked to call "the bush". But you will know that already because by this time you should have received several parcels of books, the last one with another letter enclosed. He was relieved to note that his grandchildren were receiving the education they deserved, thanks to your tutoring. He agreed with your judgment that a public school would not provide them with the proper background. He was at peace in that respect, and also pleased to note that you are living in a community with some claim to gentility.

Happily our circumstance will allow us to confirm your inheritance in my next letter. I wish you to give us direction as to how this might best be done safely. Do you wish me to leave the funds in an English bank for safekeeping? In this matter, I am carrying out William's wishes to you and to your brothers in Australia.

We do not hear often from them but thanks be to God, they are both alive and well when last we heard, two years ago now.

All is progressing here as it should. Samuel is a fine young man with all his wits in place. Willy Too is well and is going to be married shortly. We do not expect any issue from this marriage as his intended is an older widow. I believe they will suit one another admirably.

It will be up to Samuel to carry on the family name in Cavan. He tells us that he is ready to marry as soon as the period of mourning is over and the young lady he has his eye on

*is very agreeable to our family. He is ready for marriage;
circumstances have caused him to mature rapidly.*

*Give my best love to Mary and to all my little
grandchildren. How I long to see you all before I die but we must
take comfort that we shall be reunited in the hereafter, if it
pleases God.*

Your loving mother, Sarah Caldwell

How like his mother to put the best face on everything,
to comfort Forest rather than hint of her own needs. But it did
little to relieve his guilt.

Mary could see Forest was sorely affected. After several
weeks she decided to take action. One evening when Forest was
out working at the edge of the forest, Mary sent William inside
to look after the young ones. She went close to where Forest was
contemplating a large tree and called to him. He looked up and
watched her approach.

She took the axe from Forest's hand and said, "We are
going to have a talk, Forest. It is time you told me what is
grieving you so sorely. It is about your father is it not?"

"Yes, Mary. How could it not be? I am convinced that
our departure hastened his death and I am the one responsible for
that."

"That may well be true, Forest. If we had remained in
Ireland, he might have lived another year, more or less, or maybe
not. When we die is in the hands of the living God, is it not?"

"Yes it is, but Samuel as good as told me he never
recovered from our leaving."

"You are asking yourself if we did right to leave when
we did?"

"I am almost sure I was wrong to leave."

"But you prayed about it and prayed and felt that God
was directing you to take this path, did you not?"

"Yes, Mary, I did."

"Do you think if you had delayed and then your father
died, that you would have stayed in Ireland?"

"Yes. I could not have left Mother. I would have had to
stay."

"It seems to me that God told you to go when you did
for it was to be then or never. And since you felt it was right

202

then, can you not feel that God wanted you to take this path? He provided the way and the time. Can you not accept that?"

Forest was silent for what seemed like a long time. Finally he turned to her and said, "You have shown yourself to be a good teacher, Mary. You are right. If I had waited, we would not have left Ireland at all. I think I knew that then, but have somehow forgotten it. If it was right then, it is still right now. Thank you."

Forest then straightened up and said, "I'll think I'll quit for tonight and say goodnight to the children with you." Hand in hand they returned to the shanty.

CALDWELL

FOREST PETITIONS FOR LAND 1824

Toward the end of 1824 Forest became restive about assuring himself that after all his toil he would not be deprived of the home he had wrenched from the forest. By this time he had cleared five acres, which was half of the required settlement duties. Accordingly, he approached his neighbours and asked them to help him put his petition down on paper. They tried to assure him that it was best not getting entangled in that legal trot, but when they saw he could have no peace, they reluctantly gave in and on December 2, 1824 they put pen to paper.

"Mind now", Melrose warned him, "you are getting the authorities down on you. If there's one thing they hate is being asked to put their name to any document. In person they'll tell you to do nearly anything you wish out here in the bush. They'll think they have seen the last of you in any event. But being asked to write down in a ledger that they have given their consent to anything, now that's a different matter." A few of the others agreed with him.

"Well, write down just what I have done. Don't ask them to do aught about it. I just wish to give them a little warning about what I'm up to here so when I ask for title to the land it won't turn out that I'm an upstart and be shown the gateway of the property."

Here is their letter:

Township of March
2nd December 1824[17]
TO WHOM IT MAY CONCERN
Forest Colville Cauldwell came to this country April 1823 from the County of Cavan Ireland — was told by Col. Burke no Land could then be Located in the Military Townships — he must wait — was recommended to go on Lot No. 6, 1st Concession which had formerly (about 18 months before) been Located to Mr. Robert Maxwell, who has never been on this Lot or enrolled in the Militia or heard of since in the Country —

F. C. Cauldwell has cleared five acres and built a House on the lot. He is now among his Relations and Friends and has a wife and Six children the eldest 12 years old to support, therefore hopes to be Located to said lot –

We the undersigned Neighbours of the said Forest Colville Cauldwell Certify to the correctness of the above statement.

> *Thomas Morgan   James Melrose,*
> *George Morgan   Moses Wilson,*
> *Wilam Erskine   Harold Foster*
> *Evan Graham   G Fenton*
> *Henry Whitley and William McMin*

Moses Wilson weighed in on the matter and advised Forest to deliver the letter in person, "so that he can see what sort of a daicent character you are to be sure. And besides, the Justice of the Peace will find it harder to say no to you in person than he will to a letter dropped onto his desk. But whatever you do, don't push him." All were in agreement on that sensitive subject.

With this faint encouragement, Forest, Wilam Erskine and Thomas Morgan went to the Land Office, letter in hand. They were given a great many dubious looks. Finally the clerk

---

[17] Forest Caldwell, Public Archives Canada (PAC) Upper Canada Land Petitions (U.C.L.P.), Land Book M, 1824 - 26. Call (Reel) No. 1724, Vol. 107, Bundle C 14, Petition No. 217, pp. 503.

suggested, "Why don't you just claim the land and say you have lost your location ticket? Never say I told you to do that now." This piece of advice failed to allay Forest's concerns, for to make use of it he would have had to compound the first lie by presenting himself as Mr. Maxwell. He waited patiently to be admitted to see Mr. Stephens, who was expected in the afternoon.

Mr. Ross Stephens, Justice of the Peace, a heavy set, ponderous sort of fellow with little hair and heavy jowls, seemed equally unwilling to take a stand. Finally he said that he would acknowledge receipt of their letter and he would add that they all seemed to be respectable folk. On second thought, he thought it best if he could get someone else to sign a statement to that effect as well for the rumours now were getting stronger that no more lands were to be given away in that part at all. It would never do for him to be seen to be going against what the Lieutenant Governor had to say, now would it? No, he thought he could not do anything until Justice Hertig could see their letter too and then they would see. They were to come back next week and never let on he told them to. They were just to show up on the doorstep and he would take it from there.

Forest, Wilam and Thomas found themselves on the doorstep, their letter in their hand and nothing to do but go home and wait until the following week. Forest, however, was not discouraged. He had not received a definite 'No' and until then he would hope.

Next week saw them back in the same place going through the same rigmarole. The Sheriff took his time in getting them in to see these two very important men. When they were admitted, Mr. Stephens allowed himself to be introduced to each man, to read their letter out loud and then to pass it over to Mr. Hertig who was altogether a different sort of man, tall and spare if not thin, whose equally sparse hair shot out in wisps which he neither noticed nor cared to notice.

He wanted to get the matter over with in a minute flat and asked, "Well, what do you want? Owt wi' it."

"Well," Forest said, "I would like a letter saying that you have received our letter and that you — well, that you have met me — " He trailed off lamely.

Hertig stared at him very intently for a few seconds and then said it would be hard to see how they could do less and

206

whipped off the following note to be entered into the ledger after their letter. Then he handed the ledger to Mr. Stephens for his signature and was out of the office and away.

Township of March [18]
District of Bathurst
13th December 1824

We the Undersigned Certify that the persons whose signatures appear to this document are Respectable, Landholders, Neighbours of the said Forest Cauldwell. That he himself is of Good character and likely to become a good settler.

A. H. Hertig J. P.

Ross Stephens J. P.

Mr. Stephens, who had not said a word on their behalf, rubbed his hands in pleasure and said, "That looked after everything very well, didn't it? Guid day to you gentlemen, guid day."

This seemed to be as far as things could progress and Forest had to cool his heels until the following summer. At least his name was on record.

---

[18] Ibid. Several of these entries were lumped together. A few were at later page numbers but all in the same Land Book.

ARGUE

A YEAR OF CHANGE 1825

George stood at the threshold of the shanty he had lived in for the past three winters and noted a few changes the last six months had brought, chiefly that there were more cabins now than last April when they went back to Goulbourne. He had come in mainly to assure himself that his place was in good order for his family when they returned the following week and was pleased to see it was not so bad. As usual there had been a few lumbermen camping out but they had left nothing much behind other than a broken chair and a heap of bottles. George assured himself that he could repair the chair or make a stool out of it at least; he was relieved the scene did not reveal more damage. The newcomers seemed to respect that this place was occupied. He guessed he could thank his friend John Burrows for watching over the shanty from time to time.

In less than a fortnight the whole family would move back to The Landing. In the meantime there was to be a wedding party at their place in Goulbourne, of the sort now common where several marriages would take place at the same time. Rev Ezra Healey would perform the ceremonies, which had been planned for many months now. Friends would be coming from as far as Huntley and March Townships. It would be good to see his friends again, but preparations were so intense in his house that George was glad to get away for a couple of days while the women fussed about stitches, flounces and whatnot.

George mused over the accomplishments of the past four years since they had arrived in this rough country. He had completed his homestead duties a year early[19] and had obtained clear title to his land in 1823. He was proud that William, who had applied for his 100-acre allotment on his eighteenth birthday in 1822, had received his grant this past summer. They had come through the worst years, George thought. Their cabins in the woods were still isolated, but each family had more animals in their barns, and greater variety on the table. They were making their own cloth and a few had started to tan their own animal hides. Their small community ground their own flour and worked all hours of the night and day to avoid dependency on the local storekeeper. There were more settlers now, Catholic as well as Protestant and so far they all worked together to grind the flour. No problem when they worked on community projects, but George noticed that work crews on given days were mostly Catholic or mostly Protestant. There was never any discussion of it; it just worked out that way.

He had hoped that by this time he would be able to spend his winters in Goulbourne too, but he knew now that time was far off. He turned resolutely away from this discouraging note and thought instead of the additions he had made to their second shanty in Goulbourne. Their original shanty had become a barn and their new shanty was larger and boasted a stone fireplace built of stones from their own land. He had a surprise for Mary this winter. He had finally ordered stovepipes and sheets of tin from Philemon Wright and after they returned from Goulbourne, he was going to put a pipe through that hole in the roof and attach a skirt around the bottom of the pipe over the fire to gather the smoke up the stovepipe. He still could not afford the stove to go with the pipe for he would have to convey it back and forth to Goulbourne every summer or it would be stolen for sure in their absence. And such an enterprise was not to be thought of with the roads being what they were. He would not

---

[19] Public Archives of Canada Vol. 421 microfiche reel C739

pp 70x George Argue, Goulbourne , granted 100 acres Aug 23 1823.

pp 70n William Argue, Goulbourne , granted 100 acres 25 June 1825.

pp 70f George Argue, Huntley, granted 100 acres Sept 21 1824.

pp 70d Thomas Argue, Huntley, granted 100 acres Aug 23 1824.

For explanation of the last two entries, see Afterword.

even install the pipe and hood over the fire until they were living here for it would be easy to remove and very much in demand.

A whistle and a hello interrupted his thoughts. He looked up and saw John Burrows striding over the rough path to his door. What a welcome sight. The first words out of Burrows' mouth, "What a welcome sight you are, George. I've been coming by here as oft as I can, hoping to see you and at least make sure your shanty is still standing."

"I was just thinking the very thoughts you uttered. It is indeed good to see you. You look well and prosperous. I thank you for looking out for this place, very good of you indeed." Burrows waved away his thanks and inquired if he was here to stay.

"Nay, I'm just here for a day or two and then back to Goulbourne in time for a wedding hurrah at our place. You know how it goes. It is right hard to get a hold of one of the Methodist ministers who are always off riding around their circuit, so when you can get him, you make the most if it."

Burrows raised his brows in question and George said, "No, there have been no funerals this year. The Lord has been good to us. Tell me, how goes it with you?"

"I have been busy, George, and glad of the work. Lord Dalhousie has hired me to re-survey a big swath of land on the upper part of The Landing that he bought in 1823. He is convinced that the canal building is going to start soon and he figures they will need land to house the workers, barracks for soldiers and munitions as well as land for the canal, locks and so on. He was making these plans a few years back and I think he was a wise man. I am glad to get the work, as it has been very slow in this direction. Dalhousie is Church of England, you know, but for all that he does not seem to mind hiring a known Methodist for this job. He says he thinks he can trust a Methodist in his work if not in his religion and I intend to show him that he can."

"I'm right pleased for you, John. It's a big compliment to be noticed by the Governor General to be sure and I'm right pleased that you will be around these parts this winter. I look forward to our chapel evenings together. If you are heading over to Wrightsville now, I'll go with you. I aim to order a few lengths of pipe and a few sheets of tin. It is well beyond time that I made a better dwelling for Mary and the family."

They started to walk to the Point where Burrows had docked his small craft. Burrows nodded, "I think you are wise, George. It should make your place warmer and more friendly like. Yours is always the gathering place for chapel evenings, so I am sure you will have lots of willing help to put it all together. I have a few tools for cutting the tin and I'll be glad to shove my oar in as well. Maybe you should have two fires for such a big shanty."

This offer of help was very pleasing to George for by this time he knew that John Burrows had started out as carriage maker, then turned his hand to making furniture, then musical instruments, teaching music, drafting and surveying. He could turn his hand to nearly anything required, and in this country as soon as a person practiced a skill he was entitled to claim the trade, not like it was in the Old Country.

George arrived back in Goulbourne the evening before the wedding, and found that he was needed to take the oxen to Mitchells and bring a few boards over to make trestle style tables for the feast the next day. The women had been working for days to make special delicacies and these makeshift tables had better do the job.

The reasons for the multiple marriage ceremonies were practical. As they had found from their own experience a few years ago, it is difficult to find a minister to marry a couple when they wanted to marry, with the result that many marriages were initiated without benefit of clergy and without censure. He recalled ruefully that when his own daughter Annie married two years ago, it took many months before the Methodist circuit rider came to make things right and tight. This time round there were to be seven marriages or more and a baptism or two as well. His own granddaughter, Mary Anne Wilson, not yet a year old, was to be baptized. Often as many as fifteen or twenty marriage ceremonies were conducted at one time, with the children of these unions being baptized at the same occasion. Such a haphazard system did not suit these God-fearing families and they petitioned Rev Ezra Healey to come to Goulbourne on the second Sunday in October for a church service, six weddings, and baptisms as needed.

October was one of the two good times in a year for a get-together, the other being around Christmas and New Year's. Once harvest was in and the men were not yet off to

211

the woods for the winter, there were a few weeks when work was not imperative. Of course heaps of chores were always at hand, but opportunities for meeting with kith and kin who did not live next door were rare and not to be missed. What better occasion for celebration than a wedding? This gave the young people a chance to meet other young people and perchance to find one's own mate. The children simply rejoiced at the chance to do something different from the endless chores and their parents were not loath to lay down their work and prepare the best feast they could.

Inside the house his daughter Annie, now a confident young woman of twenty-two, was taking the new brides under her wing. She remembered her wedding to Thomas; it had not been called a wedding, but a union, but she'd had a new dress of brown homespun that she had made herself; she had been given a feather tick and pillows for their bed, just like a proper wedding, and she had held her head up proudly when Archie Magee pronounced their union to be blessed by God. Now she had a fine baby girl and everyone had said, 'Never you mind, lass. The next one will be a boy for sure.' Time to hold her head up again to be sure.

The dresses at these weddings were of homespun too, but one dress was of a lighter hue; Essie Scott had rose coloured wool, the envy of all the other brides. Most brides felt fortunate to have a new dress at all, one with a few pleats and ribbons, if possible, and one which they expected to wear until it was threadbare. Several brides did not have a new dress, and had to make do with a new homespun apron. Cotton was considered a luxury and therefore out of sight.

As the bride provided the feather tick and pillows, the groom was to provide the cabin. Thomas had taken Annie to his very own shanty, but when winter approached a few precious weeks later, he went off to the bush with the other men and Annie went to The Landing to stay with her parents. Not every groom had his own land or shanty and the usual plan then was for the bride to live with her husband's family. Not much privacy in those one-room shanties, the site of their all too brief honeymoon.

One of the couples on this day was James Wilson and Essie Scott; another couple and a surprise to some, was Sam Halliday and little Hattie Foster. There was a great disparity of

212

years between Sam and Hattie, but Hattie was one of these young women who felt ready for anything. She was less than five feet in height and packed every inch of her frame with energy and determination. She had wanted Sam to notice her and decided that the best way to do that was through his children. She spent much of the past two years helping Amy Mitchell, with the care of Sam's children.

It was true that Sam Halliday had been in and out of the Mitchell household for the past four years, and in that time, Hattie thought that she had come to know him well. She knew him to be gentle with his children, considerate of her and still grieving for his wife, Jessie, but she thought that if she could accept that she did not hold first place in his heart, she could be happy enough as his wife. When he had asked for her hand in marriage she showed her delight so openly that Sam felt he was cheating her by not giving this fine young woman his first love. Some of the girls felt a little sorry for Hattie and thought that they would not like to have to marry a much older man and look after two children right away. Hattie had no time for this condescension. "At least I know what I'm getting and he pleases me." With this she smartly turned her back on them.

Essie Scott, who had waited long and hard for her wedding to James Wilson, said, "I think we all feel ready for managing our own households. Our mams had to learn new ways when they came here and we learned right along with them. I don't feel afraid of that part at all, but I am glad I'm not going to be stuck out here in the bush all winter long."

This was a tactless thing to say aloud as a few other brides, including Essie's own sister Sarah, shared exactly that prospect. Several brides knew they would be established in their mother-in-law's shanty, and how well that would suit was unknown. There was no help for it, but one could see a hint of uncertainty on their faces as they contemplated many changes in their young lives. Ironically, Essie's own expectations were soon to be reversed when James Wilson and John Scott announced that they were going to start making wagons and live in Goulbourne. That Essie had known nothing about it was perhaps not unusual, as many husbands saw no reason to consult their wives about a major change in earning their livelihood. That was men's business.

George had been looking out especially for Forest Caldwell and his family. It was more than two years since the Caldwells had come from Ireland, and since their arrival both Forest and George had been too busy, each on his own farm, to take time for a reunion. Now at last Moses Wilson proudly led them forth.

"It is God's own blessing to see you here, Forest and Mary. Thank you, thank you for making the great effort to get here, for that it has been, I know. We have so much to learn of how you have fared and are going on."

"Yes", said Forest, "we have the advantage of you there, for we can see how well you have done to make a new and bigger cabin and moreover, as in Ireland, you continue to be the host for so many gatherings. For our part you can see we brought the whole family with us thanks to the kindness of our neighbours who are acting as keeper of our animals. Without their help I would have been hard put to get Mary to leave William, our eldest, in charge of all that."

"Ah yes, and Moses would have been hard put to get you to leave Mary," said George as he held out both hands to greet Mary, who was holding their latest child in her arms. Maude strode over, embraced Mary warmly and, taking the child from her, led her to the women, many of whom she knew from Cavan.

George then turned to Forest again and asked, "How is it going Forest, especially this business of getting your land claim settled?"

"It is hard to say, George. The hard part is that after all this time I don't know for sure how it's going. We have worked all the hours possible to fulfill the duties of a settler and written to the Military people and still no definite answer. It is a very different country now than when you came over. It was well for you to come when you did and to have made sure you completed your settlement duties in good time. But then you always were prudent, George, and I can see it has worked well for you."

George replied, "We pretty well had to come when we did, so our present situation is not due to prudence but happenstance and God's direction. Aye, that too. We are happy now that we came when we did, but even with that good fortune, the first years were severe. But we don't need to tell you that, I'm sure. You and Mary shall have the prayers of our whole group for a successful outcome to your affairs."

214

"Thank you, George. I greatly appreciate that and I daresay it will help more than aught else. Thank you."

They moved together to join the other men who had gathered into their own little group off on one side of the clearing and saw very sober faces for such a happy occasion.

James Blair came out with it: "What do you think of the direction things are taking?"

George Argue asked, "Are you speaking of the land grants, James?"

"I'm speaking of the 'no land grants', that I am. What passes for government in this country has been shillyshallying about for two years now. They don't say no outright, but they don't give you a free land grant either. A new settler nowadays can't know where he's at. What hope is there for the young men?"

Moses, shook his head, "As you say, James, it's a right muddle, and the poor man caught in the middle of it. I know of a few who have been in that kind of situation for the last two years, working and slaving away and hoping it won't all come to naught." He glanced toward Forest as he said this, but Forest shook his head almost imperceptibly and said naught.

Andrew, who was just seventeen and had been planning on applying for a land grant on his eighteenth birthday, looked very downcast, as did many other young men. This was not at all what they had expected in the new country.

He spoke up, "What did they mean by saying there is no more free land? There be land aplenty all around us."

His uncle, James Wilson, answered, "Aye lad, but that land is anything but free. It is already reserved for the Clergy, Church of England Clergy that is, or the Crown. It's not for sale."

James scratched his whiskers and added, "When we first got here we wondered why they kept these empty lots in between the lots given to us settlers, do you mind?"

"Aye, we wondered right enough," said John Scott, and others nodded.

James nodded, "Well now I reckon we know rightly enough what they were up to. The value of these here empty lots which have ne'er had an axe taken to them will be more valuable because they be next to one of our lots."

215

"I wonder why we did not see that for what it was right at the outset?" mused Robert Mitchell.

"Because you're a man without guile, Robert. And it is more than can be said for the likes of them as what govern us," said James Blair with a scowl.

There was silence for a while as the men absorbed this unpleasant bit of wisdom. Then Fred Mowat said, "Well at least there will be one good thing come out of it when those empty lands are sold."

"Aye, and what will that be Fred?" asked Sam Halliday.

Mowat replied, "Why the new owner will have to do his road duties and if we can get a road forced through that would be a great boon to all of us. Maybe we would get our milk to market before it spoils."

Halliday agreed, "Aye, so it would, so it would. Myself I'm thinking it will be a quair long time before we see the likes of a road we can get a cart over."

John Scott and James Wilson looked to each other and gave a small smile. They had been talking for some time now of building wagons with extra large wheels which could negotiate the corduroy roads more successfully. Now they were poised to start making them.

Robert Mitchell wasn't finished with the land issue. "There is vacant land that is neither Crown nor Clergy land. What about the lots left behind by those who can't stick it out here? We all know people who bought more land than they could manage and lost everything. There are quite a few of those." He paused, "What's more, we have no word at all about when the lots will be up for sale, at what price, and if there are enough settlers who can afford to buy them."

"No, we don't have word, but there are some who get the word right early." Archie Magee spoke up for the first time, "The Sheriff knows when a settler cannot pay what he owes to the store and he passes the word right quick to his friends. Before you know it the sheriff or one of his friends has snatched up the lot. Of course, the storekeeper himself knows first and more times than not, he is the one who takes a hundred acres to pay for a paltry debt. Sometimes he gets it for less than a shilling an acre."

He raised his voice, "Into the bargain, if it goes to the magistrate to decide, the poor man finds that the magistrate and the storekeeper are one and the same person. It's a bloo' — a flamin' disgrace." He flushed a little as he narrowly averted a swear word in front of all his friends. The near gaff was readily understood and shared by everyone present.

"All too true," said George, "and that's why I am determined not to be in debt to the storekeeper by so much as a shilling. Don't count on charity from that source or from the courts either." [20]

All in all the talk from the men was enough to cast a pall over the festivities, but their gloom was ameliorated greatly by the sight of the feast laid out for them. The tables were loaded with roasts of fresh meats, corn, new potatoes, carrots, beets, cucumbers, melons and even a few tomatoes. There were desserts too, since the women had learned how to use maple syrup for sweetening, but it was the fresh vegetables that every person craved and knew would soon be out of sight until the following summer.

When the feast was over, Rev Ezra Healey gathered them all together for a sermon directed at the young people starting their married lives, but also it was to be his only sermon to them for the next two months or more. The mothers wept as they realized full well how little these young people knew of each other or of what was ahead of them. But that was life. It had to be endured. The fathers of these young couples were relieved, either happy that their daughters were no longer their

---

[20] The greater portion of British immigrants, arriving in Canada without funds and the most exalted ideas of the value and productiveness of land, purchase extensively on credit....Everything goes well for a time. A log house is erected with the assistance of the old settlers, and the clearing of the forest is commenced. Credit is obtained at a neighbouring store...During this period he had lived a life of toil and privation... On the arrival of the fourth harvest, he is reminded by the storekeeper to pay his account with cash, or discharge part of it with his disposable produce, for which he gets a very small price. He is also informed that the purchase money of the land has been accumulating interest....he finds himself poorer than when he commenced operation. Disappointment preys on his spirit... the land ultimately reverts to the former proprietor, or a new purchaser is found.
Patrick Sherriff, Land Grant System, 1835.

responsibility or that their sons had someone to look after them. Each marriage was a load off their shoulders.

They were thankful to Healey for his instructions and encouragement, and thankful too when he finished with enough light remaining for a few of them to get home before dark. The Caldwells, the largest group of all, were asked to stay at the Argue shanty. Moses stayed for the evening too although he had an invitation to sleep at the Mitchells. The Fosters, who had as far as ten miles to go before they were home, were invited to bed down with Archie Scott's family and go the rest of the way the following day. That was how it came to be that Sarah Scott-Foster spent her wedding night in her parents' home before she left for her in-law's shanty in Nepean Township.

That night in the shanty, Moses, James Blair, George and William continued talking about their futures. Forest Caldwell sat with them but was reluctant to say much until he knew exactly what his circumstances were.

George said, "I have it on pretty good authority that the Rideau Canal will finally be built, maybe even starting next year."

"Who is your authority, George? We don't know anyone who is really an authority, do we?"

"Well, maybe not," George admitted, "but John Burrows has told me that Lord Dalhousie has bought land to be used for the canal building, and that is good enough for me. He has spoken directly to Lord Dalhousie."

"We have heard rumours of the canal for years now. But one thing is sure. If they do start to build it, you are in a right good place to be one of the first to get some sort of job. You have been smart to hold onto that shanty, that you have," said Moses.

"If we are to be there most of the year, I'll have to make a few changes in the shanty, for sure. It will be hard not to be in Goulbourne at all, but you see, I've found in the time we've tried to grow crops here, that most of the soil on my hundred is pretty poor, as far as we've cleared at any rate. It will not make much of a farm, that's for sure."

"Yes," said Moses and James Blair agreed, "It can be poor on one farm and the next farm may be much better. You never know in advance, until you've broken yourself clearing it, and then you learn what you've got."

George concluded, "It is well to give thanks for what we've got: our health, our families, our friends and not yet, by God's grace, not yet in debt to any man. We'll make it through I believe." And that concluded their chat.

In a few months the situation was made clear. There would be no more free land.

CALDWELL

CLAIMING THE LAND 1826

By spring 1825 it was becoming more definite that the clergy and officers who had been granted large tracts of land were winning their petition to the Lieutenant Governor Peregrine Maitland that the government cease giving away free land, at least in that part of the country. Forest became more determined to present his situation more clearly and obtain a promise to consider his case.

4th July 1825 Township of March, U.C.
To His Excellency Sir Peregrine Maitland RCB and Lieut. Governor of Upper Canada in Council[ii21]

The Petition of Forest Cauldwell — Humbly Sheweth,
That your petitioner came from the County of Cavan in Ireland April 1823 that your petitioner proceedeth without loss of time to the Township of March where several of his friends resided in hopes to get located to some Lands near them, and was much distressed and disappointed to find an Order had been issued to the Land Board not to locate any more persons to the Vacant lots in the Military Townships — but your petitioner being given to understand that the prohibition would soon be taken off as no more of Mr. Robinson's settlers were to be located in these Townships, to keep himself employed and to do

---

[21] Forest Caldwell, Public Archives Canada (PAC) Upper Canada Land Petitions (U.C.L.P.), Land Book M, 1824-26. Call (Reel) No. 1724, Vol. 107, Bundle C 14, Petition No. 217, pp. 503

something to support his numerous family (a wife and six children, the Eldest 12 years old) was induced, or more properly speaking was obliged to commence improving some Land immediately adjoining one of his friends, which happened to be a Lot to which a Robert Maxwell had about 18 months before been located to, who never to this present time (4th July 1825) has done any work on the Lot or been heard of in the Country —

Your petitioner wishes further to show that he has cleared and farmed Seven acres of Land and built a House — Therefore most humbly and most earnestly solicits the favour of being located the S.W. half of the lot in question (No.6 1st Concession Township of March) and thereby retain for the support of his family the result of two years labour — And your petitioner as in duty bound will ever pray — Forest Cauldwell

This time Forest went on his own with his letter and with the prayers of his neighbours supporting him. He was greeted by a new Justice of the Peace, Thomas Malhizhy, who added the following note to his letter:

Township of March
5th July 1825
I certify that the petitioner Forest Cauldwell is known to me, that I think him to be a pious, Industrious, good man — and have reason to believe that everything stated in the petition above is true
T. Malhizhy J. P.[22]

Encouraged by this letter of support, Forest started to build another home for Mary, one without a barn as he had promised. This cabin had three good-sized rooms: a bedroom for the boys and another for the girls, with Mary and Forest still sleeping in the main room. More than that was not attempted until there was further news.

In August there was another entry in the Land Book. The entry following Forest's letter was very hard to decipher:

---

[22] The signature is not very clear but this is my best guess at the spelling. The same would have to be said for Mr. I. Hertig.

Aug. 1825

*I do not find that the Petitioner has received any Land.
The North West half of Lot No. 6 in the Concession of March,
100 acres is located in the Name of James Armstrong, an Irish
Emigrant, and the South East half of the said Lot in the Name of
Robert Maxwell also an Irish Emigrant as returned by the
Military Superintendent to the 25 December 1822*
(Indecipherable lines, then)*...become entitled to.....*
Grants
*I do not find any evidence of the performance of the
Settlements duty in favour of the before mentioned persons, and
no description has.... found for any part of the lot.*

*I beg leave respectfully to suggest that Mr. Baustion
(sp.?) Late Supervisor be written to on the Subject of this
location.*

F. Ridout

Finally, in December 1825, with the ban on further
grants of land less than a month hence, there was a final entry. It
was recommended that:

**Caldwell, Forest, Irish Immig. Twnshp March Lot 6,
100 acres, Sept 7, 1825**[23]

The last entry was found in the Land Book for 1827 -
1829 but was backdated to Sept 1825.

The dates of these entries indicate a bit of bureaucratic
footwork. Archive papers indicate that the meeting of the
Executive Council was not held until December 1825.
Technically the Land Grants for those Townships expired in
January 1826; therefore to be well under the legal wire, the final
entries, which did not show up until the Land Book of 1827,
were backdated to September 1825. This preceded the
deliberations of the Executive Council in December 1825 by
three months. These Executive Council recommendations were
not signed and no single person could be held accountable for
any irregularities. No one was very concerned about Forest

[23] UCLP. Land Book N 1827-29, pp. 279.

Caldwell's success in obtaining his land in this manner and it may have been quite common after all, but it does appear that he had a little help from the authorities who backdated his claim in order to grant him the land well before the deadline when no further grants were to be made. Other documents of this period indicate that the authorities could do pretty much as they wished providing it could not be traced. The important thing was, 'Don't get the authorities down on you.' Pretty much as Forest's friends had advised him at the outset.

On a spurt of euphoria Forest added a floor and fireplace to the cabin, making Mary very pleased with her new home. Mary and Forest still had their feather tick on a cot in the main room.

Forest attributed the favourable resolution of his claim to God's blessing and he wrote a letter to George Argue c/o Richmond's Landing to thank him for the outcome of prayers.

CALDWELL

A LETTER TO DRUMSHIEL 1826

January 14th, 1826 Township March, Upper Canada
Dearest Mother and Samuel,
  We hope this letter finds you both in good health, as are
we here. This time of year is one in which we have the most
leisure and I therefore wish to tell you of our good fortune in
acquiring full title to 100 acres. The course of acquiring title has
not been without vagaries and the subject of much prayer. It is
therefore a profound relief to have this matter successfully
behind me. I now shall be able to better plan a future for Mary
and the children. We are of course much indebted to our friends
here for all the assistance, both material and spiritual, which
they have so readily given to our family.
  The funds you have sent I have set aside for the purchase
of more land when the right time comes. We have another post
office here now, not far from our home. I hope it will make our
letters travel more quickly.

Forest found to his dismay that it was almost as hard to write letters home now as before when his father was alive. It was so hard to convey the reality of living in the bush without making their lives seem deplorable. The growing gap in their daily experiences simply made letter writing too difficult. It was best to describe the children's activities and to emphasize their growing maturity. He was just as keen to give comfort to his mother as he had been to his father.

When this challenging task of letter writing was done, Forest turned his attention to his children's education. Mary assumed the responsibility for teaching the youngest ones their basic alphabet and simple arithmetic; Forest was to give the three older children exercises in penmanship and reading aloud. Forest, usually the mildest of men, was a stern taskmaster when it came to his sons' learning. He told them that they were soon to receive books from their grandmother and he wanted to be able to report that they enjoyed and benefitted from these books. Moreover they would be writing letters of thanks to their grandmother Caldwell and letters to their Smiley grandparents too. He wanted them to show that they could be pioneers in Upper Canada and still acquire an education, which meant they could write a fine script. Since paper was scarce they were to practice on their slate boards until they were skilled enough to use real paper.

The children hoped they would be pleased with the books they were to read, although they were a little dubious on this point. They groaned aloud at the thought of so much writing. William, now almost 14, thought he should be out of the schoolroom entirely and certainly not sharing lesson time with his younger brothers and sisters, even if his lessons were much more advanced. Instead he was expected and required to set an example, in attitude at least.

CALDWELL

SMILEY FAMILY ARRIVES 1826

With much sweat and anxiety Forest had achieved his goal. Joy, if joy was what they felt, is always a fleeting thing. Ironically, the more acres Forest cleared, the more surely he realized that the land, which they had wrested from the forest and from the Government, was poor land. It amazed him to see how these huge trees had grown from little more than rock in some places. Of course they'd had countless years of growth to achieve their stature. He did not have such a time frame. There was barely enough pasture to feed his animals during the summer months and he was too often having to buy fodder to get them through the winter. They were managing but only just. Each year the thin soil yielded less harvest. They certainly were making little progress. When he thought of the soil of Cavan he realized he had taken too much for granted. But how could one judge the soil to be poor when you saw the size of those trees?

A few of their very close neighbours were doing better. Erskine's land had good patches in it at least and he was able to sell his lumber for a good price to Hamnett Pinhey for his ever-expanding estate. Moses Wilson talked about moving to Huntley to start over, but thus far it was only talk. No one wanted to move away from valued friends even though better land was much needed.

Often Forest's thoughts strayed back to Cavan. Samuel, as promised, wrote to Forest regularly, mainly about his decisions for the estate. Although the speed with which some of the letters were delivered was improving, thanks to the second post office being opened up not far from them, it certainly was not fast enough to offer or receive timely advice. While a few of the decisions surprised Forest, namely the decision to put more of the land into wheat and less in grazing for the cows and horses, he made no criticism. He was pleased to see that Samuel was brave enough to take charge; only time would tell just how clever a decision turned out to be.

Of more interest to Forest were Samuel's brief tidbits of family information:

More and more families are leaving Cavan; often the entire family leaving at once. We have heard a rumour that a Smiley family plans to go too.

For Mary this was exciting news. A letter came soon from her father telling her that her cousin Harold Smiley was coming to Upper Canada, and wanted Forest to look out for a suitable piece of land. Harold was a merchant in Fermanagh; Forest was no wiser about his intentions in Upper Canada. Mary was ecstatic to think that one of her own kin was on the way and said that it felt as though she were going to have a brother living close by. He was bringing his whole family: a wife, four girls, two boys, and a servant girl.

Any thought of moving to Huntley to find better land was put on hold for two reasons: first and most important, Mary was expecting another child; no more upheavals were to be allowed. Secondly, Forest decided to make no decisions about a good place for Harold's family to locate; he was not sure where his own family might be located in a few years. Harold would make his own judgments when he was on the spot.

In matters concerning Mary, Forest could show a more militant bearing, surprising everyone, even himself. This baby would be her first to be born in Upper Canada. All around them women were giving birth to their babies without the assistance of a doctor, or even an experienced woman. Forest knew that Mary had not had problems in the six births thus far, but there was a crucial difference this time. In Cavan she'd had much more support: a cook, plus a maid of all work, her vigilant mother, indeed two sets of grandparents who were covetous of the opportunity to look after their grandchildren. This was a very different situation. Here her only help came from her eleven-year-old daughter, Margaret.

Each time Mary told Forest she was to have another baby, he blamed himself for not being able to stay away from her. Mary would not hear of his fretting and told him, "I'll be fine, Forest. You are not to worry about me." He ignored this useless advice and worried steadfastly.

Forest consulted with Hettie Erskine and a few of the other women about what was the best diet for her before and after birth. The women were amused at Forest's interference in what was a woman's business, but Forest was not at all deterred.

Mary gained one concession from Forest. She was allowed to hold a few tick-making bees. She wished to be able to provide a feather tick for Harold and his wife, another bigger one for the girls and one for the boys. She canvassed her neighbours for any feathers they might spare and for several weeks the whole house was decorated with feathers of all colours and hues, accompanied by sneezes and itching. There were no beds for the guests but at least they would sleep on a tick, a great deal more comfortable than that which many enjoyed in their first year. Forest agreed to this industry for he was reassured that she would be off her feet for most of the day, only to find her working long into the evening.

Of greater service to Mary was Forest's addition of another bedroom for themselves and the baby. It was another girl who squalled and roared her way into their midst in early August, bringing the family to four boys and three girls. They named her Elizabeth. Margaret was called "the little mother", a term of approbation to her parents, but one she came to loath when her brothers used it. On top of it all, Forest insisted that "Mother is to remain in bed for the first two weeks after the birth; Margaret will be in charge." Forest maintained his vigilance on this matter but his plans were disrupted by events beyond his control.

One week after Elizabeth's birth, word came that Harold Smiley and his family were at The Landing. Mary was delighted; Forest was ambivalent, but there was no help for it. Forest took his large four-wheeled cart with three rows of seats,[24] into The Landing to fetch them. When Mary judged that they should be arriving soon, she posted William out at the road to give a signal

---

[24] A later version of this cart was called a Democrat.

of their arrival so that she could go out into the yard to welcome them.

At the sight of her cousin, Mary wept. Mary was not at all prone to express herself so openly and Forest wondered if this was some new manifestation of childbirth. Indeed it might have been so, but Mary was having no more alarms from Forest. She wiped her eyes and said,

"I am that glad to see you. A thousand welcomes to our home, which shall be yours for as long as you need it." She then turned to Forest and said, "I am very well and overjoyed to see my family and I shall not rest until all have eaten."

Harold was about ten years older than Mary, and his wife Frances about five years older. Both had attended chapel with the rest of the Smiley family, but were less inclined than Mary to seek modest adornment. Frances was wearing a wine coloured cape over a dark brown cotton dress, both of which screamed style and money. The children's clothes were nothing remarkable and of dark blue or brown colours; it would indeed have been amazing to see them in aught else as they had just come to the end of a very long and dirty journey. They too had taken a cabin on the ship, but they were far from fortunate in the duration of the voyage or the weather. Frances, formerly a plump matronly woman, looked much thinner than Mary remembered; Harold had not lost as much weight but he looked grey and exhausted and had acquired many white hairs. His bushy brows and strong jaw bespoke determination, but it was also apparent that he was as glad to see Mary as she was to see him. The Caldwells represented a haven at the end of their journey.

When they had eaten the best meal that could be provided, Harold and Frances eagerly gave presents to all the family: cotton by the yard, scarves and muffs for Mary and her eldest daughter Margaret, dolls for the younger girls and heavy wool suits for the boys and Forest. The boys looked at the suits and wondered when they were going to need such fine clothes. It looked as if Harold had brought with him the beginnings of a small store, short on toys, but long on essentials. He had heeded well Mary's advice about what was needed in this raw country. The greatest treasure was a large box containing packets of tea, enough to last for many months.

What was of greatest value as far as the children were concerned were six new cousins close to their own age. It was an injection of strength to have such a number of close kin nearby. As they all bedded down for the night, six boys in one room, six girls in the other, Harold and Frances in the newest bedroom and Mary, Forest and baby Elizabeth in the main room, Mary breathed a sigh of deep satisfaction.

She confided in Forest's ear, "You cannot know how happy I am, Forest, to be able to welcome Harold and his family, with floors under their feet and room for everyone. Thank you, thank you for all your hard work, my dear, dear man."

Forest replied, "It was for your comfort, Mary, and I can see that it is a comfort for you although not quite as I had expected. Here we are out in the main room again. But it matters not as long as you are well and content. I will not have you waiting hand and foot on visitors, mind you. You are to accept all help offered and I am sure it will be forthcoming. That will make them feel right at home. By the by," he added as he turned over to sleep, "where is this servant girl we heard was to come?"

Mary replied, "I have not yet heard the full story there. Frances looked annoyed when I asked her and said she would tell all later, when her spirit was up to it."

"From our point of view one less body is just as well", said Forest, "but the tale will provide some interest I daresay."

The next day Forest took Harold around to meet a few of their neighbours and observed Harold looking about quite intently. Nothing remotely like a village presented itself as they walked from one homestead to another by foot. Harold became more silent as they progressed; Forest decided to broach the topic he guessed must be uppermost on Harold's mind.

"Are you wondering how to make a living here, Harold?"

"You have it, Forest. I don't see signs of much activity. We have not met one person outside his or her own yard since we started out. Do people need a store? How do they get provisions? It was impossible to imagine a place just like this when I was in Ireland making plans."

"No one yet has ever been able to imagine it. To me now, it is beginning to appear quite civilized, but I can see it is going to take a while before you are able to make sense of what's ferns't you." He was silent briefly; the image of many signs of activity at The Landing came into mind.

"You may best try to establish yourself at The Landing,

Harold. The rumours of canal building I believe are well grounded. Lt. Col. John By arrived at Montreal earlier this year and is expected to be at The Landing any day now. Merchants are now hoping and believing there may be opportunities for various businesses there. It is fair certain there will be a great influx of workers all over The Landing come next summer. I think right now is a good time for you to find a spot and set yourself up in business. Mayhap you can see now why I did not scout out any particular spot near our home. It's no center of commerce, is it?"

Harold admitted, "What I see of March Township is very picturesque and better organized by comparison with what I saw of The Landing, but I can definitely see your point of view. Although it is early days to be off and looking for a place of business, when we have barely set our feet down on the soil of Upper Canada, I think I had best not put it off. Can you or one of your neighbours take me back to The Landing soon and perhaps point me in the right direction?"

Forest nodded, "I'll take you tomorrow morning, even leave you at Firth's Tavern if you need to remain for more than one day. I have a friend at The Landing, Argue by name, who's planning to live year round there from now until the canal is completed. His homestead is in Goulbourne, but if he is about, he may be able to give you good direction. We'll try to find him tomorrow. In the winter he hauls supplies up to the lumber camps on sleighs and that is another business you can hear about from him. As for getting settled, I think you are right not to delay. Everything in this country is a matter of timing, as I have found to my chagrin. You are here at the right time for setting up a new business, to be sure."

The following morning Harold and Forest set out when the birds were already at work, providing nature's symphony. Harold prudently tucked a package of tea in his pocket to give to George Argue. It was past noon before they reached The Landing and Forest headed straight for George's shanty. By a stroke of good fortune, they found him at home. George explained that he was not busy at this time, but he had needed to come to The Landing early to catch the first opportunity for work when the canal building started. Mary was delighted to receive the treasured package of tea and immediately made oat scones for everyone to have with their tea.

231

Harold soaked up every bit of information George imparted about life at The Landing, in particular how one might go about setting up a business. He wanted to hear all about hauling loading too. What kind of foodstuffs did George need? Where did he get his supplies? After an hour or so Forest decided he had put Harold in good hands. It even began to look as if each of them might bring business to the other.

George, sensing that Forest wished to return home before nightfall, invited Harold to stay the night with them, provided he could sleep on a tick on the dirt floor. Harold bravely said, "There'll be no trouble with that and I thank you very kindly."

Forest said, "Shall I return for you tomorrow or do you wish to remain here another day?"

Harold said, "It is a big job to get me to and fro your place. I had better stay at least a whole day if I am to learn something about setting up a business here. Of course I don't wish to be a burden on George and Mary. I can easily find my board at the Tavern, much as I dislike the drinking part of it," he added.

Everyone could see the sense in his staying at least one full day and with George's reassurance that he was welcome to their hospitality, Forest agreed to pick him up in the afternoon, two days hence. He felt that he was shunting his responsibilities onto George somewhat, but George assured him,

"I look forward to helping Harold find his way. It may be that Harold and I will be able to assist one another as I expect to be picking up supplies during the winter months at least. It all depends on what sort of establishment you want to set up here, Harold. All kinds of businesses will be needed."

From George's point of view, he hoped he might find a God-fearing Methodist as a storeowner, and not a merchant who cared only for his own immediate profit. Further acquaintance would better inform him about Harold's bent in that respect.

232

CALDWELL

SMILEY GETS ESTABLISHED 1826

From the time the Smiley family arrived, life at the Caldwell household underwent a sea change. Forest, who was busy for the first two days conducting Harold on his tour of March and The Landing, worried that Mary was not engaging the Smiley family to help her. On the morning of the third day he was ready to tackle the situation.

On a daily basis there were many chores to do but William, even though he was still not fully developed, was becoming a brawny fellow, quite the opposite of his father, whom he proudly outstripped at most of the farm chores. Samuel, at eleven years, tried hard to keep up with William and between them, they took over most of the chores on the farm.

William, already very capable at looking after the animals independently, proved to be equally able to show the new boys how to work. The visiting boys were only 8 and 6, but did their best to ape William and Samuel at the chores. They were now trying to bring hay into the barns; William alone wielded the scythe and the younger boys followed Samuel's example in gathering the hay into bundles. Assured that there was no trouble on this front, Forest turned his attention to what was going on in the house where sixteen people, plus a newborn had to be fed several times a day. What he saw displeased him.

Frances sat in the only comfortable chair in the house, with her eyes closed, taking her rest. Well, maybe she needed it; she did not look too spry. Any time Forest had looked in during the past two days, Mary had been on her feet preparing food at the table, as she was now. Margaret was at sixes and sevens, distracted from her work by the presence of the other girls; it seemed that neither the Smiley girls nor Margaret knew what to do. The younger ones were playing house with the dolls brought by the Smileys. Forest felt himself coming as close to losing his temper as he could remember. Mary was being abused. He would not have it.

Trying to get himself under control, he sat down beside Frances and gave her a fair warning of what was ahead. It seemed best to begin with the girls. He explained to her that the sooner her daughters learned how to prepare a meal, the better fed the whole family will be.

"I understand, Frances, that your oldest, Lydia, is twelve, right?" A nod from Frances, who was looking a bit bewildered.

"Margaret will teach her how to make bread; that will be her job every day. With sixteen hungry mouths to feed, at least six large loaves are to be baked every day and twice that number on Saturday. Matilda, your next girl, will be in charge of gathering the eggs and feeding the hens twice each day. Margaret will show her how to do that. Our young boys, along with Fanny and Mabel, will bring in vegetables, clean them and get them ready for the pot. All the girls will set and clear the table and wash dishes. When they are finished with these chores, they can..." Frances' mouth gaped open and her brows rose in astonishment.

Forest continued, "Even baby Elizabeth will have a job; her job is to keep her mother at the feeding station and off her feet."

Mary was more than a little embarrassed at Forest's imperious manner in things belonging to the kitchen; she hardly knew what to say or where to turn. Truth be told, she needed more help and was in fact getting a great deal less. Since she was unable to stop the flow once Forest got the bit between his teeth, she found to her surprise that she rather enjoyed seeing her husband in this new light.

Margaret found her new role as teacher and general manager very agreeable and showed that she was well able to take charge now that the law had been laid down. When Harold saw how industrious his four girls could be when put to it, he expressed his pleasure openly. Frances did not deliver a verdict;

she was most often seen with her eyes closed as if she had not the strength to think of it.

By the time the Smileys had been at the Caldwells for a week, both Forest and Mary had a better appreciation of the challenges ahead for this family. As they themselves had found, letters could not prepare anyone for the realities they were to face in Upper Canada, although letters to the Smiley family had not pretended life was easy. Nevertheless, Mary had not emphasized how hard she worked on a daily basis, lest she worry her mother. How could they blame the Smileys for lacking the imagination about life in the bush in Upper Canada?

Forest canvassed his neighbours and learned that Thomas Morgan was going to make a trip to The Landing soon. He would be glad to take Harold with him if it pleased him. On his second trip to The Landing, Harold decided he would have to take a shanty soon; he observed more people there than had been around the previous week. He believed that if he could obtain the supplies he could have a thriving business. Nothing was to be gained and much lost if he did not act swiftly. He tried to buy a plot of land but no one was selling. He knew there was no point in consulting Frances when the best shanty he could find was well below her notions of what was her due.

With all this in mind, he rented an old shanty he could convert into a store. It had ample dimensions, providing room to store extra supplies, but not one of the shanties he had looked at boasted of a floor or even a stove. Frances had been the proud owner of an up-to-date stove in Ireland and had let Harold know that she was unable to cook on anything else; in fact she had rarely cooked on anything back home. Harold did not look forward to telling her that stoves were a luxury in this country and would be out of sight for a few years to come. Nor did he like to tell her that they would have to live in a shack that was roomy but drafty, with a dirt floor. Worst of all he was to inform her that he had already chosen the place. He decided in favour of taking the one close to Argue's shanty for he hoped he could count on George to haul supplies for him and be glad of the business.

Frances had been cosseted in Fermanagh and was expecting to continue the same here. Actually she expected better. Word had been passed on to her that in March Township there were quite a few retired military families and it was altogether a genteel community. From her conversation it was clear she expected they would live in March where her merchant husband would become landed gentry. Just how this transformation was to take effect was not detailed in her imagination.

In Fermanagh Harold had run a haberdashery, much like Mary's father. When Frances was made aware that they would be moving to The Landing where her husband would run a general store it was clear from her raised voice in their bedroom that this was a most unwelcome shock. Forest, still not recovered fully from seeing Mary, only a week past childbirth, serving her cousin's wife, was out of patience from the outset. Mary, recalling that her whole first year seemed to be one shock after the other, was more sympathetic. Harold was to have the unenviable task of persuading, nay, insisting, that his family move to The Landing with him.

Frances was distraught when she first saw the prospective store, and at the thought that she was expected to live in any part of it. In her short time in March Township she had heard someone speak disparagingly of The Landing as a disorganized mess of poor shacks. Was this to be her life in Upper Canada? In their little town in Fermanagh, her standing as wife of a storekeeper was not as high as she would have liked, but this! This was scarcely to be imagined.

It was borne upon her that she really had no choice in the matter. Harold, while less than happy about the near future, relied on Frances' pride to ensure that she would put the best face on the situation. She might howl at him in private but in public she would hold her head up high.

When the Smiley family were removed to The Landing it was inevitable that Mary would see less of her family than she would have liked, but Forest was quite content.

ARGUE

WORK AT THE CANAL 1826-27

At Last! Rumours became reality. Lt. Col. John By of the Royal Engineers and Superintendent of the construction of the Rideau Waterway arrived at The Landing September 21 1826, in the company of Philemon Wright, and three other men who came with him from Montreal. Lt. Col. By had been appointed by the Colonial Office on the recommendations of the Duke of Wellington and General Mann who had worked with him more than a decade earlier when Captain By supervised the building of the fortifications for Quebec City.

Lt. Col. John By was a tall, strong man in his mid-forties, calm, decisive, confident and patient, but unyielding in his commission which was B*uild the Waterway with all speed and economy possible...*

His advice from the Duke of Wellington: *Don't wait for the annual authorization of funds from Parliament to the Ordnance Department, but proceed forthwith and the funds will be forthcoming. Ordnance will be responsible for getting the funds to you. You are not to bother your head about this detail.*

In that year, 1826, the Duke of Wellington was Master-General of Ordnance, the supplies and munitions Department for the Military, under whose provenance was the building of the Rideau Canal and Waterway. With the Tory Party securely in power, Wellington's assurances on this matter seemed sufficient to Lt. Col. By and he proceeded confidently and quickly. These instructions were to cause Lt. Col. By a great deal of trouble, both in the course of building the Waterway and after it was completed, troubles which started at the top and filtered down to the lowliest ditch digger.

One of his first orders was a survey of The Landing. Lord Dalhousie recommended John Burrows for the job and Burrows and his helper could be seen in all the daylight hours somewhere at The Landing with no time for chat. When Sunday chapel meeting came at George's home, John was obviously a very happy man, eager to tell the company his impressions of this very worthy man, Lt. Col. John By.

Lt. Col. By was apparently satisfied with Burrows' surveying skills and energetic style, for, along with a couple of Royal Engineers and the essential native guide, he took John on the initial exploratory trip of the whole Waterway. John observed that Lt. Col. By could cope with any diet, sleep in all circumstances, never lose his temper and endure any setback with patience and humour. He received the devotion of all who worked under him, John included.

The word went out that Lt. Col. By was hiring men, and those who had their own accommodation and were willing to sign on until the end of the project, would be hired first. This put the Argue family and their Cavan friends in advantageous positions. They were confident that the British Government would be a reliable employer and there would be no problem in getting paid from this source. Steady wages for the duration of the canal building were viewed as a Godsend, for outside of working in the bush during the winter, jobs were very hard to come by and all too often promised wages failed to be paid. The men from Cavan were among the first to sign up.

In 1826 William was 22, Andrew 19, Robert 17. They had been hauling loading every winter from freezing to spring breakup on the river, and maintaining their lease on the shanty at The Landing while working on the farm each summer. They now turned to canal building each summer and farming was temporarily halted.

Work at the entrance to the Canal began almost immediately and involved a great deal of back breaking labour with shovel, pickaxe, and wheelbarrow. George, now fifty-seven years of age, knew he had better find a more manageable occupation. Hauling supplies to the work sites might be a possibility, providing he could get a head start.

George and William each rode a horse to Goulbourne to visit James Wilson and John Scott who had set up their wagon-making business. They ordered one wagon and rode another

238

wagon back to The Landing.

This turned out well for both wagon makers and the Argues, who now were in a position to haul foodstuffs and materials to the worksites, and haul rock and soil away from the excavations. Their services were snapped up immediately, for reliability of delivery counted for a great deal and their reputation for avoiding taverns was quite well known. They made deliveries of all kinds, but chiefly food for workers. Their wagons proved valuable, for the roads, where they existed at all, were still very rough corduroy roads. Only a very large strong wheel could roll from one log to the other without getting stuck in a trough between the logs or plagued with breakdowns. Livestock roamed freely over the area and there was no such thing as a planked walkway.

George had encouraged Smiley to set up a general store and Harold lost no time in bringing in supplies from Montreal. His location was good, in the vicinity of Isaac Firth's Tavern, but not too close. He only wished he had more arms and legs, for he knew he could sell as many loaves of bread and meat pies as he could lay his hands on. Lydia was willing to bake bread but could not keep pace with the demand. For a short time he contracted with a few local women to bake for the store and he employed Lydia to serve in the store instead. Fanny had to join the work force as well, but she contrived to do so behind the scenes. Soon Harold concentrated on larger items, such as bags of flour for bakeries and eateries which were springing up beside him. His store became known as the supplier for many other businesses, the place to go for everything from string to animal feed.

By the spring of 1827 The Landing was a scene of indescribable activity. While the swamp in the Lower Town was being drained, other workers were building barracks for the soldiers on the hill, then called Barracks Hill and later Parliament Hill. Men looking for employment were coming into the area from all directions. At the outset there was lots of space, but few dwellings. The workers and their families squatted in tents on any piece of empty land; trees came down rapidly as people tried to build shanties. Presently the space between these dwellings shrank, and George was glad that he had a good number of friends close by.

Quarrels between French Canadians and Irish

239

immigrants increased as their numbers grew and they competed for jobs, housing and status. More taverns sprang up and the demand for ale and strong liquor was heavy. Bakeries, tanneries, and gristmills sprouted up and where the soil allowed, farming expanded now that a market for produce was at hand.

The Landing had neither postman nor policeman, neither magistrate nor sheriff. Officers of the law were based in Perth and did a circuit over the territory every so often, but their services could not begin to cope with the new situation. Lt. Col. By found that he was spending a great deal of his time presiding over disputes. He wrote to the Government at York demanding that they appoint five magistrates to the area. In the meantime, and that turned out to be no mean time, he had soldiers breaking up quarrels and fights and trying to maintain the peace. In addition to building the Canal, Lt. Col. By assumed responsibility for law and order in a shanty town that made the Wild West seem comparatively civilized. Those in the Military settlements, such as Richmond and March, who fancied themselves to be a cut above most of the population, called Bytown "that place of ditch diggers", referring chiefly to the large numbers of Irish so employed. In 1827 the area began to be called Byville and then Bytown. This was no misnomer, for the force of Lt. Col. By's personality and industry seemed to have taken over the district, and Lt. Col. By only had to give the order and work started in a military fashion.

Lt. Col. By saw that he urgently needed more land to accommodate workers and asked that the Crown and Clergy Reserve Lands be made available for sale or lease up and down the proposed Waterway. There was a relatively quick response to this demand as the Government at York needed money. They turned the Crown Lands over to the Canada Company for sale in 1826, but the prices were high. The Clergy Reserves were opened for sale in 1827 at lower prices. The Argues and many others were quick to take advantage of this opportunity lest it be reversed shortly and without notice. At last the common settler felt he was able to make some progress.

As the spring changed to hot summer, the worst complaint was not the hard work of digging and lifting heavy wet clay, but the insects which gathered round every waterhole, especially the vast area known as Dow's Great Swamp. Most men working on the Canal at any of the locations came down with malaria. They did not know that it had anything to do with the mosquitoes. They called it the ague or "sweating sickness" as it was characterized by bouts of heavy sweats, severe chills and weakness. The air stank from the swampy conditions and the best knowledge of the day thought that this sweating-sickness came from the bad air.[25] George and William both came down with it, William being afflicted worse than George. Andrew, who appeared to lead a charmed life, avoided the ague altogether.

It was not luck that protected Andrew. He and a few other young men observed the natives, who stood about the work sites watching and wondering at the white men digging large holes in the oozing mud, and noticed the natives were not troubled by these voracious insects. By means of gesturing, mostly scratching, they came to understand that the natives covered themselves with grease and berry juice. These young men pestered cooks for as much grease as they could get. It was not clear what use the berry juice was but the grease helped greatly. Soon more of the men started to imitate the natives in this manner. It was not the first or only time that the natives taught these newcomers something important to their welfare in this new country. Andrew was quite happy to put up with scorn from other workers as long as he could avoid this plague, and Robert had enough sense to follow Andrew's example.

Lt. Col. By also thought the condition was caused by bad air, known in other countries as 'mal-aria', the Italian word for bad-air, and in order to help with the scourge he ordered trees to be cut down at each swampy part. Lt. Col. By suffered from malaria himself, but continued his exhausting schedule undeterred. In all, about a thousand deaths were attributed to this sweating sickness and related diseases such as dysentery and typhoid. At the "sickly season" nearly half of the work force was off sick. Fortunately this season covered only the six-week period from the beginning of August to mid-September. There were remarkably few deaths due to accidents despite the dangerous nature of such work, such as blasting heavy rock and

---

[25] As the region was drained and waters flowed more rapidly, this illness left the country entirely and the meaning of the word ague either disappeared or was thought to refer to a flu-like condition, often called "the grip". In our generation, malaria has been considered to be a disease of the tropics and not part of the heritage of North America, but it was quite common wherever the mosquito flourished in North America.

winching large boulders into place.

Waste occurred even under the best management; approval of the larger lock size required for the naval vessels was slow in coming and some excavations had to be redone. This sort of wastefulness agitated John Burrows who was coming to think that Lt. Col. By was a prince among men and not sufficiently appreciated by the government in Britain.

As John was bringing George up to date on the situations faced and dealt with by the great man, he confided his own story to George, "You may have wondered how it is that I have sometimes been called Burrows and sometimes Honey?"

"I certainly have," said George. "Is it possible you are going to tell me after all this time?"

"It was because of something that happened back in England before I ever came to Upper Canada. I was just 17, scarcely old enough to be involved in politics, but I hated to see the way things were going in England. Men were elected to Parliament who did no good for man or beast; they were absolutely useless. They were elected because they had land and influence and did not have to do anything whatsoever in order to get a seat in Parliament. They did not even have to sit in it. It all depended on whom you knew. People such as my family had no vote and no influence and yet we were the backbone of the country."

George raised one eyebrow and could not see anything to be wondered at here. "Is it not the same everywhere, John?"

"Maybe, maybe, but that don't make it right. People were starting to demonstrate against this system which favoured only a few and Father allowed me to go to demonstrations. I think he felt I was too young to be noticed. He discouraged my brothers from voicing their opinions too loudly in public, not if they valued their chances for employment in the district. We had a good trade in making carriages, you see, and who needs a carriage but someone with money? So I suppose he was right enough. Anyway, anyway, one day I got brave enough to step up to the front of a small group and say my bit. I don't know what I said. Nothing much I'm sure, but it so happened that one of the smaller landowners was at the edge of the crowd and did not like what he heard. He came round later that day and cancelled an order for a carriage that he had just placed with us and after that we had more cancellations. I guess they thought the son's views reflected his father's. They did too, but my father had more sense than to say aught outside his own home. We became known as Dissenters. At that time it was a bad word.

"I tried to get work at something else. I even thought about joining the navy or leaving the country altogether in the hopes that the family's fortunes would turn around again. My father did not wish me to do something as drastic as joining the navy. After the way we were being treated in Plymouth where we had obtained an excellent reputation as carriage makers, father, and my brothers too, said they were all ready to leave England if an honest hard working man could not make a living without being a toady, or free to worship as he ought. We had to delay a bit for my mother was not well, and sadly for our family she died soon after. I was sure that all our troubles, especially mine, hastened her death. After that we were all the more eager to leave England as quickly as possible. And that is how we came to Upper Canada."

"It sounds like a bad business to be sure, John. I can see how you wanted and hoped for a fresh start in a new country...." he paused, "but what has this to do with your name?"

"Ah, yes, the name. First of all we went to Montreal and thought we could establish ourselves there as carriage makers. With a large family, three grown sons and two daughters, to feed and house, my brothers and I took on any job we could get. If a man wanted his house painted, we became painters, or window glaziers. My sister taught music and I started to make violins or violas; I even taught music; I could not bear to hear the awful noise being made on the poor violin so I tried to ease my ears a bit. We made anything people were ready to buy and after a bit we became comfortable again as far as income went.

"But gradually I began to notice that there was a group of people running things in this country just as they did in the Old Country. Different people, different accents maybe, but all with the same idea: get money, get power, and keep it to yourselves. You know how it goes, George. They spend public money to set up a school for their sons, but don't spend a cent for your sons to be educated. They reserve land for themselves to buy up at cheap prices and sit and wait for land prices to rise rather than do a hand's turn to make this country a better place. They want to be the cream of society and they make as sure as possible that the milk is not shaken and the cream spread around.

243

They want no new ideas from the likes of you or me."

John kept pulling his hair, flinging his arms about and tugging on his collar as he warmed to his theme. George did not interrupt. John was taking the long way round as usual.

"I decided to become a farmer although I knew nothing at all about it, but I thought maybe I could be my own boss and people always need food. In 1817 I came up river to The Landing and applied for a land grant; I was granted two hundred acres and I cleared a bit of land and built a small cabin. I soon learned that I was unlikely to make a go of farming on this soil, as I told you before." George nodded.

"I kept going back down to Montreal to see my family as it was pretty lonely up here that many years ago; a few lumbermen were around but no one was staying any length of time. My father had heard from cousins in England that some other Plymouth families had come to Canada too. Honey, that is my father's name, is not all that common, so I decided that just in case the name Honey meant something to someone out here too, I was going to use my mother's surname, Burrows. My father and brothers did not change their names as they were getting along all right in Montreal by this time. But when I came up here to start afresh I started to sign my name as John Burrows. I would slip an odd time and introduce myself as Honey and quickly add Burrows and that is how some people called me Honey-Burrows. I am glad I chose this route as now I am working for Lt. Col. By and my name might be listed in the reports sent back to England, as a surveyor or whatnot. I feel more comfortable to be known as Burrows rather than Honey, the Dissenter. I aim to change it legally as soon as may be."

"Well that clears up that mystery. I admit I share your feelings about how things go in this world. Mary is even more of a rebel than I am. In fact, I still hold out hope that the Church of England will be reformed and become Methodist. Mary thinks I'm completely daft in that respect, and has no time for what I call hopeful thinking and she calls wishful thinking. I am slowly coming round to her way. Everyone here knows me as a Methodist, but I still hold out hope of another Reformation when the Church of England and Methodists will be one. That was what the Wesleys wanted you know."

"Aye, I know all that but I personally won't be waiting for it in this lifetime. In fact I have started building a chapel down in Lower Town. But you know about that I'm sure."

"Well yes, you mentioned you hoped to do that, but how are you getting the building up when you are so busy with canal work?"

"I'm getting lots of help. Quite a few of the soldiers are Methodists too and they are volunteering to help when they can. Also, I pay a few other workers to keep at it. It is a plain chapel, not too grand, but will do for a time. During the week it can be used as a school, if I can find a teacher."

"That is capital, John. One thing Mary and I agree wholeheartedly about is the need to get a school going for our own people. With little or no education our children and their children will always be at the beck and call of their masters. You notice how the Irish are the low man here on the job. Even though my education is as good as or better than many a Scot, they seem to get better positions than we do."

"Yes, that is true. But the Scots have a powerful friend in high places, Thomas MacKay. He is the Colonel's right hand man in all things masonry. He built the Commissariat, By's house and he is in charge of building the first eight locks. He hires Scotsmen to assist him. He hired a Scot weaver to oversee masonry at one of the locks, even though he had only walked on stones before. And another Scot is set to become a timekeeper at the lock, all because he has a watch. Ha! All because he is a Scot more like it. Still, I admire them. They don't bend their knee to the English. They have had their church recognized as a proper church, and so it is. That gives them a right to Clergy Reserved Lands and the Catholics too, although I doubt either of them will see much of it."

"Well", said George, "I can see this is a day to become better acquainted. You needn't fear I shall represent you as a radical. That would be rich coming from a Methodist and with more than one firebrand in my own family. As for me, I shall bend my efforts to getting schools established in Goulbourne. Much of our land is poor for farming so I might as well offer up a corner of it for a school. If we propose to wait as long for schools as we have for roads, we are right eejits indeed."

The two men parted in complete accord and looked forward to the next chapel meeting. John was not always on hand for chapel, but as often as he could, he attended chapel, and some soldiers started to come with him too. They now had quite a crowd in Argue's shanty.

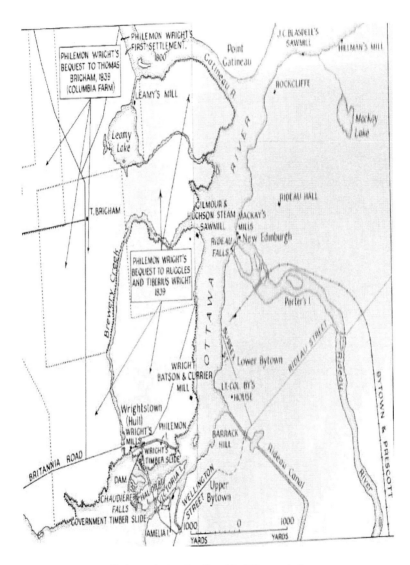

Bytown during the Canal building period.

ARGUE

BYTOWN 1828

1828 saw many changes in what was now called Bytown. The population had risen from 580 in 1826 to 2,758 in 1828. Streets were being laid out in Lower and Upper Town, both of which were bustling places. The Argue shanty sat in the centre of a cluster of log cabins, mostly occupied by the Cavan group, and George was heartily glad of it. Further down the hill families and workers squatted on any empty piece of land. For the most part the absentee landlord paid little heed so this was not a problem. The only very active landlord was Nicholas Sparks, who had already had some of his land seized by Lt. Col. By and was kept busy trying to make sure the Ordnance Department did not grab more.

Burrows was not overly sorry to see that Sparks did not have everything going his way as he realized that he had sold his two hundred acres for a pittance. In fact there were at least two thorns in Sparks' flesh: one was Ordnance which refused to pay him anything for the appropriated land, saying, 'All land claims will be settled after the Canal is completed'. The other was the fact that he did not have title to the land he thought he owned. It transpired that Burrows had not owned the land outright when he sold it to Sparks, and dealing with the defunct Land Board caused the paperwork to go on and on for several more years.

One day James Faulkner and Jock Kennedy arrived on horseback at the Argue shanty and asked to see George. Mary explained that George was out delivering victuals to the workers down near Dow's Swamp, "but he'll be home shortly. Will ye bide till then? I can give you a cup o' tea, real tea that is. George usually stops in after lunchtime to have a bite to eat and you can

247

see him then." She was happy to ask after Jock's new family and Rose Faulkner and the time passed swiftly.

When George came in the door both men rose up and put their business to him without delay. James spoke first, "I see we have found you at a busy time, George, and don't mean to keep you from your lunch."

George waved away their protests and said this was a slack moment and would they join him in a bowl of soup or whatever Mary had on hand? Mary had been busy calculating what she had and was able to second his welcome. The men agreed, reluctantly at first but soon felt more at ease. Hospitality was a strong rule: 'Never turn away anyone, stranger or friend, without a sup to keep them on their way.'

"We'll get right to the matter, Mr. Argue," Jock said. "It's this way: we find not much work at Richmond these days. At first it was busy enough. There were houses to help build and always some blacksmithing to do, but now there's not enough work for us. It is a slack time there and busy here."

"Yes," Faulkner interrupted, "and we thought to ask you how things go here and if there is any way we can get some work round about here?"

George said, "I'm pretty sure you could work if you can find a place to live. That's the hardest part right now. As you can see, there is not much empty space for a man to build some kind of place. But if you can deal with that, I expect you could get some work. Two men as skilled as you are should have no trouble."

"We look to you for direction. Where do we go to ask?"

"Come with me after lunch and I'll see if I can introduce you to someone. Do you think you can manage the place to stay?"

"Yes, I think we can manage something small for just the two of us. We brought a tent with us. It will be hard on the womenfolk to stay by themselves, but it is only for the summer and we'll be home for the winter."

"Take care now that you don't wind up being too close to Dow's Swamp. That is not where you want to be. Although I daresay it is better now. It is nearly all drained and a great thing that will be indeed when we get rid of that bad air."

They finished the bean soup and bread in front of them and were out the door in a trice. Before the end of the day they both had assurance of work if they could find a place to live. The first place they tented was not far off the swamp.

The following morning George went down early to the area to see how they fared. He found them both toiling back up the hill with their belongings on the back of James' horse. When asked where Jock's horse was, they shook their heads.

James Faulkner said, "Maybe the mosquitoes drove him off. It was enough to drive the saints crazy. We thought Richmond taught us all we need to know about mosquitoes, but we've had a new lesson now. I don't think there was a moment I was able to sleep and still I did not have enough hands to swat all those beggars. If we have to live down there I think we had better not plan on staying at Bytown."

They looked very dejected and exhausted; both men had large blotches on their faces.

George decided that without consulting Mary, as was his usual wont, to offer both men a spot at the back of their lot. The lots in that part were long and narrow and he figured that they could pitch their tent there in comparative comfort.

"You can have a place at the back of our lot. You saw it yesterday and I am sure you will find it a great deal better as far as mosquitoes are concerned. There is a breeze most nights, but no place is entirely free of the beasts, I'm afraid."

Neither James nor Jock had anticipated such hospitality and tried to protest, "We'll be cheek by jowl with you and I daresay that will be too much, although we thank you kindly."

George said, "Wait until I talk it over with Mary and if she is in agreement, then I hope you will think on it."

In the men's presence George told Mary of his offer. She responded quickly, "If we could get through that voyage in such cramped quarters, I daresay we can get along here for a few months, and who knows, something better may come up for you. There are always people who leave the works. Bide here a while until you get the lay of the land."

James and Jock looked at each other and nodded; they were very relieved. "We cannot thank you enough for your offer," Jock said very formally. "There is more to the story of what it is like down there near the swamp. The tents are jammed together very closely although most men are trying to set up a better establishment when they have the time and the strength. This sort of living is not so bad for a man on his own, but there are lots of families there too and the nighttime noises are hard to imagine. Felt like screaming myself, come to that."

James nodded again and added, "We think that there are not a few fights too as French-Canadians and Irish are not rubbing along together very well. It seemed like a fractious place altogether and we are much indebted to you and George for offering us your back yard. We'll try to see you don't regret it."

That night they both went down to the swamp to see if they could find the errant horse. They found him all right, being ridden by a young lad with a few more lads waiting for their turn. Jock's whistle pierced the air; the horse perked up its ears, swerved quickly and trotted right up to Jock to put his nose in his hand.

"Well you old devil," said Jock, "what were you about, running off like that?"

"He's my horse mister. We was just taking him out for some exercise."

"Oh he is, eh? What do you call this fine horse?"

The boys sensed a trap here, so they prevaricated and said they had not yet trained him to come when he was called.

"Oh aye," said Jock. "It's a good thing then that I have or it's clear I'd lose him every time I turned about."

Then he turned away, whistled again and said, "Come on, Bolt". Bolt lost no time in coming right to Jock's hand again. At Bolt's plain preference for Jock's company the boys gave way sheepishly and said he was wandering around all by himself so they were only trying to keep him until his owner turned up.

"And now I have," said Jock, as he and James turned to lead Bolt back up the hill.

The arrangements they made at the back of the Argue shanty suited everyone and from that time on Mary and George had two extremely capable men at their back door. They even contrived to add a room to the back of the shanty complete with fireplace which was open two ways, and James and Jock were to stay there when the nights got cold in the fall. It turned out to be a very amiable arrangement for all concerned. James and Jock felt that they were returning hospitality when they made improvements to the shanty and they found a home in a place that seemed least likely. On chapel nights they contrived to keep to themselves and were relieved when they were allowed to do so without comment.

As for the staunch Methodists who came to chapel each week, each one made Jock and James welcome in their own way. They remembered full well the way in which Jock and James had helped their community at the beginning. Jock had made two coffins for John Wilson Sr., one on the day of the disaster and another finer one when he had better tools and more time. James had fashioned iron tripods for every fire and put himself out to assist with all their needs every time they went to Richmond. They were made welcome. Occasionally Mary made a meal for several families and invited James and Jock who saw to it that they always brought meat for the table and tea for the pot.

Both Mary and George were surprised and pleased to observe that neither Faulkner nor Kennedy seemed to have a weakness for liquor, as was the reputation for many of their countrymen. One day James and Jock raised the topic with George.

James spoke first: "Have you no wondered at the fact that neither Jock nor I have a fondness for the drink?"

George said, "I have wondered a bit but am more relieved than curious. Not my business to ask why."

"Well", said James, "there's good reason for that. My old man was a good blacksmith but quite a drinker. He was sober enough some of the time to show me whatever I've learned as a blacksmith, but more and more of the time, we were dirt poor. And we should not have been with a good trade like that. I swore as a young man not to touch a drop, just in case I should wind up like he did. He died when he was only forty-two and I took over the blacksmithing. All my brothers and sisters worked hard too, just to feed ourselves.

Jock nodded, his lips pursed tight. "My da' did not drink every day, but when he did he was a demon. Mam was black and blue more often than I like to think on. I swore when I got big enough I would beat the livin' daylights out o' him. And I would have too only me mam got there first. One time when he was coming after her, she picked up the frying pan and let him have it over his head. He dropped down like a stone and we thought maybe she had killed him. He did not come to for three days. When he did he was never the same in the head again. Well, he wasn't good in the first place. But there was no more drink. My mam had to clean and do laundry and all manner of work to feed us and him too for he never worked again. She said he was far

251

less trouble with only half his wits. I reckon she was right and I decided to take the pledge. It has nothing to do with religion I tell you. Just want to keep my wits about me."

George smiled and said, "I daresay there's little danger of either of you men losing your wits."

George, Mary and Maude enjoyed the company of these two men very much and often reflected on the fact that in Ireland they would not have had anything to do with one another. Yet here, as they came to know them, they could see no reason for dissension or quarrels. Perhaps this mixing up of people of all sorts was for the best after all. Maude summed it up one day, "We have been blessed to learn about our Catholic neighbours, have we not?"

Bytown, that place of "ditch diggers", finally acquired a postman in 1828, three years after March had its second postman. A courthouse was built in Lower Town but there was still no magistrate on hand. Long before the magistrate appeared the courthouse burned down as well as the chapel John Burrows had built.

The Courthouse was not much missed, as people seemed to wish to avoid arrests and found a more popular method for settling disputes. They built a fighting ring in Lower Town and every Saturday afternoon and evening those who had a quarrel could settle it in the ring. The winner of the fight won the dispute and that was the end of the issue. But not the end of the fight. The spectators who had gathered to enjoy the fight would get caught up in the fun and carried on fighting outside the ring and into the evening. In fact there were fights on the streets every night including Sunday. The Irish got most of the blame for the fighting, that and the drink. But French Canadians were not inclined to back down from a challenge either. Lt. Col. By's soldiers still had to find time to enforce some sort of law and order but for the most part, a certain amount of fighting had to be ignored. Bytown was either lively or terrifying, depending on your viewpoint, but no one called it dull.

CALDWELL

HELP FOR MARY 1828-30

For the Caldwells, the years between 1826 when the Smileys arrived and the year 1830 were peaceful in the main. To supplement the meager harvest from his own fields, Forest rented some good pasture land close by and soon came to realize it might be better to lease land in Huntley until he knew just what sort of land he was getting. Anxieties about the move diminished somewhat as he learned that people were still leaving their homesteads in sufficient numbers for him to acquire land at a later date. Most were leaving to escape a debt owed to the local store, but others just to satisfy an itch to move to a new frontier. Many went to the American states.

Forest had sufficient income to avoid going to Bytown to earn cash at the Canal or going to the bush during the winter months. He even hired out most of the land clearing to men in the community who needed the work, selling most of the wood to cover his cost. Of course, it also reduced his net income.

In this way Forest began to acquire a small reputation as a gentleman farmer. This notion was supported when Mary's close friends made sure to mention casually and frequently how much they enjoyed being served tea from Mary Caldwell's sterling silver tea set. It was further enhanced by the regular shipments of books and tea from Sarah Caldwell. Not to be outdone, Mary's parents also sent trunks of cotton, soft woolens and fine leather to the family.

It was a reputation Forest neither sought nor desired; indeed it was one he scarcely noticed. It came naturally enough to him to hire labour as he had done in Ireland. His decision was

253

supported strongly by Mary who implored him to leave tree felling to others and his earliest experiences of clearing the land were sufficient to make him agree.

Forest may have shown some of the attributes of a gentleman farmer, but the wherewithal to live leisurely was not among them. While men like George Argue were accumulating cash and purchasing more property, Forest knew his situation was actually worsening. If he were to leave a legacy for his sons, as his father had in Cavan, he knew he had to leave March for Huntley, following the example of Moses Wilson and a few other close friends — and sooner rather than later.

He girded up his loins for the big push to move to Huntley in 1828 only to learn that Mary was pregnant again. How could he ask her to start all over again in a new part of this rough country? The following year they had another baby girl, Jane Maria, bringing the family to four girls and four boys, and many more white hairs to Forest's beard. Surely eight children was sufficient for any family. Certainly William and Margaret thought so.

Trips into Bytown to visit the Smiley family were limited chiefly to the winter months and then infrequently. It was more usual for the Smileys to make excursions to the Caldwells at least twice in the winter, bringing the whole family to share a meal on a Sunday afternoon.

It was pleasing to see the change in Frances. As Harold had foreseen she made the best of her situation in Bytown. Very gradually she began to realize that the judgments on social standing in Upper Canada were different from those at home. A storekeeper in Bytown was looked up to, and if she did not live amongst the nabobs of March Township she could hold her head up very well.

Upon their last visit, Frances was in great spirits and said she had quite a tale to tell. Everyone was ready to hear it.

"You mind when we first came, we were supposed to bring our servant girl, Lettie, with us and you saw neither hide nor hair of her?" Forest and Mary were a little nonplused at an expression usually applied to livestock, but nodded for her to continue.

"Well, when we were on the boat there was no room for her in our cabin, for you know how small they are and we were eight people already. That was what caused the rupture, no

254

doubt. She was no very happy in the hold what with the dreadful conditions there, but a young man who was coming out here, with no prospects for the future whatsoever, except not to spend it in Ireland, persuaded her to hitch up with him and they would try their fortune together. He told her, as if he knew, there were no servants in this country. So off she went, as saucy as you please, after us paying her passage." Frances paused and shook her head.

"Well he was right enough about there being no servants out here as we found when we wanted to hire a girl to help in the store or to help me in the kitchen. Our Lydia had to do that sort of thing, and Matilda too, as soon as she was tall enough to see over the counter. All in all I was pretty provoked, as you know. Well, you can imagine who turned up the other day: Lettie, a good deal older and wiser too. Her husband, if ever he was her husband, had gone off and left her to fend for herself with two young ones. She was wondering if we wanted her assistance. I was pleased to be able to tell her we were managing just fine, thank you, with our girls becoming more capable every day."

"What has happened to her, Frances?" Forest asked.

"Well, I cannot be sure, but if she wants to be a servant once more, she will have no trouble finding work. She could always apply to Firth's Tavern and so I told her."

Forest looked at Mary and she gave a slight nod. He asked, "Frances, as you can see, Mary could do with more help in the house. Do you think you can find out if she would like to come and help out in our home for a while?"

"Well I'm sure I don't know. Don't be surprised if she leaves you high and dry as she did me." She paused and said, "Perhaps Harold will be able to find where she's gone, for I am sure I don't plan to trail after her." Frances seemed to be less happy with her story at the thought that the Caldwells might take the servant she had shunned.

"And mind, you'll have her two bairns as well to feed and have under your feet. Better you than me, I say."

"Nevertheless Harold, if you can locate her, she might be a help for Mary, who never asks for help but could certainly use it, and the children can play with our young ones and rub along together I think."

Harold agreed to look out for her and as his store was a community centre of sorts, he traced her very shortly. She was working at the bakery close by, but her living quarters were half of a small room at the back of the bakery and her two children were proving to be an obstacle to getting a better place. Harold was able to assure her that she would be well treated at the Caldwells and as a result Mary and Forest found a reliable and willing helper for the next few years. There was no thought of asking for a commitment of any length, for long term planning seemed foolish, but the thought of leaving a young woman to fend for herself and two young children was a prospect too grim to be ignored. There was no telling just what she might have to resort to in order to feed them.

When Frances and Harold next visited there was a small period of unease when Lettie served the table and then sat down to eat with the family. Frances strove to make herself comfortable and nodded at Lettie as if she were another guest at the table. With considerable effort, she hid her regret at not having Lettie for her own servant, but then happily her eyes lit upon Lettie's two young children and she felt a little better.

ARGUE

TROUBLES AT THE CANAL 1830-31

The years 1829-1830 saw many changes in Bytown, and the Argues did not escape all of them unscathed. They could avoid the street fights, they coped with ague, but another problem came to their door.

One day George came home at midmorning and said to his astonished wife, "I don't know what to do."

"Whatever do you mean, George? You should be doing your rounds. Why on earth are you here at this hour?"

"Well Mary, that's the problem. I went on my rounds to collect the victuals to take to the workers and no one would give me any. It seems the storekeepers have gotten together and decided not to provide any more foodstuffs on credit. Every one of them to the last man standing, including Harold Smiley, said they could not carry on extending credit because they had to pay their bills too and no one would give them more credit. So I came away empty handed. I went down to the work site and I told the boss the news. He looked flummoxed and vexed but I don't think he was as surprised as I was. Apparently the storekeepers had been to see Lt. Col. By and told him that the time of credit was over. Promises will no longer suffice."

"Well I never! Who would have thought that the British Government would not pay its bills?"

"The storekeepers are not the only ones not getting paid. We have only had half pay for a few weeks now and some of the workers are getting none at all. Today I saw more than a few put down their tools and walk off."

Just at that point William came in the door grime up to

257

his eyebrows. Not far behind him were Jock Kennedy and James Faulkner. They looked at one another and William said, "It looks like it's time to walk. Everyone has left the workplace."

"Everyone?" said George.

"Aye, pretty well everyone," said Jock. "Working for half pay is one thing. Working for no pay and no food is something else altogether. I reckon we might as well be poor in our own homes. At least we'll be less like to die of malaria or dysentery. What say you, James?"

"Well I'm inclined to agree with you, Jock. Let's give it a rest for today and see what tomorrow brings."

William agreed with their view, and asked his mother if she could give them something to eat as they were well-nigh famished.

"Of course I can, William," and she called to James and Jock who were disappearing in the direction of their tent, "and you two as well. I have a big pot of pork and beans on the hearth; after you've washed come back and sup with us."

Smiley came over to see George that evening. He sat down wearily, gave a deep sigh and for a few moments said nothing at all.

Then, "Well this is a pretty pass, isn't it George? Did you ever imagine the likes of this? I know I didn't. The British Government refusing to pay its bills. And them sittin' on a pile of money. What to do? I had to get out of the house. It is not a very comfortable place to be right now. It's getting to the point where our larder is bare too." He paused and then added, "And if I ever do see a shilling I owe it all to the local farmers. They won't give me a dried bean until they see some hard cash."

George was silent for a moment, then said, "I have been thinking it over, Harold, and I am going to go directly to some farmers I know to see if I can get food. I guess first of all I shall have to see if there are going to be any workers left to feed. But of course that is not going to put any money in your purse, Harold. In fact it may make it worse — unless maybe you can do something similar. Maybe they will give you something on a written promise from Lt. Col. By himself. Who could have thought we would come to this?"

A few men on the site decided that they would keep on working without pay providing they could get food and the promise of pay in the future. So George went directly to a few

258

farmers whom he knew had been supplying the stores. They were further out on the Richmond Road and he had to leave home two hours earlier to go the extra distance. They reluctantly agreed to give some vegetables and meat directly to him providing he obtained a written promise from Lt. Col. By that they would be paid at some date. George used his leverage with John Burrows to meet Lt. Col. By and get this promise which was readily forthcoming. By this time Lt. Col. By was using part of his own salary to keep workers on the job. Harold could not use this approach as he had given his word to the other suppliers not to break ranks.

Monies from Ordnance in England slowly trickled in and as it did, the storekeepers, workers and contractors all along the line were paid. But sometimes it was too little too late. Some contractors went broke because they had underestimated the costs. They could not pay their workers and many workers 'went walking', the expression for men who laid down their shovels and left. They left without their owed wages, but then they were not being paid anyway. Jobs were needed but when cash was not forthcoming —!

All this, of course, upped the costs as the new contractors demanded and got a better price for their section of construction. Refusal to fund the enterprise adequately led to higher costs. Those who stayed on the job without pay refused to pay their rents. Lawlessness increased and Bytown's reputation as a wild shantytown grew apace.

George's own family was split on what to do. Andrew said, "I've seen enough mosquitos to last me a lifetime. I think I can get a carpentry job in March, working for Hamnett Pinhey." Off he went.

William went back to Goulbourne for a week hoping to make some headway on his farm but returned, saying, "The victuals are very poor with no one to cook for me. I guess I'll take my chances here for a while longer."

James Faulkner and Jock Kennedy went home for a visit but returned in less than a week. No explanations were needed. It was a choice between being at home with no income or at the canal with little income except for food. Gradually enough workers returned to the sites to ensure that the work progressed.

The most momentous milestone in Bytown was the drainage of Dow's Great Swamp in 1830. They achieved that by flowing water into the swamp at one end and out of the swamp at the other, effectively converting it into a lake. There was a huge celebration featuring a roasted ox. Everyone hoped for better health because of improved air over this area and the drainage achieved exactly that, although not for the reasons believed.

Late in 1830 there was an election in England. The Tory party was thrown out and the Whig Reformers surged into power and they were determined to exercise it. Everything that the Tories had approved was suspect and that included the Rideau Waterway. All accounts were to be thoroughly scrutinized; only then would monies be approved, and slowly and reluctantly released. Conditions in Upper Canada had been bad before and worsened considerably. Eventually all costs were approved because Lt. Col. By had sent meticulous accounts to England, but Parliament did not rush and what previously had been a two month delay lengthened considerably. Parliament wanted to let Ordnance Department know they were not the ones to authorize expenditures. That was Parliament's prerogative. Unfortunately for Lt. Col. By, because the Tory Government had appointed him, he too was suspect.

The Rideau Waterway was designed to keep the soldiers on the spot for the maintenance of the British Empire in North America and for the semblance of law and order. Members of the British aristocracy who found themselves in Upper Canada trying to hold the country for the King, felt marooned in the wilderness and abandoned by their friends in England. Petitions were sent to the Lords of the Treasury in England begging them to send the King's money as promised. One written by Lord Bellomont said:[26]

I am more wearied by the complaints of the victuallers than all other business. (They tell me) they were out of pocket 7000 Pounds Sterling. They have been fed with hopes but that artifice will no longer satisfy them. I fear that unless the subsistence is paid in England we will be broke and the soldiers turned a grazing"

Another claimed that:

---

[26] Lt. Colonel By and the Rideau Canal: PAC. Bundle 3500.

Eleven men had three quarters of the province granted to them and there was not a gentleman among them nor three well affected to His Majesty.

and:

People here have such an appetite for piracy and unlawful trade that they are ready to rebel as soon as the government puts a law into execution.

John Burrows came by to see George frequently to unburden himself to a friend who he knew would keep his mouth shut. He passionately defended Lt. Col. John By and said, "He is the most honourable, incorruptible man I have ever known, excepting yourself, George."

His rant included a denunciation of the Whig Party, the Ordnance Department, lazy civil servants and worries about Lt. Col. By's health, "The Col. came here a strong, vigorous man, George. Now he suffers the ague too often. He shows up at the site even when he ought to be abed with the fever. His wife cannot make him slow down. He is driven to get this Canal built as he promised to do. Too bad others cannot keep their promises to keep the monies coming." As John relayed his worries, accompanied by punching the air and tramping back and forth, George began to worry for his friend's health too.

Lt. Col. By appointed John to be Clerk of the Works and as his own responsibilities increased he also started to suffer poor health. Now he was the one to have to try to keep the work moving forward with only promises that the funds would come eventually.

This sort of thing went on without much change for the next year and more until the Canal was completed. Eventually the payments to the storekeepers and contractors were made although there were many outstanding land and compensation claims for years after.

Harold Smiley confided in George and Forest: "It was a near thing. I hope I never have to sail as close to the wind again as I have done these past two years. And who knows what is ahead?" There was certainly no answer for that.

The Bytown portion of the Canal was completed late in 1831. The Argues remained in Bytown to haul loading for that winter, but when spring arrived they returned to Goulbourne. It was as well that they did, for in the summer of 1832, cholera became rampant in Bytown. Their first friend at The Landing, Fanny Firth, was one of many to die from cholera that summer.

ARGUE

BACK TO GOULBOURNE 1832

The move back to Goulbourne in the spring of 1832 marked a major milestone for both Mary and George. Mary was very ready to leave Bytown and get back to Goulbourne so that she could be close to her mother. Anne had come to live with them in Bytown several times during the canal building period, but for some unaccountable reason, each time, before she had been away from Goulbourne for more than a month or two, she declared her wish to return, and although she said little of her reasons, she would not be budged.

Anne, now approaching 80, was beginning to be frail. Whether in Goulbourne or in Bytown, John McFadden stayed by her side, her welfare his special concern. Ever since John had returned from the bush an invalid and Anne Wilson had said that she wanted him to bide with her in Goulbourne, he had started to mend. For a few months he had not spoken, even to Anne, who appeared unconcerned, simply carrying on as if all was well, speaking with him as needed and taking his assent for granted.

Presently he began to smile and show some liveliness. Eventually he spoke to Anne and they could be seen happily conversing together. He started to do chores to relieve Amy around the cabin, but never far from Anne. As Anne grew older he began to be protective of her. When she went to Bytown, he went too, rather like Ruth to Naomi; 'Whither thou goest, I will go.' The family no longer questioned this, nor did they learn what had happened to him in the bush that caused such a dreadful collapse. If Anne knew she said nothing. John had tried to make it on his own in the New World and seemed to have

263

learned there was nothing more to be desired than to be a member of the family once more; Anne was equally determined that it be so. There was nothing Anne needed that John would not do for her; indeed he seemed loath for anyone else to take over his role. One wondered what would become of John when Anne died. But that was in God's hands; no need to worry about tomorrow's troubles.

Maude had returned to her own shanty in Goulbourne. Mary missed her presence but with more land cleared all about them, it was easier to see her more frequently than it had been ten long years ago. For the first time Mary sensed a community around her, for the distances between the occupied lots were shorter. Much of the Crown land and Clergy Reserve land had been sold and settled. George had been swift to buy up more lots, as he thought that the opportunity might be very brief and he was right. This meant that there were more roads and less wilderness. The roads were still poor, of course, but at least there was a semblance of continuous road from one side of the township to the other, although most people still preferred to do most of their travelling in the winter. When one's neighbour was within a fifteen-minute walk, it made an enormous improvement.

George was more ambivalent about the move. He was not sure that he had made the right decision or even that he had made the decision. He had told everyone that he would return to Goulbourne when the Canal work was over and here he was. After little more than ten years in the country he was 60 years old and virtually at the beginning of trying to farm his land. The promise to do something in the future is not the same thing as doing it right now, and he was unfamiliar with this feeling of being pushed. Of course he wanted to spend more time close to his neighbours, people he had known all his life, but, on the other hand, life in Bytown was lively; something was always happening, and he had enjoyed those jaunts into the bush, driving his well-matched team. He had experienced a feeling of freedom, and while that may have been an illusion, he'd felt it all the same. It was all the more pleasant for being something he had not known before coming to this country. In Ireland he had always taken responsibilities and that pattern followed him to Upper Canada as well. People would turn to him for leadership, and he had accepted it as a duty. He realized that he had been escaping that role for some years and wondered, if this time of

264

freedom was all behind him.

More alarming was the prospect of farming just in order to feed and clothe one's family and it was by no means certain that he would able to do even that. Strange how he could happily contemplate driving for two days into the bush in tandem with other sleighs and not feel oppressed, but in Goulbourne the sight of the huge stumps, which still littered his property, depressed him. And he did not like to admit that. He felt that whatever was wrong with him revealed a weakness in his character and he was determined to shake it off. He had never heard the word 'depression' used, except in a topographical sense.

George was far too hard on himself, still too hemmed in by the fact that he was the leader who ought never give way to discouragement or exhaustion. Of course, the bush around the lumber camps did not bother him; it was not his responsibility to do anything about those trees. On his own farm he had to do just that, turn a forest into a working farm, and to add vinegar to the cup he was to drink, what little land he had cleared was poor land.

Happy or not it was not his habit to be still for more than a few hours, if that long — whether he was getting anywhere or not. He borrowed Robert Mitchell's team of oxen and started to pull stumps and asked himself why his family thought he was too old to haul loading but not too old to pull stumps.

Fortunately at this juncture, his sons requested a family meeting. The meeting gradually revealed their concern about seeing him at such hard labour. Indeed they did think he was too old to be pulling out stumps.

"Thinking I'm too old to be pulling my own weight, are you? Is that it? What kind of thing would you have me do? I am not ready for a chair."

They had rehearsed for this conversation and William led the way. "Da', we think it would be well for you and for us if we go to that lot you bought on the 7th Concession. We'll cut the trees and you and some of your friends can start building a school there. You have been talking for a long time now of wanting to get a school going. What is there to stop you now? You'll have to admit that you'll never make a woodsman and that we all have more experience with an axe than you have. We'll cut and stack the logs and you organize a work crew to build the schoolhouse."

265

George could see that there was a shift here. They were telling him he was still the leader but they were taking over and giving him a graceful exit. He was happy to take it. Mary looked on serenely. 'I daresay she knew all about their plans,' thought George.

When it was clear that the schoolhouse would be completed by fall, George began to canvas families in a three-mile radius for youth who had missed learning their essentials. They were to come into the classroom at least for part of the year; younger children were to be included too. He started with the families he knew best, his Methodist friends. Immediately other parents started to come to him. The first group was three Anglican men who wanted spots for their children. On the whole it was good news; more families meant more to contribute to the teacher's salary.

Almost before these men were out the gate George saw three more neighbours, Earl Houlihan, Jack Rooney and Joe Monaghan, waiting to see him. These families were within easy walking distance of the school. Monaghan came right to the point.

"Mr. Argue, is there any prohibition to our children attending your school?"

George was momentarily floored and could only splutter, "The school is not mine; it belongs to everyone.

"Well, Mr. Argue", said Joe Monaghan, "You did not ask Houlihan, or Rooney or me if we were interested, did you? And the thing is, we are interested, very much so."

George was put very much on the defensive, realizing he had acted very much as he would have done back in the Old Country. Protestants and Catholics did not consort and that was that. Even with James Faulkner and Jock Kennedy living right by them at Bytown, he had reverted quickly to the old thinking and had not even considered asking these men about schooling. He was wrong footed and nothing to do but admit it.

"I apologize. I could have and should have asked, but do you think you will like the teaching?"

"Just how do you figure that, Mr. Argue? Is it a religious education you're giving?

"No, no. It's not that, although they do say the Lord's Prayer each morning and a scripture is read. I assume your priest may not care for that sort of thing. But after that there is no time

266

for much but learning to read, write and cipher."

"Mr. Argue," said Earl Houlihan, "we're not asking the priest for permission about this sort of thing. And if we ever see him, which is no very often, he likely won't want us to ask his permission. We Catholics value education as much or perhaps more than you Protestants do, because in Ireland it was very hard to come by if you were a Catholic. So yes, we want our young ones to learn their letters and numbers as well as the next man would, and we, Rooney, Monaghan and I, are willing to support the teacher's stipend right along with everyone else. There is a common school over near Richmond we believe. We understand that is the usual way of it unless there are enough numbers to set up a separate school. And we don't have near enough children for a school of our own right now."

"Your point is well taken. Can you tell me if there are going to be more families wanting to send their young ones along?"

"We have been asked to test the waters. We think there may be more."

"And to think I feared we might not have enough families able and willing to support a teacher. I shall bring the matter before the School Board, this coming week. There is no reason why your children should not attend, no reason at all. But it is a new road, is it not?"

"Yes," said Jack Rooney, "just one more new road. Mayhap it will help make up for the lack of other roads in these parts."

"Aye, that it might, Mr. Rooney. Well, the Good Lord saw fit to place us down here in the wilderness all bunched up together, so I think it well that we learn to get along, and our children too. It seems to me we are of like mind on this?"

"Aye, that we are," they said in unison and agreed that they would meet the following Monday evening.

At chapel that Sunday, George asked people to remain behind to discuss something concerning the school. Everyone who had a child in school remained in their seats and a few more besides. What was coming now, they wondered. When they were presented with Anglican and Catholic children attending school right alongside their own bairns, only a few were surprised, but still they expressed concern. Most of these reservations concerned the Catholic children.

267

"I can see why they want to avail themselves of our school, the one we are expected to pay for," said one father, "but why don't they get one of their own?" A few others nodded their support of this important point.

George said they were prepared to give their support as well and pointed out that there were not enough Catholics to support a separate school all on their own.

"Well, we don't want to have their thinking infect our children, that we don't." said another. Then he added, "Not that there is much to choose between a Catholic and an Anglican, if it comes to that."

"Since the Protestant group is in the majority, the Catholics might fear it would be the other way round."

"Yes, I can see they might," said James Blair who had no child attending the school. "Are you no afraid of fights breaking out?"

"Yes, I expect there might be fights, but once again, I fear it may be our young lads wanting to start the fight."

There were many worried faces in front of him. They had just been studying the Bible less than half an hour ago and it had a great many uncomfortable commandments in it when you got right down to it. Just this morning they were reminded to love your neighbour as yourself. It was clear which way George was leaning.

Hattie Halliday, in the back pew, stood up. "Are our children the only ones who have a right to education? For my part I see no harm in our children learning to get along with others."

Everyone turned around to look at this woman, who, by the look of it, had not consulted her husband before speaking, and were not their two oldest children, really his children? Her little one was not even in school yet.

George thanked Hattie for her comment, then backed her up by admonishing them, "Think this matter over carefully. Try to see it from your neighbour's point of view. We won't put it to a vote just now, but come by later in the day with your vote." He had a hunch he could talk them round one by one and that is what he aimed to do.

George was pretty sure there was no alternative to offering education to every child in the area, but he felt everything would go better if all parents understood and agreed

268

about the need for a common school from the outset rather than being told they had no choice. As it turned out, most of the men had already figured this out for themselves. Moreover, they realized that, with all the children in the area attending the school, the financial burden on each family would be considerably less. They made no further objection.[27]

George's next job was to find the teacher. He thought that managing these young students, some who might be bigger than the teacher, would be a challenging task for any teacher. Now in addition the teacher had to deal with students from different backgrounds and very likely there would be fighting in the schoolyard as well. He worried about finding a man capable of managing such a challenge.

To his amazement the first applicant was a young woman, Ellen Jane Rice. His reaction was, 'This will never do.' but he found that he was reluctant to be as abrupt as all that. She had the learning; she looked healthy; indeed she was very good looking, but what struck him more forcibly was her composure. It was evident that she saw nothing untoward about her application to teach 20 or 30 students of all ages the three R's. She was Presbyterian, from Edinburgh. George stalled; he asked for her credentials which he already had before him on a piece of paper. He asked her if she was prepared to teach a few students who might be close to her own age. She answered each question with the same placid confidence that all would be well. She had taught before, one year in Edinburgh, and could foresee no problem.

George discussed it with Mary who thought it would be a grand thing altogether to have a lady teacher.

"She may even instill a few manners along with the arithmetic, George. Give her a try."

The decision was made a great deal easier because no one else applied. It was Miss Ellen Jane Rice or no one. When the Board learned the teacher was going to be a wee bit of a girl, they told George that he would need to look in regularly to see how things were going.

"I shall do no such thing," said George, "unless I hear there is some problem. Do you expect any?"

---

[27] Common schools were the norm for many years. By 1847, there were 8 common schools in Goulbourne. The cost of schooling was born by the parents.

"E-er, no," said Earl Monaghan, the Catholic trustee, "but it stands to reason that there's going to be some shenanigans, right?"

"I hope not. And I am not going to stand at the back of the class, unless someone tells me there is trouble."

After a few weeks of school Miss Rice requested an interview with George, who went promptly to the school after the children had been sent home. He asked her how things were going and she got right to the point.

"I've not been in this country long enough to know how things go, Mr. Argue, but I have at least one problem, and I would like your help in solving it."

"Oh, aye," said George, "pray go on."

"It's the big boys, Mr. Argue They are no very comfortable here in the classroom with children as young as seven."

"Acting up are they?"

"Och, no-o, not at all. They are as good as gold, Mr. Argue. Never a peep out of them. That is part of the trouble. I want them to participate but they are too embarrassed to open their mouths. I feel for them, I do."

"And?" said George.

"Mr. Argue, it's this way. I know that you went to every parent who could afford to send their offspring to school and for some this is a big sacrifice for they could use that young lad on the farm. Right?"

"Right."

"I would like to suggest that the older ones don't come every day of the week. They could have their own days, days for the upper grades. I can give them my whole attention on the days they are here and they won't be embarrassed because they cannot learn their letters as fast as the younger ones. Then on the other days, I can teach the young ones who are getting on at a great rate."

"Do you mean to say there are some lads who don't know their letters at all?

"I do say that. Although they try to hide it."

"Well" said George, "I can see you have been giving this matter some thought. How goes it with the older girls? Anything to add there?"

Miss Rice nodded vigorously. "The girls are quite happy

270

to be learning alongside the younger ones. At times it seems to me they act as little mothers to them instead of tending to their own learning. But there is nothing there that cannot be managed. Dinnae fash yourself on that account."

"How are things out in the schoolyard, Miss Rice? Are the big boys getting along alright?"

"Oh, aye, Mr. Argue. They were a bit cautious with those boys they did not know well at the beginning, but after a few games of ball, things seemed to loosen up a bit. All boys want is a bit of fun and ball is played pretty much the same by all, is it not?"

George was pleased with this bit of news and said as much, adding, "I think it best that we continue this conversation after I have thought things over. There is much to recommend in your suggestion. I'll think on it. Good day to you, Miss Rice."

George was mightily relieved that there were no problems with discipline or in the schoolyard, from what he could learn, and although Miss Rice had a few good ideas, he thought to go one better about how to divide the classes. On Saturday evening he went to the Halliday home where she boarded and presented his thoughts.

"Miss Rice, I like your idea of separating the older and younger children. I can see with more than thirty young'uns of all ages in front of you, you hit upon a good plan to divide and teach to their level, so to speak. But come wintertime I think a great many of the oldest ones will be off to the bush and will not be able to get their learning for yet another year and it is nigh on too late for some of them now. These are the lads and girls whose mams were not able to teach them when they were little. So how would it be if they come by themselves five days a week or even six days for the fall months and come November you won't see them again until the springtime? Even then you won't see too much of them for their fathers will need their help to plant the crops. In the winter months you will have the smaller ones and I hope they can learn what they need from November to Easter. What think you?"

Miss Rice thought it was a great deal better than what was currently in front of her, and while it was far from ideal, she gave her full agreement to the idea.

She added, "Perhaps a few students won't remember much from November to Easter, but I can understand that this is the best that can be done for now and I thank you for it mightily. And I thank you as well for seeing to it that every child has a slate to work on, and for the blackboard too. Such aids are a great assistance, and the children progress much better with these aids."

George said, "Tomorrow morning after chapel I shall recommend the new arrangements to the Board. I think there will be a good reception to this plan. At Sunday School I may give a little homily to the young men about the great advantages of learning that I hope will bear fruit. Let me know how it goes in a few weeks' time."

The following morning at Sunday School Class, which now took place in the schoolhouse, he painted a picture to the youth where they were no longer considered smart young men but pointed to by others as "poor lads" who cannot read, write, or cipher, who would have to be told by the storekeeper how much to pay and how much they still owed, and if it did seem to be a mortal lot, how would they know where they were at.

"If you don't know your figures, you'll rue the day you did not grab the chance to learn them. Learn as much as you can so you will not depend on someone else to tell you where to go, when to stand up or when to sit down. Learning is at the foundation of being your own man when you grow up. Grab it while you can. For some the next few months may be your last chance. Apply yourselves and God bless."

The Board, which now included one Catholic and one Anglican, were relieved that their fears of pandemonium in the classroom and fights in the yard were not realized and more than a little amazed to think that this little bit of a thing had such good mastery over all those children.

"The thing is, they seem to be that fond of Miss Rice, that they all want to please her more than anything," said George, who was feeling very proud of having obtained a first rate teacher.

Jack Halliday stood up and told the Board, "Miss Rice brought a couple of balls and a bat with her. On the first day of school, she gave them to our oldest, saying, 'You might find some use for them in the playground at recess time, providing everyone can join in the game, mind.' My boy said it worked a treat, and she never let on that the ballgame was not all his idea."

George now had only one task, that of reminding parents

to put the promised stipend in the pot. So far there had been plenty of promises but very few pennies.

MOVE TO HUNTLEY 1832

It is hard to know exactly what was the final catalyst that caused Forest to fix a firm date for their move to Huntley. Perhaps it was that more and more of his friends had left for better land and seemed to be reaping a better reward for their industry than he was in March. Forest asked them to keep a lookout for fertile land when it became available and they were eager and happy to him help in this way. He told them he wanted to get his hands on at least 250 acres all told, but the acres did not all have to be in one lot, providing they were fairly close together. He was prepared to buy or rent, although he was uncertain if he could manage the whole amount outright. Several of Forest's friends thought this was a very uncertain way to go about obtaining the land, but Forest was adamant. Now was the time to move.

Whatever the reason, both Mary and Forest made a firm decision that they would move to Huntley in the spring of 1832. Mary was determined that this time nothing should stop their move. It was no surprise to learn that she was pregnant again for it seemed that every time a move was planned, Mary was either pregnant or had just delivered a child.

Forrest Smiley was born in February 1832 and the transition to Huntley went off smoothly in May. Mary continued to be blessed with an excellent facility for childbearing and claimed that the three years between each child gave her ample time to recover her strength. It appeared to be not enough time for Forest whose beard was totally white by this time.

It turned out that the land Forest rented had deep rich soil. At last Forest was on land he could understand and he was ready to put down roots. Firmly intending to purchase these fifty acres as soon as possible, he commenced to build a better home for Mary.

He started out with a log dwelling, but it was a more elaborate affair, boasting two main rooms with wooden floors, a staircase to a second storey for bedrooms, a roof of cedar shingles and a plan to add a summer kitchen at the back. The original buildings on the land were used to house animals and their fodder, a vast improvement over the original shanty with animals attached to the rear of the house. They called their new home *Cavandale*.

They now had nine children, ranging in age from one year to twenty years of age. The oldest members of the family, William and Margaret did not greet the advent of yet another baby with pleasure and were not at all confident that the end was in sight.

For the past two winters William had gone to the lumber camps and each time he returned he felt the congestion of so many people in such a small space. Even with the extra space and before the arrival of the last child, William decided he'd had enough. He expressed this aloud in Bytown one day, saying he was thinking of trying to go west with the fur traders if they would have him.

Archie Magee heard of William's intention and said to him, "What makes you want to go?"

William confided that he could not put up with one more bairn. "They just keep coming and *Coming*. It is even worse for Margaret. At least I am outdoors for most of my waking hours. We have a helper for Mam now too, but Lettie has two children of her own. No matter how many rooms we build there is just never enough room."

Bit by bit, Forest found a few more 50-acre parcels of cleared land near his homestead. A man named Campbell had owned much of it, but he had left and now Edward Malloch owned it. He was not prepared to sell it to Forest but they agreed upon a rent with a view to purchase at some future date. This was the best he could do.

For Mary, the housekeeping was still never ending. Even though Forest was able to afford a few purchases at the local store and Harold always brought Mary something extra when they came to visit, the days were long and arduous. When Mary prepared a picnic for everyone to enjoy in the woods, under the shade of the big trees, it was always part of a bigger excursion to gather berries and herbs. After such a day, which represented a treat for the whole family, Mary, Margaret and Lettie stayed up late making preserves and jams for the winter. The general rule was work for all and never an idle moment from dawn till dusk.

Around the house there was not a tree left standing. One unexpected pleasure of more open space in the clearing was the revelation of glorious fall colours at the edge of the woods, a marvel to behold and all the more precious for being so fleeting. Forest's promise of better times for his family included the establishment of an orchard, the planting of a tree or two for shade, and a rose garden for beauty, a beauty they yearned to behold once more before they died.

ARGUE

SUMMER OF DISCONTENT 1834

Mary and George expected to find Goulbourne less exciting than life in Bytown, but for Mary the presence of four grandchildren nearby and the expectation of another grandchild from their daughter Annie, proved stimulating enough. In addition, there was a marriage to arrange for Jane, who had attained her twentieth birthday in 1831. Mary had insisted that Jane not marry before her 20th birthday and Robert Cherry, a gentle man and their close neighbour, bided his time patiently for her.

Andrew, four years older than Jane, had to wait three more years for his chosen bride, Sarah Wilson, until she too achieved her twentieth birthday. Unlike Robert Cherry, Andrew was not at all patient and dealt with his frustration by a vigorous life style. Andrew and Sarah were second cousins; Sarah was the younger sister of Thomas Wilson, Annie's husband. Once again two families, which were already related to each other, would be knit more closely together.

Annie had provided Thomas with a healthy child every two or three years. The blessings of weddings, healthy babies and safe childbirths were quite enough for Mary, but George had other matters on his mind. Progress in the things that mattered to him seemed woefully slow since he returned to Goulbourne, and he had many occasions to exercise mental discipline, forcing himself to count his blessings.

One: their school was up and running. Two: there were fewer vacant lots, for many of his friends had been canny enough to purchase Clergy Reserve Land when it became available a few years back. Three…?

He stalled. What other improvements? Their small band of Wesleyan Methodists had grown, but still there was no chapel for their worship. It seemed as if one small step forward was followed by a large step back. The British Government had reversed the decision to allow the sale of Clergy Reserve Lands — no surprise there — and despite the fact that quite a number of the vacant lots had already been purchased, there were still many stretches of road which were all but impassable for almost eight months of the year. People tried to stock up on yearly supplies before the snows disappeared, and in this climate, that could happen with great rapidity.

Even a man like Hamnett Pinhey, a member of the ruling elite from the military settlement in March, was reported to have said at a meeting in 1832, 'I have known Richmond for thirteen years, in 1819 then a rising place; it has been falling ever since and is now almost nothing. Not a house has been built. If you get into Richmond in the spring, you cannot get out until summer, if into it in the fall you will not get out till winter. And whose fault is that, but the Magistrates and Gentry of Richmond, that is to say the Shopkeepers?'[28] But Pinhey was like a voice crying in the wilderness and while there were quite a few crying in the wilderness, they did so with less effect.

When the families gathered together for chapel meetings on Sunday and Wednesday evenings, it took a very short time to move from Biblical readings to grumbling about this and that. There was no lack of this and that. Occasionally George wondered if most of the appeal of Bible study was the social time itself. At least it enabled him to take a pulse on what was going on around him. He overheard some of the younger lads wondering if they should start up a local branch of the Orange Order. George, Archie Magee, Archie Scott and quite a few of the older men were appalled. Did these young lads think it was exciting and would make them feel strength in numbers? God alone knew. They had been in Goulbourne for nigh on 14 years now and although there were fights whenever there were numbers of Protestants and Catholics at the fairground, on an

---

[28] Library and Archives Canada (LAC), Hill Collection, vol. 2, p 3236-9

everyday basis there was no trouble whatsoever. Well, there were often brawls at taverns of course, but George hoped he would not have to worry about those young men who were daft enough to frequent such places. What in the Sam Hill was the point in starting up the Orange Order? Then the Catholics would have to start up some order of their own, the Defenders of the Faith perhaps, and they would be off on the old merry-go-round.

These thoughts went round and round in George's head until one day a possible solution popped up. Maybe an idea would be to start up a campaign for a Town Hall, something Americans liked and the Colonial Government didn't. Generally George was reluctant to side with Americans on any matter opposed by the British, but he was beginning to think they might have a few useful ideas. A Town Hall might serve to deflect interest and energy from the Orange Hall.

Archie frequently dropped in to visit George on a Saturday evening and kept him up to date on what the young folk were doing.

"I tell you, George, I am having a hard time talking some sense into my young ones. Matthew is twenty and thinks he is old enough to go to the Richmond Fair, which of course he is. He is also at pains to remind me, 'It's only four times a year, Da.' As if I don't know that. Now I hear there will be fairs at Bell's Corners and Huntley too. Pretty soon there will be one every weekend and most of the younger ones are ready to go as far as it takes to get to one of these fairs.

"It is fine during the day when we farmers exchange cattle and other animals, but after the sun goes down, it turns into a Donnybrook. I suppose it usually starts out as a brawl between Catholics and Protestants but after a bit the whole fairground is into it, everyone swinging at everyone else and having a lovely time, to hear Matthew talking about it." Archie shook his head. "Fair reminds of Auld Ireland, it does." After a pause he added, "At least our youngest, Charlie, bides at home and you are lucky, George, that your son John shows little interest in that sort of carrying–on."

"I know all about it, Archie. John does not want to go. He is the most scholarly of my sons; maybe because he is also the least robust, but I hear about it from Robert. I can see the drop in attendance the next day at chapel. If they do show up, they tend to look bruised and battered, but unrepentant and proud."

George went on, "I think myself they ought to aim their frustrations at the Government, but it is nowhere to be seen. Bashing your neighbour's head seems to be a very acceptable substitute. The fighting in Bytown occurred every night of the week, with wonderful regularity, but seeds of discontent are closer to home too."

"Do you think the young ones are discontent, George, or just happy to have brawl?"

"I cannot speak for others, Archie, but I have my own grievances. The Government finds money to support private schools for their children, such as Upper Canada College, but cannot find a shilling for the common schools such as ours. 'To them that have, shall more be given.' A truism no doubt, but one which should be turned upside down. Wealthy families should pay their own tuition."

How satisfying it was to share one's convictions with a close friend by the fireplace without having to bash heads about.

ARGUE

MORE CHANGES 1835

George was not the only one to be discontented. Archie Magee, the first of their members to come to Goulbourne, came to see George one Sunday afternoon and asked to have a private chat. Archie and George both were lay leaders for the Methodist group in that part of Goulbourne. Rev. Ezra Healey, the circuit minister, depended on them to lead the services in his absence, absences which were the norm. George expected Archie wanted to discuss the plans for Bible readings for the fall and winter. He could not have been further off the mark. Archie wanted to tell him about another set of plans.

"George, I have been in this country for going on 18 years now. At first, I'll admit, I saw only possibilities, and things are better now than they used to be. We eat better. You have a school going and more schools are starting up. I guess this should be enough for me, but it's not. I have been thinking on it for some time now and I have a mind to go with the fur traders to the West. I'd like to leave this spring before I'm a year older. I can still handle living rough in the bush and I'm going to give it a try."

George could scarcely have been more surprised. Archie was a pillar of their group, a pillar yes, but an adventurer too. He had been the first to leave Cavan for the New World when he was a young man of 18 years and now at 36 he was ready to go off into the unknown again. His wife had died in childbirth and the child too. He had not remarried and had been alone for some years now.

"How long have you been thinking on this, Archie?

"I have been longing to go ever since we went to The Landing to build the Canal. I envied those traders who stopped at The Landing on their way up the Ottawa to hunt for furs. I wanted to know what it was like to travel on the water, to be so free. I also wanted to get to know the native people better. The fur traders seemed to get on with them just fine. I badly wanted to go with them, but felt I owed it to the community to stick around. Now I realize I have no one to tie me here and I am ready to go."

"You have a brother here. Is he going to go with you?"

"Nay. William does not fancy the idea at all, but there is someone who does, and I think we might tie up together and try our luck. You know him, but I don't know that he has talked with his family yet, so I can't say more, except that he is from Huntley and comes from a good family."

George was quietly absorbing what a big hole Archie's absence would make in their small group, for he had assumed he would pass the leadership to Archie in the next few years.

Archie added, "I want to leave a wee piece of me here in Goulbourne and who knows, maybe one day I'll be back. I'm transferring the title of my land over to William on the understanding that he will donate an acre of it to the building of a chapel. I hope you'll help him out when the time comes. I'll leave the timing of that to you, George. There's no rush. William has agreed that he will donate the acre. The rest will be up to you and those who can help you."

"It shall be as you wish, Archie. It will be called Magee Chapel. You're a natural leader, and I am confident that God goes with you wherever you go. You will be like Joshua going into the Promised Land, but you are going to be badly missed Archie; make no mistake about that. I cannae see who will take your place in chapel, but then, God will provide for us as well as for you."

"I'll go as soon as my partner gives me an answer, George, for I'm all ready, but I'll see you again 'ere I go", and with those words, he clasped George's shoulder and turned quickly lest he weep. He knew this was to be the last time he saw George alone, and parting from his friend and mentor was the hardest parting he would face.

Archie's intended partner was William Caldwell, now a tall, handsome, well set up young man who, having spent a few winters at the lumber camps, felt horribly confined each time he returned to the homestead. The last time William and Archie had discussed their plan to go west was when William began to suspect another bairn was on the way. He decided it was time he was gone. He had no wish to settle down; rather he was keen to join the fur traders, if they would have him. His parents had been reassured to hear that Archie Magee was going too. Together they left for Bytown on April 1st 1835. When there was no word from them or of them for two weeks, their families knew they had started on their adventure.

George used their departure as an excuse to make a longed for trek into Bytown to see if they were off, but the real reason was a wish to see his old friend John Burrows and have a change of scene. He was fortunate to find John at his home in Lower Town with his wife and three young children. John seemed to be a happy man in his domestic life, but George thought something was eating at him. Gradually he learned what John's work entailed.

"Lt. Colonel By has left me in charge of settling all the claims against the Ordnance Department, both land settlement claims and other injuries. I feel I am able for this work and grateful to have it, make no mistake, but it is a grueling task. The land settlement is very bitter. The completed Waterway took up much more land than had been allocated; large areas had to be flooded and every shilling that has to be extracted from the British Government is hard to come by. I need the stamina and determination of a goat, and it is considerably more than I possess at times.

"It is also hard to judge how to compensate a man for the loss of a limb during the canal building. Especially so when I find that the man has died destitute, and his widow with four children has remarried out of necessity. I share their deep sense of injustice.

"What bothers me as much and sometimes more than all this, George, are the vile insults and calumny the Government in Westminster has heaped on Lt. Col. By. I have written a letter about it to the Kingston Patriot newspaper. Here, I have a copy you can read right now if you will." He waited while George read it through.

A Notice in the Kingston Patriot, (under Notices of the Rideau Canal), by John Burrows, entitled — "Friend to Justice and to Merit" —.

The following notices of the Rideau Canal, in which is made clear, the exalted worth of the superintendent of that stupendous work, Lt. Col. By, of the Royal Engineers: who for its grandeur of design, its indefatigable execution and rapid and successful completion, amid, not only, natural difficulties, most untoward and unparalleled, but also artificial obstructions, caused by intrigues of envious men, has merited and enjoys the gratitude of the present, and secured for himself a renown, imperishable in future ages, are respectfully dedicated to the public, by its obedient, humble servant, the author.

George read it through and handed it back to the author: "I know the great opinion you have always held of this man, John. As usual, you have not spared the superlatives. I hope you have sent him a copy of this article. If not, you should do so as soon as may be."

John nodded and asked, "Do you think he would like that? I'll do it tomorrow. They ought to be thanking the Colonel and honouring him for the greatest piece of engineering ever seen in the Empire. Instead they are driving him to his grave. I hear his health is very poor and he was always a lion of a man. Nothing bothered him. To have his honour impugned is more than he can bear.[29] What with concern for him, all this work and in addition, recurring bouts of the sweating sickness, I admit I am worn down at times."

He made an obvious effort to be more cheerful. "Of course I am grateful for the work, grateful for being able to purchase more lots in Bytown and make up for my earlier lack of foresight in selling prime land for a few pounds. Most of all I am grateful for my wife and children. Elizabeth and I have set up a school here in Lower Town. She is a teacher you know, and it's an honour to have her as my wife." He sighed.

---

29 Lt. Col. John By was found to be guiltless of all accusations leveled against him. He had hoped for promotion and accolades for his achievement. He received none and the Whig government never publicly exonerated him. He died in 1836, a broken man.

"Well, that is more than enough about me. How goes it in Goulbourne?"

"Like you, John, I know I should not complain. Me and mine are well enough, but I long to hear what goes on in the country at large. Do you hear of what they are thinking of in York when you're up there trying to get money out of them?"

"Aye, I hear a great deal of unrest by the farmers. There are quite a few American settlers around those parts and they have not forgotten The Rights of Man. Moreover, there is a fiery Scot up there by the name of Mackenzie. He owns a newspaper so he is able to be a vehicle for all the criticisms of the Government. He does not hold back. Fair lays into them he does. He is either a brave man or a fool, maybe a bit of both. I hear he's had his printing press destroyed once already. He keeps getting re-elected to the Assembly, and is kicked out time and time again."

"Well, from what I can understand, the Legislative Assembly has no say whatsoever anyway, so a man is wasting his time in that body, to be sure."

"True enough, George. We'll see what happens and I shall try to send you a note if anything ever does. I cannot interfere with it, for I value my job. But it goes against the grain, it does, when I cannot join the battle for what I believe.

"Here's a story you'll like. Not long ago some members of our fine government were down here for a meeting, and beheld the lawless state of this town. The fighting went on all night, and no one could get any sleep."

John chortled, "It's the best thing that could have happened. The great fathers of our land, as a result of a poor night's sleep, finally promised us a few magistrates. We ourselves have established a Society for the Preservation of the Peace. There are 200 volunteers who patrol the streets at night. This town long ago reached the point when it was not safe to poke your nose outdoors after dark, and a few policemen cannot handle it. The smart policeman goes off in the opposite direction. The Irish Shiners are out there ready for a brawl in all weathers. Sorry to have to lay it at the door of the Irish, but there you are George. Your countrymen are ever ready for a fight and the French are not loath to give it to them for that matter."

George learned at Firth's Tavern that Archie Magee and William Caldwell had been in Bytown for only one day when they met up with some traders who took them both in two canoes. The good news was that they went together and the bad news was that no one knew when there would be news of them again.

On the whole George was well satisfied with his visit. It was good to have a friend like John Burrows who could tell him what was going on beyond the borders of Goulbourne.

George took a roundabout way home, stopping in Huntley to stay overnight with Moses Wilson, his brother-in-law, then on to see Forest and Mary Caldwell to give them news of their son. The Caldwells made him very welcome indeed, and were grateful for news of William. With such a large household, George did not prolong his visit, but went on to spend the night with his daughter Annie, who was far advanced in her fifth pregnancy. He was pleased to see her, but when he observed her fatigue, he vowed to get himself home to Mary the next day and send her up to Annie's right away.

ARGUE

A TIME OF SORROW 1835

The year 1835 was to bring more vital changes for the whole community. Presently George began to wonder why he had been so impatient for change, which will surely come, desired or not.

Anne Wilson died in her sleep that summer. Mary, who had seen her become increasingly frail, was not surprised to find her dead, but she was surprised at her sense of great loss. Anne had been lucid up to her death and had remained a steadying influence for her family and for the whole Cavan group. She said less and less as the years and months passed by, but her calmness and serenity comforted all those who came in contact with her. Mary suspected Anne spent a great deal of her time praying and concentrating on an outcome she desired. When friends gathered in their home for chapel meeting she was sometimes found to be looking at a given person, often one of her sons or daughters, who presently found themselves taking a position on an issue that they had not planned on taking at all, not at all. Then they looked to their mam and found her to be regarding them with placid satisfaction. Made you wonder. Sometimes others in the group acted in much the same way. She was regarded as mother to all. Was this the reason she had been loath to leave Goulbourne, especially when George was absent so much of the time?

It struck them now that they had provided no special resting place for their mother. George seemed to feel this most keenly, but then he was always prone to thinking he was the one who should take the lead in every matter affecting them all. Odd, but some now sensed it may have been Anne who had been taking the lead all along.

Maude said with her usual brisk speech, "Anne has left a great deal of herself in all of us and we shall see her everywhere." Then she broke down and sobbed harshly.

"I don't know where John's body lies. I know it is somewhere on our property but when we returned from Bytown the grave marker had disappeared, I know not how. I know I ought not to think of his mortal remains but it's hard."

Everyone was stunned. No one in all these years had seen her show her grief. Some were relieved to know she could cry, and some thought she had taken a precious long time about it.

Mary, who almost invariably let Maude take the lead in all decisions, said with great composure, "We shall bury Mam in the Church of England cemetery over Ashton way. Mam was brought up in the Church of Ireland and I am sure she will not mind resting there. At least we shall know exactly where she is and can visit at any and all times." Maude looked at Mary gratefully.

Before two days had elapsed, the Scott family suffered their own tragedy. Charlie Scott, at 18, was the youngest and quietest of Archie's family. He looked most like his father of all the four sons, with a shock of thick blonde hair, skin inclined to burn, and a stocky build. In temperament he was least like his father. Archie bristled with never-ending energy; Charlie was calm, methodical, a steady plodder, one who attempted to keep up with his brothers in all the work, but clearly had little stamina. This was a handicap among his energetic brothers and his mam worried about him from an early age. After the first winter the Scott family spent at The Landing hauling loading, Lydia decided she would remain in Goulbourne and asked that Charlie remain there also to look after the animals and assist her with the needed chores. Archie agreed readily, for although he did not express his concerns to his wife, he too felt Charlie could not keep up with the demands of long days required in hauling loading. Lydia observed that he was best off if he had a wee sup of tea and oatcake in the middle of the morning, an early supper after the chores and then early to bed. They muddled along comfortably together.

During the summer months it was arranged that Charlie had the least taxing work to do. Often he was asked to take the cart to Richmond for supplies, or deliver grain to the mill for grinding. Benjamin, the eldest, could easily see the reason for what seemed to be his parents' indulgence of Charlie and said naught. Matthew, who was only a year or so older than Charlie, occasionally complained of this favoured treatment, for which of them would not like to make a trip to Richmond and have an easy day of it? His whingeing was soon squelched by their father who neither made explanations nor saw the need to do so.

On the fateful day Charlie was driving the gig[30] home from Richmond in the early afternoon. A neighbour, Thomas Muldoon of two farms away, was following at a little distance when suddenly he thought he saw Charlie sway sideways, then forwards and disappear off the front of the gig, down, down under the hooves of the startled horse, which leapt forward and then sideways. Muldoon was horror- struck. He was not even entirely sure what he had seen. Did Charlie fall because of the rough road? But surely he could have held on.

The horse's antics left Charlie on the middle of the road clear and free of the gig and that was a blessing. As he came alongside, Muldoon was able to see that Charlie was in a bad way. His head was lying awkwardly to one side. It fair made his bowels loose just to behold him. He started to panic and broke out in a sweat, then forced himself to breathe and not gag. For God's sake, here he was a Catholic, the only one to witness something horrible, something unthinkable, happen to a Protestant. And no witnesses. What in the name of all the Saints was he to do?

He couldn't leave Charlie here. He needed, he needed, Oh God, he needed to get Charlie onto his own cart and somehow tie the horse and gig to the back of his cart and get all back to the Scott farm. He had better move Charlie first. Muldoon was a skinny man, not up to Charlie's dead weight, but desperation enabled him to get Charlie onto his cart. For a mercy Muldoon's horse held still. As soon as Charlie was more or less safely on the cart, still immobile, the first horse took off, the gig swaying dangerously behind and bumping hard over the rough road. Muldoon's horse took this as a signal for him to follow, but

---

[30] A light two-wheeled cart pulled by one horse

at Muldoon's frantic cry he slowed down again until Tom got up onto the cart and had the reins in his hands.

There were still three miles to go to Scott's farm. Lots of time for him to worry about how in hell he could tell the Scotts what had happened when he did not even know himself. He had a bad, sinking feeling for he was sure Charlie was dead and he was the only one to see what happened. May the Saints preserve him!

The next three miles were a nightmare, and by the time he drew into Archie's yard he was a mortal wreck of a man. He had almost stopped at Rooney's and asked him to go with him, but managed to have enough wit to know this would not provide any help. All his neighbours knew he had gone by himself to Richmond. He was the only witness — he and the horse — which would have arrived at the Scotts' yard 'ere now.

The whole family was out in the yard when he drove in. When they saw Charlie on his cart they slowly moved together toward him as if they were held in a nightmare. They asked no questions. Archie slowly picked up his son, and turned to his wife who gazed at Charlie, with both hands in her mouth. Then, a guttural howl slowly rose in pitch to a high keening, unbearable to hear.

No one had any questions for Thomas. That was just as well for by this time Thomas Muldoon was beyond speech. In fact no one paid much heed to Thomas who badly needed a stiff drink. He was at a household where nothing stronger than tea could be offered and even that was well beyond anyone's ability. After what seemed to be an age in which no one spoke, Archie turned and, still holding Charlie in his arms said,

"I have you to thank for bringing our son home to us. You'll have some tea before you go on." He didn't know what he was saying.

Muldoon drew a breath of relief and said what he had been practicing on the long trip home.

"I don't know rightly what happened, Mr. Scott. I was well behind your son, but I thought I saw him fall off the wagon. The horse was not going too fast. I don't know why he fell or even if he did. God help us all." And then he muttered under his breath, 'Mother of God and all the Saints help us.'

"I better go now Mr. Scott. I am that mortal sorry I am. Shall I come back tomorrow?"

"That would be a kindness Mr. Muldoon."

As Thomas turned to leave, the family dog started to howl; Thomas could hear him far down the road.

Benjamin and Matthew followed Thomas out of the yard on horseback on their way to fetch George Argue. When they got there, George said immediately, "Go and fetch Maude on your way back. Mary and I will go directly."

When they got to the Scotts and saw Charlie, it was pretty obvious from the shape of his skull that he had been kicked in the head by the horse. Lydia was still moaning softly by Charlie's side and saying, "He ought to have had more food by him. He should have had more food. It's all my fault."

George put his hand into Charlie's pocket and drew out a piece of oatcake still wrapped in a piece of cloth.

"He did have food, Lydia. He still had what you gave him. For some reason he forgot to eat it. It's not your fault."

"I keep telling her it's not her fault, George, but she won't hear me. Maybe she'll listen to you."

"I knew him better than any of the others. He was always the closest to me," moaned Lydia.

Mary stayed silent and held her hand. She knew better than most that Lydia would hear nothing that was said. Maude gave her a draught of something to drink and insisted she lie down. She refused, saying she would take the first watch. Everyone left her to do so. When Archie got up at 4 am in the morning, she was lying across Charlie, half in and half out of sleep, but maintained she had been awake all night. Neighbours came and took turns at the watch.

A grim cloud pervaded the house and yard. It was the young people's first experience of death in a member of their family. At the abrupt removal of their quiet brother, they realized how important he had been to all of them.

John Scott, Archie's youngest brother, and James Wilson took over and arranged for Charlie's funeral. Since Anne Wilson and Charlie Scott died only two days apart, it was decided to have both funerals at the same time. Sam Halliday and Robert Mitchell made two caskets. Gloom spread over the whole settlement. Young men and old lined up for the honour of pall bearing and since it was quite a journey to the gravesite, it was decided that pallbearers would rotate. The whole community followed on foot. Muldoon was singled out and was asked if he would be one of the pallbearers. Other Catholic neighbours such as Monaghan, Rooney, Houlihan and Hanberry walked the whole distance, although nothing would persuade them to enter the Den of the Damned, the Church of England.

The senseless and apparently unnecessary death of this young man was much harder to bear than Anne's death, for she had lived a long life and had died peacefully and inevitably. Nevertheless, not much time was to pass before everyone missed her presence and mourned the loss of Anne Wilson.

As for the Scott family, it was to be a while before either Archie or his wife knew how they were to go on. Archie blamed himself for not realizing that someone should have been with Charlie. His wife blamed herself even more so, for she knew better than anyone that their son's frailty had grown worse as he matured. Why had God allowed him to die? Why? Why? He of all people was an innocent young man.

Archie, always the convivial centre of their gatherings, now avoided all but chapel on Sunday mornings, and he left before anyone could do more than tip their hat to him. During the week he moved through his chores in a daze with his sons keeping careful watch over him. Most often he was seen standing by himself in a field, facing the woods. After a while he would nod, walk a few paces briskly, then slow down and repeat the whole process. When Benjamin was asked what Archie was saying, he answered, "When he nods, he says, 'That's it then.' and off he goes. It's always the same. Pathetic." Then Benjamin walked off, paused for a few moments, shook his head and walked on again. Was he giving them a demonstration? They thought not.

These two deaths reminded everyone that not only was life chancy and could be painfully brief, but that, in the 20 years since they had come to this country, they had made little progress in arranging to honour their dead within a hallowed graveyard. Not surprisingly George now became more determined to build the Magee Chapel as promised and to have a proper Methodist graveyard alongside.

Mary felt the empty spot in the house where Anne had sat, but John McFadden was openly distraught, and Mary worried about him. Knowing just how it would be with John, Maude came up with an idea. Maude had fallen or been pushed into the role of midwife for the community and she asked John if he would assist her.

John, aghast to the point of speechlessness, finally managed to stutter, "No-no-not the job for me, not the job for a m-man."

"No, no, of course not, John. I rightly know you cannot do what I do, but all the same you can help me greatly if you would. You maybe don't know this, but often these babies take a mortal long time to get born and it is either in the middle of the night or the next day before I can think to leave again. And then who am I to ask to take me home? The young mother needs help; usually there are other children and her husband needs to help out at home. If I knew that you were at hand to get me back and forth it would relieve my mind greatly. And then again, I might need to go back again a few days later to see how the mother is getting on. It is what I like to do but often cannot manage it on my own. These roads are a perfect terror to me, but if you were to drive me, you see, it would help me more than you know. I fain would have asked you before, but I knew Anne needed you so I said naught. But do ye consider it, please."

John kept refusing until one night Maude came over and knocked on the door pleading, "John, I need your help. Tom Bradley has come to fetch me to help his mam; he is only a young'un but his Da needed to stay with Millie, they are that worried for her and no woman about. Can you come with me, John, to help out with the other bairns and bring me home? I fear his Da will be quite useless at this point."

John saw he was needed and he went; thereafter he understood that this was his job.

As he grew more comfortable with Maude she suggested that he could help Amy Mitchell and Lizzie Blair too, from time to time, much as he helped Mary. They greeted his offer to help most enthusiastically; once again John was back to full time occupation. Most importantly, he felt he was needed by the whole Argue family and that what he was doing would have pleased Anne.

293

ARGUE

WHAT KIND OF COUNTRY? 1836-37

While matters of life and death took the forefront of everyone's attention, George continued to be preoccupied with the more distant future: what kind of a country was this going to turn out to be? George, now sixty-five and beginning to sense his own demise, mused more and more on the big question: Had they been right to abandon all that Ireland meant to them and come to this new country? The more he asked himself this vital question, the more he felt the need to talk to one of their members to learn how the other men felt. For the past two years he had not talked to Archie about this question or about anything of importance really.

When he had tentatively broached the matter with Archie one day, his response was, "Yes, well, I wonder you know, do you think Charlie might have been spared if we'd stayed in Ireland, George?"

George said, "Accidents happen on both sides of the water, Archie. There was no reason we know of for your son's death. We're not God. It is not our place to question His wisdom."

Archie flinched.

"I'm right sorry Archie, but sometimes I want to jolt you into returning to life. I miss our talks. You were always able to make me see the more positive side of the picture and I know, I know, I cannot expect you to be your old self, the one I counted on for courage and optimism, but I need you to be that person. I'm being selfish is all."

Looking keenly at Archie, he added, "I daresay your wife might like to have you back too," for outwardly at least, it seemed that Lydia, who had howled out her grief much more than Archie, had recovered her equilibrium better than her husband.

Archie hunched his shoulders and turned away silently, but a few days later he came back and said to George, "Right then, tell me what's on your mind. At least I can listen."

Encouraged, George said, "It comes down to this: did we do rightly to leave Ireland and come to this country? You know what we left and why we left. Has it been worth it, Archie? What d'you think?"

Archie ruminated for a while and it began to look as if he had not given a thought to this or any other matter but Charlie's death for the past two years. "Well George, I cannot say, but I know the young ones like it better'n we do. They always think the future will be better. But what do they know? I've been thinking I could do with a change of scene for a few days. Why don't you and me get ourselves up to Bytown to see our old friend John Burrows? He might be able to cheer you up. At least he will give you a good chin wag if that's what you're needing."

"Archie, that's the very thing I need. I told you I needed you at my side and already you have given me a boost. We'll go as soon as Christmas is past."

"You're not to mention my trouble. It will be a relief to me to look on a face that does not feel sorry for me and treat me with a delicate touch. Mind now."

Before the year's end they were at Burrows' door, and were warmly invited into his home.

"What a welcome sight you are and you have chosen a good time for a visit. We're about to welcome in the New Year and will be obliged if you will share our home for the occasion. Is there aught but the chance for a visit that brings you here?"

"Not really," said George, "but you always seem to know the latest news from York and I'm always wanting to hear it, even though it has given me little pleasure most of the time."

After they were settled in and John's wife had put a cup of tea in front of them, Archie said with some of his old spirit, "George is tossing and turning all night about this question: did we do rightly to leave Ireland for these backwoods? Our lives here have known no ease thus far. Our homes are crude, the toil heavy and our grandchildren can at best get only the three R's. Even with all the troubles in Ireland, were we better off there? We all ask ourselves the same question, although generally speaking we don't like to put it to our wives. We fear we know their answer all too well."

"H-mm, well, I'm no wise man who knows the answer to that question. I cannot read the future. What had you hoped for, George?"

"I had hoped, and still hope, for a country where our children and our grandchildren, will not bend their knee or their head to a 'Lord'. And look what is happening. The gentry in this New World might not have crowned themselves lords yet, but they seemed determined to learn the part and play it. Have we exchanged our lives in Ireland with the hatred and fear between Catholics and Protestants for one where our daily lives are more crude and brutish, the education of our children more rudimentary, and for what gain? Mayhap we'll have the same fear and distrust in this country too."

"It is true we cannot be sure there will not be some of the old troubles here too, but perhaps more to the point right now are rumours that are coming in about armed rebellions that have taken place in York and yes, in Lower Canada too."

George and Archie heard this news with incredulity, mixed with delight.

Very swiftly, John went on to say, "But the news is not at all good. It happened about two weeks ago or more. I hear the rebellion in York, which was led by that firebrand William Lyon Mackenzie, has been put down swiftly and everything is in tatters. He may be a good newspaperman but not much good as a general of his troops. They were poorly organized from the start, carrying only sticks, pitchforks, and few muskets. Several are in jail and I don't like to think what's going to happen to them."

"How about Mackenzie?" Archie asked.

"He's made it off to the States, or at least trying to — it's not sure yet."

"How could such a thing have happened?" George asked, his amazement turning to dismay.

"Well George, quite a number of the settlers up around York are Americans and they are a very different crew from the Irishmen around these parts. The rebels are not United Empire

Loyalists who are all Tories to the last man; these farmers came later and they are full of the 'Rights of Man', Representative Government and so on. They are very, very angry about the refusal of the Government to spend a penny on roads, and just as angry that most of them have no vote. They say that even if they could vote, the Legislative Assembly is just a group of dogs with all bark and no bite. Mackenzie has been touring throughout the whole area, setting fire to their anger and this is the result."

"There is no Mackenzie in Lower Canada", said Archie who felt his Scot kinsman should be defended. "What started things down there?"

"The same feelings of anger at the ruling group apply there too. They call it the Chateau Clique. The rebellion down there is still going on, but I daresay it will come to the same bad end."

On the whole the news was bad, and yet all three men felt heartened somehow that they were not alone in their grievance against the government. Not that they could see anything of the like happening in their part of Upper Canada, which was settled primarily by Irishmen, both Protestant and Roman Catholic. Many of the Irish Protestants came from the Province of Ulster and, as members of the Loyal Orange Order, were more obsessed with their traditional fear of the 'Roman Catholic menace' than they were to see the Government as their enemy. The Catholics knew they were not numerically strong enough to mount an armed insurrection on their own and certainly could not count on help from their Protestant neighbours. In addition, both Protestant and Catholic clergy drew back from insurrection. Both groups, for different reasons, played into the hands of the ruling elite.

Ironically enough, the rebellions, despite their apparent and immediate failure, were effective, but none of these three men would live long enough to learn the full outcome.

When the Whig government at Westminster heard about the armed uprisings, it sent out Lord Durham forthwith to study the situation and report back to them. They did not want a further loss of colonies in North America attributed to their mismanagement. Lord Durham was not long in Upper and Lower Canada before he became very unpopular with the existing Tory governments. He was too much of a reformer for their tastes and they strongly petitioned London to recall him, which they did after he had been only six months in the country, surely a record of speedy dispatch.

Durham's assessment of what caused the rebellions was the lack of representative government in the colonies. He recommended that the Executive branch of government be required to follow the directives of the elected Legislative Assembly. Ironically, that was exactly what the Whig government had advocated very strongly for the British Parliament, but thought that in the colonies it smacked of nasty words like Democracy and Republicanism, which in turn led to revolt against the ruling class. They had no wish to see this sort of thing happen and quickly rejected this recommendation.

Durham's other recommendation, that Upper and Lower Canada become one, was very unpopular among the French who felt that, although they now had the majority of the population, eventually they would become a minority in the country, under the control of the English majority. Nevertheless, Westminster approved this recommendation rather swiftly and the Act of Union passed in 1841. At the time they thought they were doing a fine thing, allowing French Canadians to become English. Who would not want to become English if they got the chance?

When George and Archie returned home with news of the failed rebellions, Mary said to George, "Why, I thought you were such a staunch Tory, George. I believe you are becoming one of those dangerous radicals." George raised an eyebrow and answered her teasing with a very sober, "Maybe I am. Maybe I am at that."

When Archie relayed the news to his wife, she responded to this extraordinary event with a nod, "Just what one might expect." She noted that Archie was looking a bit more animated and for that she resolved to thank George Argue.

Most of what was transpiring at York made little impression in Goulbourne where most settlers were unaware of Durham's report. Nor were they to feel the effect of it for many years to come. Nevertheless, it was the turning point for the country and although George did not live to see it for himself, its implementation made this country the one he had hoped for and longed for in his dream.

CALDWELL

THE FAMILY GROWS UP 1835-43

William of course had read the signs correctly. His parents were expecting another child. Their last child, Hannah, was born six months after William's escape. Forest was comforted by the fact that Mary still had Lettie to help her in the house, but this help would not be with her for much longer. Lettie had received a proposal of marriage from a farmer in Huntley, not too far from the Caldwell homestead. This time she undertook to have the bans read and the date set before she gave her final consent. She further insisted that she be available to help Mary for at least three months after the new baby arrived.

Margaret was now her mother's mainstay and she ruthlessly trained her younger two sisters, Mary Anne, aged 9, and Elizabeth, aged 6, to take on as many chores as possible, both to ease her own burden and to prepare for the day when Lettie left.

By 1835 Forest was renting four 50-acre parcels. He told Mary of his long range plan to give each son 50 acres, but he had not yet shared that bit of news with his sons, for he did not feel easy in his heart about it. He was beginning to see parallels between himself and his father. Was he trying to establish a patriarchy here in Huntley as his father had done in Cavan? Perhaps the whole idea was folly.

The one thing of which Forest was supremely certain was his love for Mary; her welfare remained his paramount concern. Fortunately she knew how much Forest cherished her and their mutual happiness neither faltered nor swerved.

Second to his determination to place Mary on the pedestal she deserved, was his love of teaching the Bible to his class at church. Students were eager to join his class and hear his conviction of God's unfailing love for each one of them. Where other men preached of Hell's fire, Forest's words were all of comfort and assurance. As popular as he was with his students, among his sons he was not always successful in achieving harmony and peace. This is not to imply that Forest was not loved and respected by his sons and daughters. The peace which eluded his table arose from the lack of respect the offspring accorded one another. The eldest boys especially carped at one another until Forest in desperation one day suggested that the place might be too small to hold all of them. Mary was not to be grieved and that was that.

William's absence may have accounted for the fact that Forest acquired only four parcels of land for his five sons. His departure left a big hole in the family but things had settled down somewhat at the table. In the barns and fields where the sons continued to work together, arguments continued about the best farming practices. Samuel favoured wheat, James favoured beef cattle and John thought he should not be hindermost in having his own position if he could just figure out what it should be. Thank the Lord, Forrest Smiley was only a youngster and had no opinion.

The girls in the family looked as though they were raised to frontier life, as indeed they were. They were tall, strong, large boned, with square shoulders, firm jaws, and just as inclined as their brothers, to respect their own opinions. Moreover, they did not know *how to flirt*. Except for their parents, they deferred to no one, least of all their brothers. Their parents were constantly amazed at the young women they had raised. They wondered if indeed they had raised them or if the country had more to do with it.

Margaret, the oldest in the family after William went west, felt entitled to order everyone about, giving her forthright opinion on any and all matters. One day as she neared her 26th birthday, she overheard James say to his brothers, *"I hope we won't have an old maid on our hands."* Brothers had an interest in this matter as they were obliged to support an unmarried sister. Straightway she took umbrage and married the first man to come her way. Her sister Mary Anne, who was only 15 when

Margaret married, vowed to follow suit as soon as possible, for she reasoned she might as well slave in her own home with her feet under her own table, as do so in her parents' home for the comfort of her dratted brothers.

None of these young women had the slightest trouble in finding a mate. What with high mortality in childbirth and the endless supply of work, women of all statures and dispositions were in demand, especially those with strong backs. There was no need to practice charm.

Early in the year 1839 Samuel decided that he too was ready to establish his own household. His chosen mate was Fanny Smiley, his second cousin. Neither family saw anything wrong with his decision, nor did the fact that Fanny had only turned 18 at the beginning of 1839 delay proceedings. The marriage was quickly arranged to occur shortly after her birthday. Forest gave Samuel his fifty acres and the other sons came to realize that this was also to be their inheritance when their time came.

Samuel was happily married to Fanny and before many months passed she was obviously expecting. Samuel did not suffer anxiety on this account for both Fanny's mother and his own had experienced no difficulty with this task, or none that troubled him. Fanny was a different candidate; she was 18, petite, delicate and frightened to death of what was ahead of her. Birthing pangs started late in her eighth month and lasted several days. The baby was coming wrong way about and the women who were on hand to assist her could not manage to turn the child. Her mother arrived as soon as she could get there, but by this time Fanny had been struggling for two days and was barely conscious. A doctor was called from Richmond, but he was unable to do more than the women had done. He calculated he might be able to save the baby but not the mother, and offered to do so. Samuel and Fanny's mother nodded, scarcely realizing what they were agreeing to. Fanny died as her small babe was taken from her womb, very much the worse for wear after the long struggle to be born. The immediate emergency was to keep the child alive. Water and honey was all that was available for the first day and then they tried cow's milk. The christening in the Anglican Church in Huntley was arranged immediately. The baby was christened Frances on the same cold day in January 1840 when her mother was buried.

Frances Smiley took the child home with her for the first week and managed to find a young nursing mother to keep the baby fed. She could see that she was going to become a mother again if she did not rearrange things very swiftly. She reasoned Mary Caldwell was younger than herself and very experienced in these matters. She consulted Mary, 'What to do?'

If Frances Smiley thought that Mary might agree to raise her son's child, she calculated without Forest. He put his foot down very firmly. Some other arrangement would have to be found. The baby remained with her maternal grandmother and began to show signs of thriving. There seemed to be little time to grieve the passing of an eighteen-year-old girl.

Frances was not idle; she heard of a young widow, a Frances Maxwell in March, whose husband had died six months ago and left her childless. She told Samuel of this young widow who *might* be prepared to help him if what he could offer was appealing to her. If not, he was going to have to find some way to raise his own bairn. She no longer had the stamina for bringing up another child.

Samuel, who had gone home to his parents' home to be looked after, was still in a state of shock and grief, for he had truly loved Fanny. He told his parents of his mother-in-law's proposal; to his surprise his father urged him to meet the young woman and, if they thought they might suit, he should consider it. His sister Margaret urged him in the same direction, as she did not want to be asked to assume the task herself.

Samuel met Frances Maxwell who proved to be a comely, pleasant and practical woman. A brief courtship ensued and Samuel began to feel hopeful that Frances might agree to his proposal, which included raising his child. His proposal was well met by Frances, who of course had known all along just what the proposal would involve, and thought she could do worse and maybe no better. The marriage ceremony was performed immediately and she and baby Frances were installed in Samuel's home on March 26, 1840.

Frances Maxwell had no children from her brief marriage to James Maxwell, but soon proved the deficit did not lie with her as she gave Samuel five more children. The first child arrived safely eighteen months into the marriage, to Samuel's relief and joy...

302

In 1840, the Smiley family was still living in Bytown, but Harold finally was able to please his wife's wish that they purchase land in March Township. Frances shamelessly said that she wished to be closer to her granddaughter, but it appeared that she did not wish to be too close. March Township still held the greater appeal of the hope of a genteel life style. Their older son took over the store in Bytown and the younger son did the farming.

In the year 1843, twenty long years after coming to Upper Canada, Forest finally acquired full title to the parcels of land he had been leasing. There is no family explanation for the long period of leasing. Perhaps it took Forest that long to be able to afford the purchase, or perhaps it took Malloch that long to decide to sell.

As soon as the land was his, Forest embarked on his final 'better house for Mary' campaign. Fieldstones were placed all around the exterior of the house to the top of the first floor, leaving a space between the inner log wall and the outer stonewall of 18 inches for sawdust insulation. The outer walls of the second story were sawn lumber, again leaving a foot and a half for insulation. No more cold, drafty rooms for Mary. It was now a house worthy of the name *Cavandale*.

At last Forest achieved his objective.

ARGUE

CHILDBIRTH 1841

Mary stood at the door of her new home basking in the warmth of the first spring-like day. It was mid-May 1841, but warmth was late coming that year and all the more welcome for it. Their home was no longer a shanty, but a two-storey log building, snug and warm compared with her first and second shanties. The spaces between logs were solidly packed with lime and sawdust and there was even an attic well filled with sawdust from the nearby sawmill. What a difference.

When they had left Bytown a decade ago, Mary had expected a quiet life in Goulbourne. Her memory of times past in the woods led her to expect much solitude and little excitement. But the years had flown past with as many changes as a body could wish for and more.

They now had ten grandchildren, all nearby; Annie was to have her eighth child soon and Mary planned to go to Huntley for her confinement. She was concerned for Annie, for each pregnancy seemed to leave her more exhausted. She hoped to persuade Maude to come to Huntley with her and be there for the birth. Maude had not yet committed herself for Annie's child was not due for several more weeks and she felt obligated to a couple of young women in Goulbourne who were depending upon her.

Mary was restless about Annie and decided it was best for her to go well before the due date. George would be looked after for John and his wife Essie lived with them and their daughter Jane lived just across the way. Maude promised to come as soon as she had word; John McFadden was to bring her.

About two weeks before the baby was due, Annie was resting as her mother insisted she should, and the younger children were outside playing. Suddenly Annie gave a sharp cry of surprise as her water broke and the birth gushed forth. Horrified, Mary called out to Mary Anne,

"Mary Anne, have someone fetch the nearest neighbour and your father. Tell Margaret to keep the young ones outside and then come and help me."

Mary Anne screamed the orders out the door and flew back to her grandmother who was holding a newborn in her arms. Mary normally would have cleaned the baby and cut the cord, but this was no ordinary time. She thrust the babe into Mary Anne's arms, much to the girl's terror, saying only, "Do what you can."

Annie was bleeding profusely and Mary raced to get rags to try to staunch the bleeding. She commanded Mary Anne, "Lay the babe down and help me raise your mother's feet."

Mary cried and prayed aloud as she struggled. Mary Anne stood rooted to the spot, unable to tell if her grandmother was praying or cursing. Nothing stopped the bleeding.

By the time Thomas and the neighbour arrived, Annie was unconscious, very pale, and still bleeding slowly. Mary was on her knees praying and her granddaughter, wide-eyed with fright, clutched the baby. The neighbour, who had often assisted at births, forced some bitter herbs down Annie's throat, assured Mary that she had done all possible and what happened now was up to God. She then turned to the babe.

Annie lingered for an hour, but never regained consciousness. The nightmare continued.

The suddenness of this death overwhelmed them all. Yes, childbirth is always risky and yes, Mary had been worried, but Annie had delivered seven babes without trouble. They were not prepared for this disaster. It would have been impossible to say who was most cruelly affected: Thomas, for whom Annie had always been his mainstay; the young ones who had lost their mother; Mary who watched her first born die; or Mary Anne, who from that time forth viewed childbirth with paralyzing fear. Shock rippled outwards to the whole Argue family and friends. Maude felt she should have been there, but nothing could be undone.

What was clear was the family situation: Thomas now had eight children, five of them ten and under. Mary Anne, who would be expected to take over her mother's role, was in a bad way herself as she relived the whole disaster.

Mary soon saw that there was no space or time for her grief. She remained to care for the newborn and little ones. It was as well for her that she was busy from morning to night, with little time to think and exhausted enough to be able to sleep. It was hard to comfort the second youngest child, Etta or any of the children, when she felt so little comfort within herself.

George came to stay briefly and to help Thomas prepare for the funeral. George was virtually overwhelmed himself and felt worthless. He wished he could comfort his wife, but was sensitive enough to know it was useless to approach her. Each bore his grief alone, yet not entirely so. A look between them was enough to let each other know the pain they shared, and then they allowed each other the space to heal as they could.

After a couple of weeks, Mary Anne, 17, and Margaret, 14, told their grandmother they could carry on somehow and their grandma, promising to return to them in a week, went home to Goulbourne.

George did not know what to do with himself, but knew he needed to do something: the greater the pain, the more he needed to act. He spent as much time outdoors as possible. He longed to be able to go for a long trip into the woods and promised himself he would do just that when snow cover made it possible. Maybe he would take Archie with him and stop off in Bytown to see their friend John Burrows.

Maude understood that Mary had to grieve in her own way, no matter how long it took, and accepted this without comment. This friendship, which needed no words, was a great support to Mary, who did not shut herself off from Maude. Once more her friends tried to console Mary that her daughter was in a better place. Mary did not respond. She thought that Annie's best place was with her young children and no one could tell her otherwise, but she did not contradict them.

Every second week Mary went to Huntley to help care for the little ones and to give the older girls a sense that their grandma would stand by them. When she returned to Goulbourne she immediately went over to see Jane, who lived just across the road. Every morning and afternoon she made visits, nearly driving Jane distracted with how to reassure her mother.

"Ma, I'm perfectly fine. How can I make you understand that I am well and you needn't fret yourself?"

"What will comfort me, lass, is your having your baby in good health", for Jane was expecting her third child in November, and could no longer hide her pregnancy from her mother. Mary determined that, with increased vigilance and God's help, her only remaining daughter would bear this child safely. Eventually Maude and George persuaded Mary to spend three weeks in Huntley and one at home. They used the excuse of the difficulty of getting her there over the summer roads, but the real reason was to give Jane a break. Only Maude's promise to visit Jane regularly enabled Mary to yield.

In November, Jane successfully ended her pregnancy with the birth of a healthy baby girl. With a desire to herald a new beginning, she named the baby Henrietta, an unfamiliar name in the family. Mary was a little taken aback, but the thrust of her daughter's jaw stopped her words before they escaped her lips. Jane had named her first daughter Mary Ann, and felt that she had done her duty to both the living and the dead. The baby was healthy; Jane was healthy; that was all that mattered.

CALDWELL

A REUNION 1843

In the year 1843 when the harvest was all in the barns and winter season was coming upon them, Forest decided to hold a council with his four sons. He told them that the time had come when he was ready to settle each of them with fifty acres and they could get on with their lives. In return he expected that they would either live together in harmony or find another solution. They were not to bring their differences to their parents any more. Mary was not to be grieved and that was that. Forest himself was looking every year of his sixty some years, but it was Mary's weariness that concerned him most.

Samuel already had his own household in a smaller cabin on the Cavandale property. That was to be his 50 acres. James and John realized it was time for them to move out. William's way out seemed drastic as they had not heard from him since he left more than eight years ago, but clearly their father would not stand in their way even if they chose that route.

A few days later a total stranger strode into the house, clad in skins and a hat made out of fur. Those parts not covered with fur were covered with long hair. They stared at him in amazement until he spoke. Then there was a great clamour and Mary hugged her first-born son while the tears streamed down her face.

"Your father and I had begun to believe you must be dead, William. Why ever did you not let us know you were alive?"

Then without waiting for his explanation she turned to Jane Maria, and told her to go out to the fields to fetch her father

308

and brothers. The older girls were set to the business of preparing a special meal of mutton and new garden vegetables. More questions were to wait until everyone was at hand.

Forest was so emotional at seeing his lost son that he did not trust himself to say anything, but his joy was clear enough without words. When they were all assembled in the kitchen questions came thick and fast from brothers and sisters.

"Where have you been and what have you been doing with yourself?"

"Well, at first I thought paddling a canoe would not be more strenuous than cutting timber, but it took a time before my body agreed with me. It was a struggle to keep up. Archie felt it too, I know, but we knew we could do it. There was not too much chat with the traders at first because we did not understand one another well, but in less than a year we were all talking the same jingle. They had to tell us what to do so we had to learn pretty quick. Of course the main thing was to have strong arms and a strong back and the will to put them to use.

"The first thing Archie and I had to do was catch enough furs to wear during the winter ahead, for we were to live in a tent, summer or winter. Fortunately we were able to find an Indian camp and the women there made the furs up for us. Without that help we could not have gone on. And the *coeureurs du bois*, that's what these traders call themselves, would not have taken us with them. A man suffering from frostbite is not much use. After that we managed just fine."

William soon tired of telling them just how it was in the woods and on the rivers. He knew they would not be able to comprehend how it was no matter how many words he used and he was itching to be out of doors again already. He summed it up by saying; "Thought I'd make enough to buy some land already cleared and think about staying in one place for a bit. So here I am."

Forest asked, "Why did you not write?"

"Nothing to write with and no postal service. I did send along a message with a trapper who was coming down the Ottawa River as far as Bytown but I guess you did not hear from him, eh?" They shook their heads. "Well maybe he didn't make it. But I have and I am back to bide a while."

They asked about Archie Magee and he told them that Archie had not come back with him. He had liked the life of a fur trader so much that he decided to go on one more expedition. William said he had to be on the way to Goulbourne to tell Archie's brother this news. This was accepted without further question. Since they had no understanding of Archie's situation, why question his decision.

William took off for Goulbourne the next day, still trying to figure out just what he was going to tell William Magee. He decided that very little would be best. He had left Archie living in a remote Cree settlement in the Northwest Territory, which was all of the land north and west of Lake Huron. He could not describe his whereabouts more than that and he decided to minimize the fact that Archie, now in his forties and still fit enough to keep pace on the rivers, had chosen to remain with the Cree tribe for a bit. More than this William would not say, and he preferred to say less, for no one would understand it anyway so why bother. He was not sure he understood it himself.

In Huntley they fussed over William as much as they could and more than he liked. He told them as many edited versions of his adventures as he thought fit, duly admired their new house and farm, but after a week, said he could not sleep indoors any more and must be off.

"I think I'll try my hand at farming after all. There is a spot further up the Ottawa I fancy. The land is still there for the taking. Don't expect to hear much from me. I'm not much of a hand with writing."

This time he did let them know that he had settled in an area called Shawville on the north side of the Ottawa River. He was managing all right in his own way and was still a bachelor.

Mary fussed and fretted for a time until Forest gently reminded her that she could help William more by praying for him and help herself a deal more by having a little confidence in the Holy Spirit.

"Yes, Forest, I know. And I will try, but I am not overly confident that the Holy Spirit and I always want the same thing."

"Then you had better leave it to the Holy Spirit to work things out, Mary. I daresay that might be for the best in the long run."

Mary glanced at him and, seeing only his steadfast regard, said no more.

310

ARGUE

A LAST TRIP TO THE BUSH 1841

Snow covered the ground to a barely adequate depth for a sleigh journey when George came into the cabin and declared his readiness to make a wee trip. Archie was to go with him, not sure just when they would be back, maybe two weeks would be the outside of enough. And could they take what provisions they might need? Mary knew of this plan and was ready to hand George a few loaves of bread, a precious pot — 'mind you bring it back now,' — oatmeal, dried meat, salt meat and a chunk of homemade cheese. If they were to be away longer than two weeks, he was going to have to find more supplies.

It had become a regular pattern for George's sons, Robert and William, to haul loading up the Ottawa every winter. They were to travel in tandem as far as Bytown and while his sons loaded up their sleighs with supplies, he and Archie would have a quick visit with John Burrows. Then they would travel with them up to the camps or at least as far as the first camp. The trips into the bush were much longer now, sometimes taking as long as two weeks for a round trip from Goulbourne and back. The pattern was to spend about a week at home before they were off again. Many men kept this up every winter until the 1870's, when a railway up the Ottawa made hauling loading a thing of the past.

When George and Archie arrived in Bytown they found John Burrows much aged. John was fifteen years younger than they were and for that matter they had aged a bit too, although they had no mirror to tell them so. They needed little urging to visit again on their way back to Goulbourne and spend more time with John and his family.

The trip upcountry showed George and Archie just how many changes had occurred in the years since they had hauled loading themselves. For most of the trip they followed packed trails, well away from the river If they had waited until the river froze over, their trip would have been much faster, but George could not wait and they were well pleased with their timing. It was less windy in the woods and they could see better the larger clearings and more shanties scattered along the route.

At the end of the second day on the trail, they still had not made it to the first camp. They were heartily glad to have the company of Robert's and William's sleighs as they tried to start up a fire to make tea and oat gruel. During the night buffalo robes kept them warm and snug in the piles of hay. They reached the first camp early the following morning and after assisting with the unloading, George and Archie decided to head for home. Their eagerness for a trip into the bush was well sated.

"You are sure you won't be too cold, for you know you won't have any hay with you now?" William inquired.

"Oo-ch, no", said Archie. "You mind we did this when you were young'uns."

George added, "We'll make swift time on the way back down, with a lighter load and all. I am sure we will only be one night on the road. Mayhap we'll spend tonight at an inn."

"That'll be a first," said Robert, and waved them off.

They were on the road only one night but it was very late the following day when they arrived at Burrows' doorstep and were glad of the warm welcome. Although it was well past time for hot food, Elizabeth Burrows heated up a pot of stew and, following a few days of oatmeal gruel, it was well appreciated. They had stopped at a store on the way to Lower Town to splurge on the wild extravagance of a whole pound of tea for their hostess. The rest of their provisions had been left with William and Robert.

It took only a short time before they disposed of family news. George was loath to mention the death of his oldest daughter, so he spoke instead of the birth of another granddaughter, who marked the twenty-third grandchild so far. Instead of looking as proud as one might expect, he kept his gaze

312

on the floor, which had a sheen that suggested fine living and some help in the house.

He then looked up and said, "We cannot rejoice as well we might for we lost our oldest daughter just last July in childbirth. It is selfish to say, for we know she is in a better place, but I miss her dreadfully; we both do. She was always such a lively one, the most like her mother, but I think child bearing in this country takes it out of these young women. She was only thirty-eight when she died but already she had given birth to eight children. She did her duty and gladly so. I don't know how people cope with this if they don't believe in heaven. It's hard enough as it is." This was greeted by silence from Archie and John, who had both suffered the loss of a child.

Then Archie said, "It is some years now since Charlie died but you know, George, I've often thought that we do our people a grave disservice by insisting that they rejoice when our loved ones die. Knowing or believing that they go to a better place did not help me at all, and I can tell you what hindered me was feeling bad that I felt so bad. I could not be happy, or even resigned, and that made me feel all the more alone." — more silence — "But there, let's not dwell upon it. We took this trip so that George could be in a different space. Tell us some news of Bytown, John. It seems middling to prospering."

John was relieved to leap into another topic. He asked if they had heard aught of Bytown's first election this past year and when he learned they had not he was happy to give them the details.

"The most interesting thing Archie," and he nodded to include George, "was the number of people who could vote and I believe everyone who could vote did. We did a thorough count and we have 3,122 adults in this town, I am pleased to say. Out of that how many do you think voted?"

"Maybe a couple of hundred", said George and Archie nodded.

"Only 85 souls were allowed to vote." This was greeted with dismay and almost disbelief.

"What was the problem?"

"The problem is that to qualify for the vote you have to provide proof of outright ownership of at least 300 acres or the equivalent of that worth if you are a merchant. Doesn't matter if you are a man or a woman; as long as you can prove on the spot that you have enough assets outright, you can vote."

"Well I can see that would eliminate a large number. I guess no one in Goulbourne could vote at all. I know you have been buying land John; were you able to vote?"

"No I was not. I have several lots and I am not what I think a poor man, but I don't have full possession of the lots. Mayhap at the next election requirements will change once again; they change the rules as often as they wish. Our Lt. Governor, Lord Sydenham, does not scruple how he rigs the election. The rules change from place to place and if that doesn't work, then he changes the boundaries and puts the polling booths beyond the reach of people he does not want to have the chance to vote. He is a scoundrel of the first water. Where does London find such a wretch to represent them in the colonies?"

"Did you say man or woman could vote?" asked Archie.

"Aye, the law says only that an individual must have net assets worth three hundred acres outright and some women do, Praise the Lord. But not many women voted here in Bytown; it goes against custom. Across the river it's a different story. There the women have always had the right to vote if they were wealthy enough and willing to take three oaths of loyalty. They don't scruple about the loyalty oaths, for not many women fancy strapping on a sword to defend the Government. And it's far easier for them to vote if they have a mind to. They just drive up in their fine carriage and four, go to the booth of the candidate they want to vote for, and no one dares interfere with a woman as they do with a man. Everyone stands back and takes their hat off."

"Well now, that will make some people sit up and take notice. Mary will appreciate this bit of news, as will Maude Wilson. Not that they will have the chance in this lifetime, but mayhap our daughters and sons will vote, and maybe not. I cannot see many of them owning 300 acres outright."

"Well there was only one woman. She created quite a stir. She was treated with respect. No one tried to prevent her voting as they do with the men. But there was anger toward those who make the decisions about who can vote and who not. They came in for a great deal of criticism."

"Criticism will run off their backs easily enough," grumbled Archie, "and the blessed eighty-five who were able to vote won't try to make any changes now that they have joined the elite. What to do?"

"Archie, I hear bits of news from England: it seems that merchants now have a great deal more say about how the country is to be governed. They are telling the Lords they don't want to be taxed in order to assist the colonies. They want Free Trade for they can get lumber cheaper form the Baltic countries than from Canada. Why bother with preferential treatment for overseas colonies and paying higher taxes for armies to control the colonies? Let the colonials do as they please and be hanged."

After a pause he said, "If it continues this way I think Durham's recommendation to allow the colonies responsible government may get passed before too long."

"You really think it will come?"

"I do, George. It's bound to come, but I won't lay a wager on the year."

"Indeed not. But there is one last thing I need to do and something tells me I should waste no more time. I have a chapel to build. I made a promise to Archie Magee; he has to put up the land and I am to put up the chapel. It will be called Magee Chapel. You built a chapel long ago John; you tended to first things first. We have been in Goulbourne for twenty odd years and still no chapel. It is something I must do, if it is the last thing I ever do."

None of them knew how prophetic these words were to be.

This picture is not intended to portray what life was like in Carleton County at that time. Quite simply it is the only photograph of cabins and shanties in Upper Canada in that period. This picture is likely to have been taken in the late 1840's or 1850's.

Note that the shanty has no chimney but an iron pipe is jutting out of the centre of the roof. In the door of the shanty are a man, a woman and a child. The men are wearing white shirts. They are not poor. The new house is built of squared timber.

Not all areas developed in the same pattern. Lands given to the United Empire Loyalists on the waterways around 1783 to 1790 were very developed and civilized by comparison. Lands further into the hinterland continued to look like this for many more years. Little attempt has been made at farming; they have likely survived by selling timber, for the amount of cleared land is very extensive.

This picture gives the impression that not much had been achieved in 20 plus years in the country. And in some cases I am sure that was very true; it was enough to avoid starvation and survive. I suspect the men and woman in the picture are proud of their accomplishments.

317

CALDWELL

JAMES' COURTSHIP 1844

James, now 26, was courting a young woman whom he hoped and intended to make his bride. He had met Ellen Neelin at a campground meeting near Stittsville more than a year ago but he knew he could not bring his bride into his father's overcrowded household, so he held back on asking her. With each month that passed without his seeing her, he felt sure that he would lose out to some other young man. For this reason he did not make his intentions known to his family, but his siblings knew where his interest lay.

One day Forest asked James if there was any truth in the rumour that he was seeing a young girl. James said, "Yes, I am, but there has been no discussion of marriage yet. Her name is Ellen Neelin and I don't think you'll have any objection to her or her family. Ellen is the daughter of Reverend Gregory Neelin up Munster way."

"Oh, aye, I've heard of the man and his four daughters. I have not had the privilege to meet him yet, but I've heard folks speak well of him. His wife died when his girls were very young, I believe, and he chose to raise them on his own rather than marry again. Very admirable I suppose, but very difficult too."

James dismissed that with a wave of his hand, "Well that is in the past now for they are all grown up and ready for matrimony. Catherine is already married to Joseph Alderson in Goulbourne and she is younger than Ellen."

James looked undecided for a few moments and then apparently made up his mind to something. James was the only one of the family to look exactly like his father. All of them were taller than average for that time, being over six feet. Most of them acquired a little flesh to go with their height and several could be said to be very good looking, but James felt, quite rightly, that his looks alone would not be sufficient to attract a young maiden so he deemed it necessary to show himself to be a good catch in other ways. Accordingly, he decided to share his plans for the future with his father, whose help he needed before he could make much headway.

"You recall telling us that each of us will inherit fifty acres from you?"

Forest nodded.

"If it is right with you I would like to tell Rev. Neelin about my prospects. What do you say?"

This was agreeable to his father. With that security to offer his bride, James approached Reverend Neelin to ask for Ellen.

Very soberly he was told, "You have my permission to court her, but the decision will be Ellen's to make."

Ellen, flustered and anxious, asked her father, "Do I need to tell James about that… that time?"

Her father replied, "Aye, lass I think you should. It is not so much of a secret you know. You may find that he has heard the story already and there are a few people who will be glad to tell James if you don't yourself. And if it makes him think less of you for it, best to know now."

"I would as leave not marry at all and stay here and look after you, Da."

Her father shook his head and said, "I think the best way through this is to go through, not roundabout or sideways. Go ahead lass, and see what God has in store for you."

Ellen agreed reluctantly. It was easier to obey than argue. Or so she thought at the time.

The following Sunday James was to pass the afternoon with Ellen and her family. Before he arrived, Gregg Neelin gave his daughter a look that made his expectation clear and Ellen nodded, promising her father that somehow she would do it that very day. But it was a great deal easier to decide to tell all than to actually get the words out of her mouth. She asked James if they could go for a bit of a walk down to the creek; she had something she needed to tell him.

It was obvious to the least observant person that Ellen was under severe duress. Her face alternated between red flushes and pallor and her breathing was dreadfully uneven; at times she appeared not to breathe at all and then gulped painfully for air. James was becoming pretty alarmed.

Finally, while they were still some distance from the creek, he stopped and took her hands in both of his and said, "This is where we stop and you tell me all that is on your mind. It cannot be as bad as all that. You look fit to die with the worry about this. There is nothing that you can tell me that is as bad as all this surely. Unless it is that you don't wish to marry me. Is that it? You had best be out with it."

"James", she croaked and then stopped. She clenched her jaws, straightened her spine and drew herself up to her maximum height of five feet. She did not look up at his face but stared straight at his chest and said, "When I have told you what I have to say you may consider yourself free of your offer of marriage. I should have told you before what I will tell you now — before, — now."

James interrupted and implored her, "Please get on with it, Ellen. You're not talking sense. There can't be anything so bad that we will not be engaged when all is done, can there?

She shook her head as if that was not what she wanted to hear, took another deep breath and said, "I have been responsible for the death of a man."

There was no sound from James and when she peeped up to have a look, she saw only a look of bewilderment on his rather funny face, as if her words still made no sense.

"I have killed a man, James."

"But Ellen, you're hardly bigger than a walnut. How could you kill a man?"

"Well, I did. So you see I am not what you think I am and that is why you are free to break off our courtship, James."

"Ellen, I think we had both better sit down, yes, right here, and you had best tell me how this amazing event took place." With that her took her by both elbows and pushed her gently down onto the grass.

Ellen closed her lips in a firm line and said not a word.

James implored her, "Please Ellen, I'm sure you and you alone can help me to understand this. Otherwise I shall just have to think you have been having a bad dream or I'm having a bad dream. Which is it to be?"

Ellen sat silently for a while and then she looked James full in the face and said, "I wish it were only a dream that I could wake up from. It's not so much that I don't want to tell you, James. It's just that, that, the words won't come. I've never been able to speak of it, not to anyone, not even to my father. I will try. I suppose you deserve that much." She leapt to her feet, and started pacing back and forth, never looking at James.

"It was a long time ago now. I was only sixteen and I wanted to go to the Orange Day Parade near Bell's Tavern on the Richmond Road. Father did not want me to go. He said it reminded him too much of the goings on in Ireland and we should all be happy to get away from things like that and not carry it with us to a new country. But I would not hear anything about that. I did not care one whit about all that quarrelling between the Romans and us. I only wanted to go and have some fun and meet people my own age. So I got my sisters to plead too. But it was no use. Da, for a change, was quite firm on the matter. He would not attend such an inflammatory occasion and without protection his daughters could not go and that was that."

"How I have wished and wished that he had prevailed. But such wishes are useless and I am twice a fool for such wishes at this stage. I did not give up. When I realized that the main part of his objection was that a man must be present to offer protection, I simply went next door and asked James Munro if he would act as our escort. He was eight years my senior, a man Da trusted, and finally he gave in. I know now that Da often gave in against his own judgment when any of his daughters pleaded and pleaded. I suppose I knew it then too and that is why I refused to give up until I got what I wanted. On the day of the parade Catherine backed down and said she didn't want to go after all. She would stay home with Da. I was furious with her but Da said I could go provided Mr. Munro and I stayed with others and we were not too late leaving the affair. So with the promise that we would do all that he asked we set off."

She paused, and James still looked at her and said nothing. She felt she hated him for putting her through this and that made it easier to carry on. She vowed that never again would she find herself needing to admit anyone to her private misery.

321

In a bitter tone she said, "We had a grand time. I met so many people and I know that at the time I thought that this was the best time I had ever had in my whole life. We planned to leave immediately after we had eaten our supper and have lots of daylight left for getting home. I don't remember now what we ate, but at the time it seemed to be everything that was wonderful. We were to travel in the company of the Shores who had their own buggy, but when we were no more than a mile down the road, one of the axles on their buggy broke. It was beyond fixing on the side of the road, so the Shores decided they would have to walk back to Bell's Tavern, try to find a place to stay for the night and wait until their buggy was fixed the following day. All of this delayed us a little and now it was just the two of us. We still thought we would be through the Stony Swamp and nearing Richmond before dark, for the days were long, but we miscalculated on the condition of the road. It had rained since we passed over it in the morning and now the bumps and hollows seemed more dangerous. Mr. Munro felt that he had better take it a little slower or we too might have a breakdown." She shuddered, "I cannot bear to think of that place."

"We went on a bit and it was so hard on the buggy on those dreadful roads. The bumps were so bad that just to stay on the buggy I had to hold on with both hands as hard as I could, but I never complained. I could tell Mr. Munro was not very happy. We were almost out of the swamp and there was still a little light when, suddenly", she paused, "suddenly, two men jumped up out of the ditch at us. They leapt right at the mare's head and dragged her to a stop. Mr. Munro yelled and tried to lash Betsy into going ahead, but it was no use. Then one of the men came and dragged him off the buggy and they started to beat him. They were both hitting and kicking at him so hard and yelling, 'We'll teach this Billy Boy a lesson he'll not forget.' Mr. Munro fell down and could not fight them anymore and I thought they would kill him for sure for they were still giving him awful kicks."

Ellen was moaning now and bending over as if it hurt her to stand but she kept on going. She had entirely forgotten about James Caldwell. "I jumped down off the buggy and took off my boot and my stocking. I stuffed the stocking with the first big stone I could find and I swung it at one of the men who had his back to me. Neither of them had paid me any attention yet. I

322

hit him on the side of the head very hard, and he dropped down onto the ground without a sound. The other man looked up at me and I was going to hit him too for all I was worth when he took to his heels and fled."

Again Ellen stopped and then straightened her back and went on. "I was very surprised at that, for I had no idea I would have any — success. Mr. Munro was insensible on the ground and nothing I could do raised him. I was desperate. Finally I was able to drag him over to the buggy and get him up onto it. I will never know how but he was not all that heavy for a man, and all the hard work on the farm and the terror I felt gave me extra strength, I guess. All the time I kept saying, 'Whoa Betsy, Whoa' and for a miracle she stayed put. I left the man I had hit where he was. I never really gave any thought to him. I just kept praying that the other one would not come back. And then I drove Betsy home. For a time I made her go as fast as she would, but after a while I let her have her own way. I was too exhausted to urge her on. Mr. Munro was waking up and when he realized what was going on he told me not to worry none about driving Betsy home. She could find her own way there, and as swiftly as she wanted to.

"I don't remember any more of what happened on that trip. I heard later that we stopped at Richmond and Mr. Munro, who was obviously very unwell, got his head bandaged up. He told them about the man whom we left lying by the ditch in the Stony Swamp. No one wanted to go and fetch him in the middle of the night and they said that someone was bound to find him the next day. They asked Mr. Munro if he knew the men and he said no, he didn't. I know we continued to go on, for Mr. Munro said afterwards that I kept wailing that we had to get home and since it looked like Betsy could get us there we kept on going. I even insisted on holding the reins, I'm told. And that's all."

"That's all?" James exclaimed. "Why have you said you killed a man?"

"He never regained consciousness. I killed him. It took him two weeks to die, but he died because of that blow."

"What happened to the other man?"

"We never heard from him or found out the name of either of these men."

"They could have just been travelling through."

323

"The Justice of the Peace ruled that it was an accidental death and said he could have died from exposure anyway. But I know the truth of the matter. And now you do too."

"Well, Ellen, I can see that you are still fair upset about all this but I can't see myself what else you could have done in the circumstances. I suppose you could have picked up the reins and hightailed it out of there when they were both still occupied with Mr. Munro. But then they might have killed him and then you could have told yourself from then until doomsday that you were responsible for Mr. Munro's death. I think you did just the right thing and I am proud to know that my future wife has wit, courage, and gumption. You should be proud of yourself. Why do you not know that?"

Ellen said nothing at all for several minutes and when it began to appear to James as if she might be finished talking for life, she said a small, "Thank you. You're very kind."

"Surely, girl, someone has tried to tell you as much before now?"

"They may have. I don't know. From that time forth we have not spoken of it in our home. Father blamed himself for ever letting me go. Catherine blamed herself for not going with me. I have blamed myself for everything. We never speak of it, never. If anyone tried to cheer me up I wouldn't let them. And I would not have told you only Da said I must. I think I would rather have just broken off the engagement and stayed home and looked after Da. But now even if you don't want to marry me, I'm glad that I've told you. It feels good to tell someone who is not obliged to me as my family is. You have given me some comfort and I thank you for that."

"Have you heard me say I don't want to marry you? I begin to think that your greatest fault may be that you're hard of hearing. Haven't I just said that I'm proud and pleased with my future wife? Let's have no more daft talk."

Ellen looked him full in the face and saw only a clear resolve there. She began to think that James was a little better looking when he firmed up his jaw like that. She liked what she saw very much. And James was equally pleased when he saw her expression soften and take on a hint of admiration mixed with gratitude. He felt that perhaps he might be equal to this rather daunting young woman after all.

The wedding date was set for January 30, 1846. The decision to wait a full eighteen months before their marriage was not James' decision. Ellen proved herself capable of great resolution now that her self-esteem had been resurrected. She said she must look after her father until such time as he could make other arrangements. What those arrangements were to be was not made clear. It was also made very clear that no one in their family would ever attend an Orange Day Parade. After that was dealt with, the subject was never referred to again by either of them.

The engagement period was eighteen months longer than James desired but he schooled himself to wait by working until dark six days a week. By Christmas 1845 his cabin, barns and livestock were all in order and he was ready for his bride.

James and Ellen Caldwell's family on the porch of his CityView, Nepean home. This home was built in 1890's, following 2 log homes which had both burned down. These are his six children with their spouses plus a grandson, seated, who is soon to die of consumption.

CALDWELL

A TIME TO MARRY, A TIME TO DIE 1846

1846 was a momentous year for the Caldwell family. Mary had insisted on having the wedding party at the Caldwell home for, as she firmly stated, "Reverend Neelin will be doing the honours at the ceremony and we shall provide the breakfast. He has only one daughter left at home with him when Ellen marries and it is a bit much to expect the youngest one to provide the wedding breakfast with so little help."

The occasion on January 1, 1846, was a joyous one; Ellen, who had very nearly forgotten how to smile, was a new creature, glowing with happiness.

All was done as Mary decreed, and although she received a great deal of support from all her daughters, Mary appeared exhausted too often for Forest's liking. When the affair was over and the last guest departed he put his foot down and told his precious wife that she must start taking her rest each day.

She abided by his wishes, but it did little good. Each day she grew more and more tired and presently it was obvious to everyone that she was losing weight rapidly; her appetite waned, and signs of her approaching death were visible to everyone. Forest had a terrible struggle within himself to adjust himself to the incredible thought of Mary dying. A phrase from a hymn seemed to go through and through his head, 'Jesus doeth all things well.' Was this a mockery? Finally he submitted to what was inevitable and consoled himself only with the hope that perhaps they would not be parted for long.

Mary died in May of 1846. Forest was already experiencing symptoms of dropsy, a condition of edema that was not considered serious unto death. But Forest took it as reassurance that he would soon be reunited with Mary and his spirits lightened noticeably and unaccountably to those nearest him. There was no evidence of his impending death until his last few days. Forest followed his beloved Mary to their joint grave in September 1846. They were buried in the Church of England graveyard in Huntley, their unpretentious gravestone still tilting precariously in the first years of the 21st century.

Forest and Mary Caldwell's Tombstone

ARGUE

LIFE GOES ON 1845-48

George was aging fast and he now seemed to have no time for anything but to fulfill his promise to Archie to build a chapel and honour his name. It was easier to move William Magee in this direction after William Caldwell arrived and told them quite clearly that Archie was well but not planning to come back to Goulbourne in the foreseeable future. William finalized the transfer of the land from Archie's name to his, as had been arranged, and William and George set about drumming up energy to build the chapel. George also purchased the 100-acre lot adjacent to Magee Chapel so that he could donate land for a graveyard. This commitment had weighed heavily on his mind, and he knew no relief until he had the deeds to the land and his own last will and testimony were finalized.

It was as well he started on the project early, for as the decade moved along it was obvious George's days of leadership were over. He became weak in his mind as well as in body. Mary had scant time to nurse her grief at Annie's passing before she saw George leaving her slowly.

The Magee Chapel was completed in 1845, a log cabin was all, but in later years it was covered with sawn lumber and painted white.

George Argue and his wife Mary (nee Wilson), who emigrated from County Cavan, Ireland in 1819 and settled near Stittsville, Ontario.

George and Mary Argue shortly before his death, likely in 1847. George died in 1848. He does not look well here and it is quite amazing that they managed to have this picture taken as the first photograph was taken in Paris in 1826.

In 1847, when George's sons saw that he was nearing death, they were determined to build a chapel in his name. This they did on the land George had designated for the graveyard and only about one hundred yards east of the Magee Chapel. The Argue Chapel was built of fieldstone, designed to last. And it was used long after the Magee Chapel burned to the ground. It even survived the great fire of 1870, which ravaged the whole of the Ottawa Valley, but was less fierce in that particular section. Parishioners were able to save it by carrying wet mud to slather on the windowsills and doors. The years immediately following were more devoted to building up the country than with preserving its heritage; therefore in 1873 the Argue Chapel was demolished to expand the graveyard although the foundation is still visible in the cemetery.

George Argue died in 1848, just after his 76th birthday. He was the first person to be buried in the graveyard, which, considering how important he had thought it to be, was quite fitting.

His friend Archie Scott died a few months later and John Honey Burrows died in the same year, age 61.

He could not have known it, but in the year of his death the British Parliament finally passed into law Durham's recommendation for responsible Government in Canada. It took many more years before it became a reality in Canada, for the Family Compact and the Chateau Clique fought long and hard against ceding any power to the Legislative Assembly. It was to become the mammoth struggle of those great reformers, Baldwin and Lafontaine.

George knew nothing about the Potato Famine, which commenced in 1845, the full horror of it not known until 1848-49. By the time news of it travelled to Canada, George was dying. Mary however, who had not wanted to leave Ireland, now knew that coming to this land had been for the best, and George could have said, *"We did rightly to come to Upper Canada, didn't we Mary?"*

It was Mary's destiny to outlive both her daughters. Her youngest daughter Jane, who lived on the adjacent farm, bore seven children, the last three in quick succession, one every year until 1850. She then developed consumption and died in 1854, age forty-three. Mary insisted on nursing her daughter and keeping the younger ones away from her as much as possible.

She did not exhibit as much grief at Jane's passing as she had when Annie died for she assured herself that very shortly she would be following Jane to the grave.

Only a year later Mary witnessed the death of Andrew's wife, Sarah, who had given birth to eleven children in twenty years of marriage. Since women were lauded for the ability to have many children, Sarah received a great deal of praise. It was therefore considered a strange thing indeed when eighteen months after the birth of her eleventh child, she went out into the woods on a snowy January day with her babe in her arms, wearing only a shawl to cover them. She contracted pneumonia and died within a few days. There was no word for postpartum depression then, although a poem written in her honour, noted

"her home shone brightly with social happiness,
a blaze too bright to last."

Maybe they knew something of it, but depression of any sort, for any reason, had no room to thrive. One had to carry on.

Mary lived to be 85 years of age, as had her mother, gradually assuming a role similar to that held by Anne Wilson. It was Mary's destiny to outlive many of her compatriots, including her very close friend Maude. Her obituary emphasized that she had welcomed death, and considering her strong faith and the numbers of her family who had preceded her, one can readily believe it. She was laid to rest beside her husband in June 1863. Their small tombstone had almost passed into oblivion but a spate of family enthusiasm in 1980 caused a new one to be erected in their memory.

These two families were typical rather than unusual for that time. We cannot exaggerate the hardships these immigrants endured: leaving their homeland, the dangers and horrors of the voyage, the backbreaking labour, the early deaths and the daily deprivations. Yet through it all, I believe that George, Forest and their neighbours, both Catholic and Protestant, were assured of the rightness of their quest, and that assurance, which at times flickered, ran like a thread of gold throughout the dross of their everyday existence. With each cow, each hen, each apple tree and each room in their house, their hopes grew. Their rewards were small by later standards but they were real enough for these early settlers. If treasure is to be found in the struggle to achieve our dreams, then George, Forest and their friends were rich men.

The good that ordinary men and women do, lives on, unheralded, but of great value.

In the bulb there is a flower;
* in the seed an apple tree;*
...
In the cold and snow of winter
* there's a spring that waits to be,*
...
From the past will come the future;
* what it holds, a mystery,*
unrevealed until its season,
* something God alone can see.* [31]

---

[31] Words and music by Natalie Sleeth . Copyright 1986 by Hope Publishing Company. Used by permission.

AFTERWORD

This chronicle is based on family stories, written and oral, obituaries, letters, documents found in the Public Archives, and on records of other settlers of that time. One could say that the skeleton of the tale is faithful to history but it is clothed, sometimes scantily, and sometimes in full regalia.

Mary Anne, the last child born in Cavan was baptized in the Ashfield Church on Mar 28th, 1823 according to Mormon records. I think that it is virtually impossible for them to have boarded the ship before Mar 31 at that rate and then to arrive in Canada before the end of April. I think the entry in the church records was wrong as Forest's letter in the Archives, written in his own hand, states that he arrived at Quebec in April. Therefore I altered the birthdate by a few days. Still, the departure must have been quite a hurrah and the voyage remarkably brief.

William Caldwell's fear of his name dying out in Ireland came true, although not immediately. Roughly 100 years after Forest left Cavan, the Townland of Drumshiel passed out of Caldwell hands. Toward the end of the 20th Century there was just one of the Caldwell family alive in Ireland; she was an elderly spinster. Of course descendants of Caldwell daughters have been disregarded.

One of our great-great grandfathers was crushed by a falling tree within a couple of weeks of entering the country. As it was too confusing to introduce yet another ancestral family, I told the story by means of having the death occur to John Wilson Sr. Death from falling trees was not an unusual occurrence.

The chief area, in which I modified the facts to save the reader and myself extreme mental distress, was in the marriage of two of George's children, Annie and Andrew. Annie Argue married her second cousin whose real name was Thomas Argue. I named him Thomas Wilson in order to maintain the degree of consanguinity but to lessen the confusion. Thomas Argue's father was also George Argue and he too came from Cavan. He was George's first cousin, about 8 years older. He led a group from the parishes of Annagelliffe and Castleterra, Cavan, to Huntley Township. His oldest son was Thomas, but he had a son called Robert and a daughter called Ann, among other children. There was too much similarity in the names of these two families.

To create further bedlam in the reader's mind is the fact that Andrew Argue, George Argue's son, married Ann Argue, the sister of Thomas Argue of Huntley and daughter of the Huntley George Argue. Both these women died of childbirth, one at childbirth and one 18 months after the birth, as written. I found it so hard to keep it straight which Ann Argue died when and of what cause that I changed their last names, and I changed even the first name of Andrew's wife; I called her Sarah Wilson. What was even more dismaying, but not referred to here at all, was the amount of intermarriage that likely occurred in Ireland before they came to Upper Canada.

A historical figure I have used freely is John Burrows. It would have been virtually impossible for two such devout Methodists as George Argue and John Burrows, both of whom lived in the same sparsely populated area at the same time, not to have known each other. Whether or not they became fast friends is conjecture, but it is most likely that they approved of each other and shared much in common.

All of the essential ingredients of the story were predominant features of life in that time, especially the problems of debt, transportation, illness, the ruling clique, the canal building era, and the nature of Bytown as a shantytown.

I have not researched the genealogies of families other than the Argues and Caldwells; therefore any references made to other families, such as the Scotts or Fosters and others, are not to be relied upon as factual. The story of Charlie Scott's death was true of a death in the Argue family, but it did not occur in that generation. I took liberty with the time frame in order to reflect the nature of life, of death, and medical knowledge of that period and that of the next generation.

As for the spelling inconsistencies, that was the norm for that time. There was no "correct" way to spell a word. It was spelt as it sounded to the writer. Forest Caldwell spelt his name

335

three different ways, Cauldwell, Coldwell and Caldwell, often in close proximity to one another. I have adhered to one spelling unless it appeared in an Archival document. Goulbourn was spelt at least three different ways, Gooldbourn, Goulbourne and Goulburn.

The twenty-first century is still young, and the whole world is caught up in the culture of "terrorism", a time in which the differences of religion, national identity and economic injustices are frighteningly divisive. I don't doubt the single-mindedness or the strength of the religious beliefs of these men and women, but I doubt that they were unusual for that time and place. They were regarded as religious fundamentalists by Anglicans who called them "those shouting Methodists". Their faith gave them the strength to endure and to overcome very severe hardships for as long as a twenty to thirty year period before living conditions eased a bit and by then they were either dead or ready to die.

Fortunately their creed told them to pursue peace and turn the other cheek. They would have been terrible indeed if they believed in the right of might and the terrible swift sword and all that sort of thing. They wanted to leave all that behind them in Ireland where they had seen enough of terror.

Factual errors are mine alone.

FAMILY MEMBERS

Anne Wilson, the matriarch of the whole expedition, had the following children:
Moses m. Martha Bell
Mary, 1778-1863, m. George Argue
Elizabeth m. James Blair
John m. Jane Ferguson
Amy m. Robert Mitchell
James Wilson m. Esther Scott. He, with John Scott, was the first to come to British North America

Anne had a younger brother, John Wilson Sr., who married Maude Foster. Two of Maude's brothers also came with the group.

Argue Family

George, 1772-1848, m. 1803, Mary Wilson, 1778-1863
Anne, called Annie, 1803-1841 m. Thomas Wilson* of Huntley, d. 1871 - 8 children.
William, 1804-1875, m. Margaret Smith, 1800-1885 - 8 children.
Andrew, 1807-1893 m. Sarah Wilson* of Huntley, d. 1855, 11 children.
Robert, 1809-1892, m. Elizabeth Armstrong d. 1894, 6 children.
Jane, 1811-1854, m. Robert Cherry, 7 children.
George, 1813 – 1821.
John, 1815-?, m. Esther Wilson, 7 children.

* see Afterword

Caldwell Family

William and Sarah Caldwell, Co. Cavan, parents of

Forest Colville Caldwell, 1780-1846, m. 1810, Mary Smiley, 1794-1846.

William, 1812-1855, b. Ireland.
Margaret, 1814-1883, b. Ireland, m. Richard Taylor.
Samuel, 1816-1882, b. Ireland, m. Fanny Smiley; m. Frances Maxwell.
James, 1818-1903, b. Ireland, m. Ellen Neelin.
John, 1821-1900, b. Ireland, m. Margaret Scott.
Mary Anne, 1823-1892, b. Ireland, m. ___ Grier.
Elizabeth, 1826-1900, b. March Township, U.C., m. G. Fenton.
Jane Maria, b. 1829, March Township, U.C. m. William Gourlay.
Forrest, 1832-1898, b. March Township, U.C., m. Annie Alderson.
Hannah, 1835-1885, b. Huntley Township, m. William Bradley.

A DEMOCRAT WAGON

CARLETON SAGA

This buggy, or "democrat", was fancy transportation before the turn of the century. These three-seaters were especially useful for wedding guests or pall-bearers, or on picnic safaris or "Orange" walks.

MAP OF CARLETON COUNTY: 1881

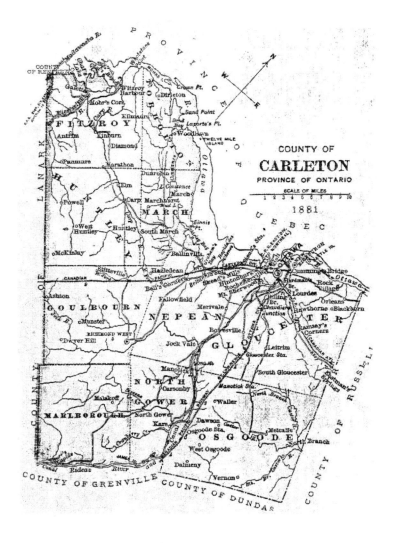

MAP OF AREA: 1832

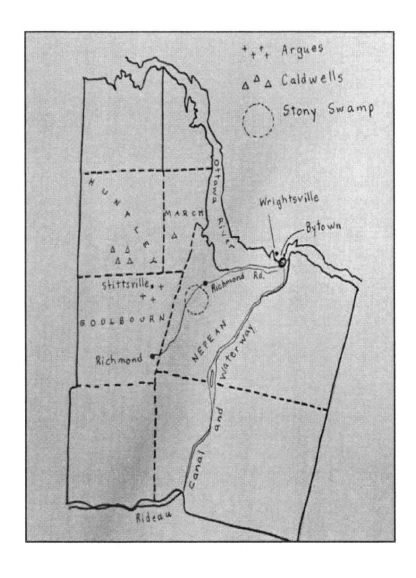

+ + + + Arques
Δ Δ Δ Caldwells
Stony Swamp

Ottawa River

Wrightsville
Bytown
MARCH
Stittsville
GOULBOURN
Richmond Rd.
NEPEAN
Richmond
Canal and waterway
Rideau

JOHN BURROWS' SURVEY SKETCH

John Burrows' survey sketch (looking south) of Cox's, Nicholsons' and Clowes' rapids on the Rideau River in 1827
John Burrows Diary, City of Ottawa Archives, Image 21338.

ABOUT THE AUTHOR

Olive Caldwell Lee was born and raised in the Ottawa Valley very close to the original homesteads she describes in this book, surrounded by the stories and the spirit of the region.

She now lives in the Lower Fraser Valley in British Columbia.

She can be reached by email at olivejungle@shaw.ca.

Net proceeds from the sale of this book will go to the following charities: The Stephen Lewis Foundation and the United Church Mission and Service Fund.
